Criminal Psychology

Criminal Psychology

R. Mishra

Sumit Enterprises
New Delhi - 110002

First Published 2006

© Reserved

ISBN : 81-8420-044-7

Published by :
SUMIT ENTERPRISES
4649B/21, Ansari Road, Darya Ganj
New Delhi - 110002
Phones : 011-30916277, 23279353
Mob. : 9810217567
E-mail : Sumit_enterprises@rediffmail.com

PRINTED IN INDIA

Published by Sri Lokesh Gupta for Sumit Enterprises, New
Delhi-110002, Typeset by Deep Printers, Printed at Rajdhani
Printers, Delhi.

Preface

Psychology is the study of individual characteristics or qualities such as personality, reasoning, thought, intelligence, learning, perception, imagination, memory and creativity. There are two groups of theories or schools of thought. These are cognitive and behavioural there are psychologists who place weight on a triological link. Conceptually it would be better to begin testing at a very young age and follow the children through to adulthood. Ideally the tests should cover not only personality and official criminality but also self reported criminality. The researcher would then be better able to assess whether their personalities were inherent, learnt from normal socialisation or were the result of a brush with the criminal justice system. The proposed methods of assessment might also show whether these personality types actually commit more crime or whether they are just more likely to be caught. There would still be problems, the perceived personality traits may be the result of earlier conflict with figures of authority such as teachers. The participants were also asked to complete a questionnaire asking the number of times they had been arrested for a violent crime whether they had ever been a gang member and whether anyone in their family had ever been imprisoned. In order to encourage honest responses they were asked not to put their names on the test for many generations some scholars have attempted to discover and demonstrate physical determinants of criminal behaviour. They have reported that crimes against property are more frequent in winter months and crimes against the person are more frequent in summer months. In considering biological theories as a whole it is unlikely that they alone can offer a convincing explanation for criminal behaviour. This book has nine chapters explaining control of crime, theories of criminal psychology and the feminist perspectives on criminal psychology.

—Editor

Contents

Contents

1

Introduction

What is Crime?

It is difficult to define what is criminal or to distinguish a crime from a tort. One cannot even declare that crimes are always more serious in their effects either on the individual or on society. For example, the negligent manufacture and marketing of a product which turns out to be dangerous may be far more injurious to both individual and society than the theft of a pencil, yet the former would normally only constitute a tort whereas the latter is criminal. There are similarities: each is a wrong, each is a breach of a legal obligation or rule. What, then, is the difference? Although it is circular, the best definition and the best distinguishing feature is that only if the breach of a legal rule (the wrong) has criminal consequences attached to it, will it be a criminal offence. An offence or a crime, then, is a wrong to society involving the breach of a legal rule which has criminal consequences attached to it (i.e., prosecution by the State in the criminal courts and the possibility of punishment being imposed). This gives a legalistic view of a crime but fails to impart the types of activity which may fall under that head. Above all, it must be re-emphasised that it is a circular definition — a crime is something the law calls a crime and uses criminal prosecutions and sanctions to deal with. Despite these shortcomings with the definition, it is essential that one never

forgets that no matter how immoral, reprehensible, damaging
or dangerous an act is, it is not a crime unless it is made such
by the authorities of the State.

Basic Elements of Most Crimes

Most criminal laws forbid certain types of behaviour,
and therefore before a person can be convicted, it must be
proved that he or she acted in a fashion proscribed by law:
this is generally known as the *actus reus* of an offence. Some
defences go to the very core of the action and claim that part
of the *actus reus* was missing. For example, the offence of
assault requires that an individual unlawfully injures
another: a claim that an injury was caused as the result of
self-defence is thus claiming that the action has not been
completed, i.e., it renders the injury lawful. Another example
arises in the offence of rape, which involves sexual
intercourse with a woman without her consent; if the man
claims that she consented he is claiming that part of the
actus reus is absent. In both cases the defence goes to the
heart of the action. Other defences may admit the action but
ask that it be excused because of, for example, duress or
certain types of mistake. In stealing, someone intentionally
deprives another person of property and thus clearly commits
an offence: but if that offence is committed because a third
party forced it at gunpoint, the offender could plead lack of
choice.

Generally, omitting to do something will not amount to
the *acuts reus* of an offence. For example, if I decide to watch
a young child drowning in inches of water and do nothing to
save its life, I am not guilty of any criminal offence though
clearly my inaction is morally indefensible. Basically, the law
usually only punishes individuals for positive conduct and
not for inaction. There are, however, some notable exceptions.
In a few instances the law requires certain types of behaviour,
for example, failure to submit the accounts of a limited
company is a crime. In others, there may be a duty to act.
This duty may arise through statute, for example, the duty
to report road accidents to the police; or it may arise out of a

persons's job or out of holding public office, for example, a police officer has a duty to prevent an assault; or it may arise out of the obligation to care for a dependent.

The second important element which is required in most cases is a mental state. There must be a state of mind with respect to the *actus reus*: this is called the *mens rea*, that is an intention to act in the proscribed fashion or to bring about the unacceptable ends, or in some cases reckless indifference to causing a particular harm. It is important to distinguish *mens rea* from motive. If I decide to kill a close relative, such as my grandmother, because she is helpless and begs me to put her out of her misery, some might argue that my motive is honourable and understandable. But if I premeditate my action and intend its consequences, my conduct is murder just as if I had shot an enemy with hatred in my heart. Both are murder; the motive does not alter the fact that the crime has been committed. Motive, however, may be taken into account in sentencing or in carrying out the sentence. In the above example, the court has to pass a life sentence on all murderers, but the time actually spent in prison may vary depending on the conduct of the prisoners and possibly also on the motive for the crime, as this may touch on the possibility of the offence being repeated. In cases where the court has a discretion, it may decide to punish the person whose motive was good less severely than where the motive was greed, hatred etc. Foucault (1988) has claimed that all too often the law gets caught up with motive rather than with intent. He also questions the idea that motive should be used at the sentencing stage, although most would have more sympathy for a merciful killing than for a cold-blooded killing, and most would prefer to see the former sentenced less severely than the latter.

There are some defences which question the *mens rea* of an offence, such as a plea of insanity, diminished responsibility and automatism.

In some cases the *mens rea* of an offence may be established if the individual intended to do wrong, though a greater harm than intended occurs as a result of the actions.

For example, if I intentionally hit someone it is an assault,
and I could be convicted of that crime, but if the person is
particularly weak and dies an a result of the injury, then I
may be convicted of manslaughter or, if it can be proven that
I intended to cause grievous bodily harm, murder. Although
I did not intend to kill, the death is the direct result of a crime
which I did intend. Although most lawyers tend to claim that
'crime', *mens reus* and *actus reus* are carefully defined and
objectively applied, and thus lead to just decisions, a number
of critical legal theorists have begun to question this.

Some offences do not require any *mens rea,* as to all or
some of the *actus reus,* on behalf of the offender. These
offences are known as strict liability offences. Many strict
liability offences are set by Parliament and are sometimes
referred to as 'state of affairs' offences or as absolute liability
offences. They often fall into the area of public welfare
offences or regulatory offences and regulate potentially
dangerous activities, like motoring, or they protect people
against other dangers of modern life. In these cases, all that
needs to be proven is that the state of affairs existed and the
crime is complete; it is no defence to say that one did not
intend this state of affairs or even that one was unaware of
it. Examples of this arise in many road traffic violations (e.g.,
driving with defective brakes, or more generally the use of
defective and dangerous motor vehicles); possession of
dangerous objects or substances such as firearms or controlled
drugs (where all that is necessary is knowledge of possession,
not that the thing possessed is a controlled drug); public health
legislation such as the sale of food containing extraneous
matter; or control of pollution. These types of activities fall
into the category of strict liability to force people to exercise
highe standards of care to ensure that offences are not
committed, especially when their activities could present a
danger to the public. Furthermore, because they often involve
an omission, for example failure to renew the tyres on a
vehicle, it would be difficult to prove the *mens rea* as to all or
some of the *actus reus.*

Lastly, for all crimes there is a legally prescribed

punishment. The punishment is usually set out in terms of a maximum and the actual punishment in any particular case is left to the discretion of the judge. In a few cases there is a minimum punishment. For example, murder carries a life sentence, drunk driving the loss of a driving licence, and there is now a minimum sentence for repeat offenders of certain serious crimes under the Powers of Criminal Courts (Sentencing) Act 2000. In addition, both the defence and the prosecution can now appeal the sentence, and the Court of Appeal can lay down guidelines for sentencing.

What Actions are Criminalised?

Why certain acts or omissions are declared criminal and others are not is a difficult question. So are the questions: what aggravating factors warrant being made the subject of a separate offence? and which mitigating factors should be recognised as defences? As with the terminology, there is an element of fashion involves in attempts to answer these fundamental issues, but the underlying rationale is largely governed by the traditional ethos and ethics of the society. In our case this relates mainly to the largely white, male-oriented, Judaeo-Christian tradition and the conservatism that accompanies the desire for stability, order and predictability. Morality and notions of blameworthiness based on harm may explain the formulation of the early fundamental crimes (murder, theft, etc.) but do not necessarily fully explain the modern social welfare, moral improvement and traffic offences created by statute. No one philosophy or cause can adequately explain why differing forms of activity are deemed criminal. Morality, economics, politics, public administration, public order and public safety all play a part. Also, there is an interrelationship with the equally complex question: why do people commit crimes? If defining crime is problematic, explaining why people participate in these activities is even more elusive. As we shall see, attempts to provide explanations have to confront such fundamental issues as: does crime occur because man is inherently evil; or because of socio-economic conditions; or because of physical or mental illness; or because of genetic, inherited defects; or are there other factors or combinations of factors which are responsible? They represent an attempt to get away from studying the principles of criminal law and the theories of criminology in a vacuum, and to enquire about their aim and purpose; whether these ends are achieved; and whether claims made by criminologists and others are substantiated by sound research. It is not claimed that such an approach gives, or can give, clear-cut conclusions, but it is strongly contended that it is essential for anyone seeking understanding of a hugely complex field.

Consensus approach

This assumes that the activities which are criminalised are firmly based on the generally agreed mores for conduct. The criminal law thus seeks to identify and control the types of behaviour which the community finds unacceptable: in this way it helps to preserve public order. Perhaps the most universally assumed aim of the criminal law, and that which is said to be the strongest unifying element in the consensus theory is that of averting harm. Mill accepted that the State could always intervene in the liberty of personal conduct to prevent one individual harming another. This basic liberal ideal has guided the consensus theory in its main aim, the prohibition of crimes which are *male in se,* harmful in themselves. This includes activities which attack the person such as assault, murder and rape as well as acts which attack property or the possession or ownership of property such as theft, arson or intentional damage. Feinberg (1985, 1988) would also include the prevention of offences. Many of these offences are criminalised in most societies and there is often claimed to be a general consensus about their prohibition.

A modern portrayal of a consensus theory should take account of autonomy. Within this Lacey and Wells explained the criminal law:

> as a set of norms backed up by the threat and imposition of sanctions, the function of which is to

protect the autonomy and welfare of individuals and groups in society with respect to a set of basic goods, both individual and collective.

In terms of autonomy the law should create an environment in which individual choices are maximised except where they might impact upon the autonomy of another individual. This requires a minimalist version of the harm principle whereby the criminal law 'should only be used as a last resort or for the most reprehensible types of wrongdoing' and individuals need as much autonomy as possible whilst guaranteeing a similar freedom to others. Raz argues that in order for individuals to be autonomous they need to be independent and free from coercion and manipulation. Neither the State nor the law should interfere with that freedom nor should it be curtailed by the actions of other individuals. It is here that the State should instigate criminal laws to protect individuals from one another. Autonomy is undermined by feelings of insecurity so that it might be necessary to criminalise activities which cause such offence as to put others in fear (for example, racial hatred). Von Hirsch and Jareborg noted that for individual victims four generic interests might be in need of protection: physical integrity, privacy, autonomy, and freedom from humiliation or degrading treatment. This would be supported by recourse to human rights as the source of criminal law and would pave the way for crimes which recognise the State as perpetrator. Schwendinger and Schwendinger went further, claiming that all violations of basic human rights were acts of criminality whether included in the criminal law or not. Here many States would be included as perpetrators of crimes rather than as the force that defines and enforces them, and human rights then become standards that must be defended by the criminal law. Autonomy and harm can be used to justify protection of the State, such as tax evasion, although here the links are more tenuous — autonomy requires that the State works to create the conditions necessary for choices to be realistic; without revenue this would be difficult so that some citizens would suffer reduced autonomy and therefore harm.

A very modern analysis of the need for crime is to answer
the problems faced by citizens as members of the 'risk society.'
Key proponents of this are Giddens and Beck, who have both
referred to a concept of 'manufactured uncertainty' where
everyone in society is forced to live with large risks. Most of
these risks are caused by successful advances in science and
technology whose effects are difficult to assess. Note here that
a risk society is not necessarily more dangerous than anything
faced in the past. Rather it means that the risks are now
manufactured in that technology has altered the natural
world so extensively and in so many areas of our lives that
there is almost no aspect of modern life which is unaltered. This
means that we cannot predict from the past what the risks
may be in the future and therefore risk becomes more
profound and for many more debilitating. Individuals assume
and expect the State, through politicians, to minimise future
risks for everyone and provide compensation, or require
companies to compensate, when they fail in this
responsibility. At times the risks encompass technological
problems, such as BSE; at others it is economic, such as the
lack of control over the use of pension funds (Maxwell), or the
use of futures markets (Leeson), or the dangers posed by dogs
(biting humans for carrying rabies) or control of criminals in
our society. In the area of crime, risks and uncertainties give
rise to feelings of insecurity which may be very debilitating,
interfering with autonomy and thereby harming the lives of
individuals. There is therefore an argument to include risk or
insecurity as a reason for creating criminal laws. This might
include the control of the mentally disordered and supervision
of disorderly juveniles in the criminal laws.

Some consensus theorists would accept a role for the
criminal law in protecting individuals from themselves, from
taking dangerous substances, participating in dangerous
activities or regulating the way we participate in such
activities (requiring protective clothing in some jobs or
wearing seat belts in cars). A number of liberals, although
largely agreeing with Mill and the autonomy theories, have
sympathy for this argument: '.... paternalism — the protection

of people against themselves — is a perfectly coherent policy.'

Consensus theorists thus recognise that protecting the safety and integrity of the individual is not the only aim of the criminal law. They accept that there are numerous aims: maintenance of public order; rasing revenues (e.g., the laws punishing those who evade income tax); regulating business (e.g., they punish the charging of excessive prices and they punish unhygienic and unsafe practices); protecting employees; conserving the environment; preserving heritage; and enforcing morality. It is interesting that the significance of this last function — the upholding of morality — has changed in recent years. In a pluristic, multicultural society Devlin's 1965 view of the criminal law as centrally necessary to prevent the moral disintegration of society is on the wane — although this has not shifted much political rhetoric away from a stress on protecting morals. Overall the basic effect of these various aims of the criminal law is to maintain society in its present form and to ensure its smooth functioning.

Today in this country there are literally thousands of offences created by statute which are designed to enforce certain standards in the practice of otherwise lawful activities. The rules relating to road traffic, to public hygiene, rules about health and safety at work and rules governing the entry into and conduct of certain businesses or professions are examples. These rules are generally enforceable by way of criminal sanction. Unlike the traditional common law notions of crime, these newer statutory offences generally punish omissions as well as positive acts.

Furthermore, they are more often than not created as offences of strict liability for which an accused may be held liable without any proof of a blameworthy state of mind with regard to one or more element of the *actus reus.* This last innovation has produced practical advantages but it means that if a minor prohibited act, omission or event occurs for which a person is responsible, that persons may be guilty. Guilt does not necessarily depends, as it must in other offences, on state of mind. People may be deemed guilty irrespective of what they intended, thought or believed. Consensus theories accept this as necessary to the smooth running of society and also as a way of permitting activities which may cause harm, whilst minimising the danger. Generally, the ordinary man or woman in society does not consider persons convicted of these sorts of offences, including traffic violations, 'criminals,' that term being popularly reserved to express moral condemnation for the acts of murderers, rapists, thieves and the like; yet these regulatory or social welfare type offences can cause no less suffering and harm. Should society and the law treat such offenders as being as blameworthy and reprehensible as the traditional 'criminals'? Why is there a consensus that they should not?

Finally, there are offences the sole purpose of which is the enforcement of morality. As indicated above the justification for these has tended to be brought more into question. Should the criminal law be concerned with matters of private morality if the conduct does no harm to society or to the participants? The abrogation or repeal of such laws would delete a mass of criminal statistics and prevent large numbers of people being labelled criminals. It would not mean that these acts and their perpetrators would be acceptable, because they may still be considered antisocial by the majority of the community. Clearly, repeal would be to those persons' advantage, but it could also be to the advantage of the community generally. Law enforcement agencies may, for example, then be able to concentrate their resources in the prevention or pursuit of serious criminal offenders: the muggers, rapists, robbers, those who cause grievous bodily harm, and the like. Are the criminal offences relating to alcohol, gambling, pornography, bigamy, blasphemy, bestiality, criminal libel, conspiracy to corrupt public morals, conspiracy to outrage public decency and possibly also controls on drugs outmoded and unreasonable restrictions on our liberty? Would individuals and society be at risk if current laws on these matters were abolished? If these laws are essential to our society, why are adultery, fornication and seduction not criminal? Occasionally, popular demands lead to legislation to withdraw certain conduct from the ambit of the criminal law. One of the best examples is the public debate following the Wolfenden Committee Report・1957) which led to Parliament passing the Sexual Offences Act 1967, which declared that homosexual acts between consenting adult males [then over age 21, altered to 16 by s. 1 of the Sexual Offences (Amendment) Act 2000] in private were no longer a crime.

The limit of the criminal law is a topic which has taxed lawyers, criminologists, sociolgists, philosophers and others for many years. It is necessarily complicated by the wide range of problems which the criminal law is expected to address. Sharp disagreements over what the law should, and should not, include thus reflect not only the enduring mysteries of the human condition, but also the variety and subjectivity of the aims and functions of the criminal law. A further set of nuances is explored in the next subsection.

Modern sociological approaches

The above approaches generally assumed that there was something about the nature of an act itself or its consequences which made it unacceptable. The present approach will consider whether the crime consists not in the act itself, but simply in it being defined as criminal. The implication is that crime is constructed by the society or group. This idea has given rise to a number of explanations of criminality but here we are concerned with how this might have affected the definitions of crimes. Virtually all societies are too large for everyone to define the rules which are thus constructed by some group or groups. Acceptance of this as a sociological fact has led to various interpretations of the ways in which such crimes are defined.

The first of these is the conflict school which views the constructs of modern society as fluid and claims that new issues are resolved, or old ones redefined, by the resolution of conflict. In this analysis society is not built on harmony and consensus but rather is constructed of competing groups who struggle for power. Conflicts between workers and employers; between the sexes or the races; between religions;

between political groupings. Each of these conflicts is resolved
by the more powerful group enforcing its views and using
the law as its weapon. In criminal terms this is done through
controlling their opponents' behaviour, by calling it illegal.
On this view the criminal laws is constructed to protect the
interests of powerful groups. Neither individuals nor their
behaviour is inherently criminal: the social order has
constructed the proscribed areas of behaviour. It is further
argued that the law is applied more vigorously to the less
powerful than to others, making criminality almost by
definition the normal response of the powerless or
disadvantaged to their position in life. Conflict theorists also
claim that public opinion is manipulated by the same powerful
groups so that the proscribed behaviour becomes widely
accepted. This might explain why certain actions are either
not criminal or are treated very leniently.

In the 1970s critical criminologists took this position one
step further. They criticised the conflict theorists for still
viewing criminality as pathological and proposed a view,
based on Marx, which studied crime as a wider subject,
including the relationships between crime, criminal, victim
and State. The areas of behaviour which are defined as
criminal are those necessary to a capitalist society. Under
these the upper classes can exploit the weak, put them in
physical danger, and transgress their human rights either
with total impunity or with only very light punishment. This
very politicised attack led some to question the *status quo*
and to confront the possibility that the criminal law was
designed to control certain types of behaviour for reasons
other than the general well-being of those in the society. The
anti-capitalist slant alienated many.

More recently the critical school of thought has splintered
into Marxist and more conservative sections. Most of the latter
group still provide socialist perspectives but do not accept the
Marxist alternative to the *status quo*. They retain the attack
on early theories but do not accept that the criminal system
emerges solely out of the capitalist domination of society. They
see power as just one element — others include culture,

personality, prejudice and even chance — in determining the social order. They agree that the criminal law tends to define the activities of those who are dominant as legitimate and those of the weak as less acceptable, but the reasons are not always capitalistic. Many activities are deconstructed to discover interactions and to understand and analyse behaviour. Law may be constructed by the powerful and in their interest, but this may often be with the blessing of the weaker in society. These writers have a wider view of the concept of crime. They look not only at the criminals and their behaviour, and the State and its need for a definition of criminal, but also at society's constructs of social control, and at the views, actions and input of the victims.

Each of these theories sees crime as an artificially constructed social reality: it is made by particular people to protect the interests of some over those of others. The thesis is that the criminal law is intended to enforce conformity with the norms of those with the dominant interest in a given society. To illustrate the point, even violent behaviour is not always viewed and treated the same way. Criminal violence is created by those who make and enforce the law rather than by the nature of the bahaviour. In the media and general discussions on the level of violence it is usually only this officially constructed area of behaviour that is considered. Thus most of the controls on violence only protect against violence on the street. Until recently domestic violence was not taken seriously. Even as recently as the last century the law permitted husband physically to chastise their wives; it still permits parents (and other carers) to treat children in ways which if committed against an adult, would be a crime. Only in the last 20 years has excessive violence against partners or children been accepted as an activity needing strong enforcement measures to punish and control it. Assaults committed by law enforcers themselves are rarely prosecuted whereas similar acts by others might well culminate in imprisonment. Corporations and governments may take decisions they know or suspect will result in death or injury and yet will not necessarily face criminal

prosecution: asbestos, thalidomide; use of soldiers to test
mustard gas or the effects of atomic bomb radiation. The
criminal law does not protect against all the dangers we face,
nor even against all the worst dangers (e.g., food, air,
environment).

Intention and Age

In order to judge whether an action is criminal, we need
to consider not only the act itself but the *intention* and the
age of the perpetrator. It would be unjust to punish people
who could not help doing what they did, so if the act was
not *intentional,* but was accidental, done under duress, a
mistake or intended for good then it is not a crime. Thus
the same action, such as cutting someone with a knife, is a
criminal act if it involves malicious wounding but not if it
was entirely accidental or part of a surgical operation.
Intention cannot be proved if an individual does not have
sufficient understanding to know what they are doing, so
we need to consider whether someone has learning
difficulties or a psychiatric illness before deciding whether
their behaviour is criminal. With respect to age, because very
young children cannot be held responsible for their actions,
the legal system has introduced an age below which people
are not considered criminally responsible – this differs
between countries but the principle is the same.

Culture and History

The concept of what constitutes a crime is also influenced
by culture and history. Some actions are criminal in one
culture but not in others. In Egypt and Sudan, female
circumcision is legal, in England and many other countries it
is prohibited. Private consumption of the drug marijuana has
been decriminalised in the Netherlands but not in Britain.
Changes over time in our ideas of what does or does not denote
a crime reflect humanitarian concerns, scientific and industrial
advances, and increasing affluence. Suicide, homosexual
behaviour between consenting adults, adultery and
prostitution are just a few examples of behaviour that has

been wholly or partially removed from criminal law. On the other hand, neglect and abuse of children, employees and animals have been added. With the advent of the car and other motor vehicles, such acts as dangerous driving, speeding and failure to wear a seat belt are actions that are now illegal. In essence then, crime can be considered a *social construct*, a product of social and cultural influences rather than a universal truth. The set of behaviours it encompasses are so diverse that they only have one thing in common: they are proscribed by the criminal law.

Approaches to Deciding What is a Criminal Act

How does any society decide which acts are criminal? Hollin (1989) outlines three main approaches to defining crime.

Consensus view

The *consensus view* states that a society's legal system is based on an agreement (consensus) amongst most of its members about what behaviours will not be tolerated and should therefore incur punishment. By defining crime in this way, actions are only criminal if they are forbidden by law, so anti-social behaviour is not considered a crime unless the particular act is illegal. Some illegal acts are uniformly deemed to be wrong and have always been forbidden – crimes such as malicious wounding. Other actions, as discussed above, pass in and out of criminal law depending on the changing values of a society. Printing a book was once forbidden in this country; incest was once a legal act. The consensus view sees the main of a legal system as a means of preserving a stable society and is more or less of equal benefit to all its citizens.

Conflict view

The *conflict view,* a sociological approach rooted in Marxism, is a very different approach which maintains that the law benefits some far more than others. According to this approach, there are many competing groups within society, groups such as unions, industrialists and professional bodies, and they are in conflict with each other because some are more wealthy and powerful than others. Criminal laws exist to protect the rich and powerful from the remainder of the population. In this way the ruling group secures its interests at the expense of the underprivileged. Even when actions are forbidden in the common interest, they are defined in an unequal way so that the powerful tend to go unpunished. An example is the English law against rape, which was only recently extended to include sexual coercion within marriage. Before that the wife, who is the partner who is usually the weaker in both physical and economic terms, was not given the option to refuse unwanted sexual intercourse even though its imposition involves physical force.

Some neo-Marxist sociologists feel that the conflict view is too extreme an approach and have offered various modifications of it, but they all agree on one point: that crime is the product of inadequate social conditions. Objectors to this approach point out that crime is a harsh reality for many working-class people who suffer considerably from its effects and is not something to be glorified in a 'Robin Hood' way.

Interactionist view

The *interactionist view* takes a middle line between these two opposing approaches. It emphasises the fact that there are no absolute value of right and wrong because these depend on the *meaning* placed upon them by the individual. Each of us has a different view: taking a life is sometimes seen as criminal but not always. When killing occurs in wartime, when capital punishment is used or when someone is acting in self-defence then the act is not called 'murder' and it is not criminal. On the other hand, taking a life in the act of euthanasia is a criminal act in most societies but one that some people would like to see decriminalised. According to the interactionist view, the decision about when an act becomes a crime is not drawn from a consensus of the whole population but by those in power. In one way, this agrees with the conflict approach; however, it differs in that it does not see those in power as motivated by maintaining their economic supremacy but more by a belief in their own moral superiority. The interactionist view is concerned with the way in which legal standards are related to changing moral values.

This leads neatly on to our next consideration, the relationship between crime and morality.

Morality and Crime

Morals are beliefs and values that are shared by a society or a section of society and are the means by which we judge what is right and what is wrong. Activities such as cheating, lying and stealing are deemed by most people to be morally wrong and we instill these values into our children, so that eventually they develop a conscience and uphold the social order (including obeying laws) through inner conviction, rather than simply through fear of punishment. The morals held by a society have a considerable influence on what is classed as criminal, but immorality and criminality are not the same thing. This means that not everything considered morally wrong is illegal (we do not have a law against telling lies) nor is everything illegal necessarily immoral (it's not immoral to part on a double yellow line but it is illegal).

The sociologist Durkheim highlighted the fact that within a complex society there is no set of moral values that are shared by everyone. Since individuals in such a society differ markedly in their social status, occupation, religion, ethnicity and so on, they are unlikely to share all their moral values. Given that these moral values, however strongly held, differ between groups, which group's moral opinions, if any, should be adopted by the law? Whereas it is easy to appreciate why the law would be used to protect persons and property, the question of whether it should reflect morality in cases where no harm is done to others is far more debatable. The controversial question is: should the law be used to direct the behaviour of private individuals simply because this behaviour violates a moral code, even though it is hurting no one (except maybe the perpetrator)? The kinds of behaviour this includes are those concerned with alcohol, sex, drugs and gambling.

There are two problems with using the legal system to punish so-called immoral behaviour. The first is that there is no general consensus as to what constitutes an immoral act; any decisions concerning what is and is not moral would be value judgements and who is to decide which set of values should predominate? The second problem is that even if there were agreement over what is moral or immoral, as long as no harm is done to others, why should such behaviour be criminal?

Many arguments have been offered as to what should constitute an appropriate relationship between morality and the law. We will consider two opposing ones.

Natural Law Approach

The natural law approach argues that law should strongly reflect morality. There is a variety of such theories so it is not possible to summarise a single approach but the one theme they have in common is the proposal that there is a higher law, known as the natural law, which should be the basis of the laws that societies make for themselves. The natural law approach argues that laws that do not reflect this code should never have been made and need not be obeyed.

However, there is no universal agreement amongst natural law theorists as to what should be the exact content of the laws and this is a weakness of their position. Usually it would encompass basic human rights; the Bill of Rights, like that in the US constitution, could be seen as being based on natural law principles.

The Approach of John Stuart Mill

An opposing position was offered by the philosopher John Stuart Mill who argued that the criminal law should function primarily to prevent individuals harming others and should not concern itself with private morality. Modern theorists of this school focus on what is known as *victimless crimes*, crimes such as homosexuality and drug use which do no harm to anyone other than, on occasions, the participant. Since they do not do harm to others, supporters of this view argue that such acts should not be illegal. Indeed, it is on that basis that homosexual acts between consenting adults were decriminalised in Britain, but other forms of consensual sex between adults, such as some sado-masochistic behaviour, remain illegal.

This view was reflected in a 1950s government report on homosexuality and pornography, known as the Wolfenden Report, which argued that the purpose of criminal law should not be to interfere in the lives of citizens or seek to enforce any particular behaviour other than that which was necessary 'to preserve public order and decency, to protect the citizen from what is offensive and injurious and to provide sufficient safeguards against exploitation and corruption of others especially the vulnerable, that is the young, weak in body or mind, inexperienced or those in a state of physical, official or economic dependence.' In other words, the argument was similar to that of John Stuart Mill: people should be free to make their own choices as long as they do not harm others.

Professor Hart, a supporter of the Wolfenden Report, argued that the law should not be used to enforce moral values and to do so was in itself morally unacceptable since it infringes the liberty of the individual. Hart (1963) further suggested that often it was not morality that prompted people to object to unusual behaviour; instead it was that such objections were often the result of prejudice, bigotry, ignorance or misunderstanding. (This is related to theories of prejudice, especially that of the Authoritarian Personality.) An opposing argument was put forward by Lord Devlin who proposed that a scoiety could only be stable if it had a set of shared moral principles and that it was only in stable society that individual freedom was possible.

The Relationship Between Law and Morality

The relationship between law and morality is a complex one, which is constantly being reviewed as new issues arise. For example, in vitro fertilisation has led to arguments on

the extent to which 'test tube' embryos should be selected.
The two views expressed above are not always entirely
incompatible and both are still influential in the judgements
that are made.

In 1992 an interesting case led to a heated debate about
the extent to which people should be punished for acts that
harm no one except themselves: the case involved a group of
homosexual men who were convicted of a variety of assaults
against the person. These men had willingly participated in
a number of sado-masochistic acts involving, amongst other
things, safety-pins, nail, stinging nettles, heated wires and
sandpaper. Although the acts had been videotaped, this was
for personal use only. Any injuries sustained were not
permanent nor serious enough to warrant medical attention.
The acts had taken place in private and all the participants
had freely consented and expressed no regrets whatsoever.
The men lodged an unsuccessful appeal to the House of Lords
and then took their case to the European Court of Human
Rights. See if you can find out the decision made by this
court.

The initial judgement made in this case was heavily
criticised, since, it was argued, these individuals had done
no harm to anyone exept themselves and had not been
involved in any corruption. Should these men have been
convicted? What is your view?

Measuring Crime

Methods of Estimating Crime Rates

There are several sources of information about the
prevalence of crime but none of them is wholly accurate. The
data used by criminologists derives from three main sources:

- statistical records compiled by the police and criminal
  justice agencies
- large-scale surveys commissioned by the government
- small-scale surveys conducted by academic and other
  researchers.

We will concentrate on the first two of these.

Police Recording of Crime

The Home Office publication *Criminal Statistics* presents a record of the number and types of crime recorded by the police in England and Wales. Offences included in the recorded crime statistics cover a wide range of crimes, from homicides to minor theft and criminal damage.

These statistics show a marked change in the crime rate over time. From the first records in 1876 to the 1930s, the crime rate was relatively unchanged but then the picture altered dramatically. There was a significant rise from the 1930 up to the 1950s and an even more rapid rise thereafter. The annual figure for recorded crime was around 500,000 in the 1950s, which doubled in the next ten years to 1 million by the mid-1960s, doubled yet again to 2 million by the mid-1970s, and had reached more than 5.5 million by 1998. There has therefore been an eleven-fold increase in crime rates in England and Wales between 1950 and 1988.

Over the last eight years for which records are available (1992–2000) there has actually been a steady but relatively small fall in each years, the longest sustained fall since records began in 1876. Despite this, the underlying trend has been predominantly upwards; this underlying trend is reflected in the fact that the number of notifiable offences per 100,000 of the population has risen from 5,200 in 1978 to 9,800 in 1998/99, a rise of 65 percent.

Crime statistics do not simply provide information on the variety and number of crimes that are committed, they also consider who the criminals and victims are. This data can be quite provocative for, as Maguire (1994) reports, many of our stereotypes of who constitutes a criminal are inaccurate. He points out that:

> "criminal behaviour is not the near-monopoly of poor and deprived young males. For example, the sexual abuse of children, domestic violence, football hooliganism, workplace theft and drug offences have all been shown to be committed by people from a wide range of age groups and social classes ... while a series of major

frauds ... have demonstrated for all to see that criminals are to be found in suites as well as on the streets."

Official crime statistics provide on important source of information on recorded crime but these greatly underestimate the amount of crime because many crimes go unreported. There are several reasons for this. People may consider the offence too trivial; they may doubt that the police can be anything about it; they may prefer to deal with the matter personally or not recognise the act as criminal. Some crimes such as vandalism and tax fraud have no responsive victim to report them. Yet other crimes such as drug dealing and soliciting have willing victims who indeed may be in trouble if they did report the crime. Even when crimes are reported they need not necessarily be recorded by the police, who may consider them too trivial to warrant intervention, for example, some minor domestic disputes.

In addition to this, some crimes are more likely to be reported than others; in general it is the more serious crimes that are reported but there are other considerations. For example, car theft is more often reported than theft of other property, because of insurance implications. Trends in the particular crimes reported may change over time. Rape, for example, is more likely to be reported now than it once was because of changing attitudes of both the police and the general public to victims of such an offence. Hence figures for rape have shown a relatively large increase, not all of which necessarily reflects an increase in actual rape.

It is worth noting that despite the fact that these crime figures should be treated with caution, they act as the main picture of crime used by politicians and highlighted in the media. They are also used in strategic planning by the Home Office and police forces.

Survey Information

The amount of unknown crime has traditionally been referred to as the 'Dark Figure,' and in order to reach an estimate of the extent of this, other sources of information are used. One of the most important of these is the British Crime Survey (BCS), a survey conducted every two years of adults (people over the age of 16) in private households about their experiences of victimisation in the previous year. The main purpose of the survey is to give estimates of the extent of household and personal crime in England and Wales and to compare these with official statistics in order to gauge the extent of unreported and unrecorded crimes. In addition, it also provides important information about attitudes to crime and punishment. As with all surveys, this is likely not to be wholly accurate. Variables that can result in bias are:

- the characteristics of the interviewer and how he or she is perceived by the interviewee
- the way in which the interview is conducted and the level of educational attainment of the respondent.

In addition, just as with official statistics, there are victimless crimes, which will not therefore be reported. Despite these limitations, surveys are still important sources of information about crime rates and attitudes to crime.

The BCS provides information on the amount of crime and concern about crime. When conducting the BCS, respondents are first asked whether they or anyone else in their household has been the victim of any of a series of crimes, each described in everyday language, since the beginning of the previous year. If the answer is 'yes' then a detailed interview is conducted.

2

The Control of Crime

The criminal justice system has many punishments at its disposal. It can sentence offenders to a period of imprisonment or it can use more lenient deterrents such as suspended sentence, a period of probation, community service or a fine. Imprisonment is a very serious penalty, which is costly for the state and extremely disruptive not only to the lives of the offenders themselves but also to the lives of their families. It is used because, besides protecting the public, it is considered to be the ultimate deterrent. But is it? In this chapter, we will consider the effects of both custodial sentences and some non-custodial sentences and assess their relative effectiveness.

Once offenders are imprisoned some of them will be part of a treatment programme aimed at improving their immediate behaviour and reducing the chances of them reoffending. Behaviour modification, social skills training and anger management are the ones we will describe and assess.

Outside the prison, there are many people and agencies working to reduce or prevent crime. The crime rate in New York in the 1980s was escalating at such a rate that the extreme policy of 'zero tolerance' was adopted. Did this policy of clamping down on every petty crime pay off and, if so, were there any significant side effects ? Would it be appropriate to adopt such a policy elsewhere, including

Britain? We will consider these questions and then assess
the effects that the architecture of buildings can have on the
crime rate. Could the design of housing estates and high-rise
apartments really increase or decrease the opportunity for
crime and if so, how ? Let's see.

The Effect of Custodial and Non-Custodial Sentencing
Non-Custodial Punishments
Fines

The levy of a financial penalty, known as a fine, is the
most frequently used punishment, with a million being levied
in 1995 (Home Office, *Criminal Statistics*). There are several
advantages of using fines rather than other punishments,
as suggested by Caldwell.
- they are relatively economical to administer
- they are a source of income for the state; some of this
  can be used to compensate victims
- they do not prevent the offender from earning a living
  or caring for dependants
- they do not stigmatise the offender or disrupt family
  life
- the offender is not exposed to the possible
  criminalising influence of prisons
- they are an effective deterrent both to the offender
  and to the rest of the population
- they are flexible—they can be adjusted to suit the
  offender's ability to pay.

There are a few disadvantages that include :
- the opportunity for others to take on the
  punishment—fines can be paid by family or friends,
  so they may not acts as a deterrent
- if fines are used to punish regular offenders such as
  drug addicts or prostitutes, they have no reforming
  effect
- often the amount levied is not enough to deter people
  from criminal acts that involve a financial gain, such
  as drug dealing.

Fines have been found to be more effective than either probation or imprisonment for first offenders and even for a considerable number of recidivists. However, there is always the possibility that if they were used more widely as an alternative to prison, then the crime rate would increase because offenders would remain in the community, free to reoffend.

Probation

Probation is the main type of community penalty and involves the suspension of sentence while the offender is still under the control of the courts and is supervised by a probation offenders under surveillance and providing them with help, although the exact aims and objectives have always remained ambiguous and vague. The probation service has traditionally been viewed as the 'decent, caring, face of the criminal justice system' whose significance, Mair argues, is underestimated by researchers and the general public, yet it serves a vital role. It deals with far more offenders than the prison system does (almost twice as many in 1995) and is far less expensive than a custodial sentence. Besides its relatively low cost, probation has the advantages of not exposing the offender to the criminalising influences of prison or removing his or her ability to earn a living and care for the family.

One of the most significant in the development of the probation service was the massive rise in crime from the 1950s onwards and the consequent rise in the prison population which led to serious overcrowding. By the mid-1970s the idea of keeping offenders out of prison was seen as a major objective of the work of the probation service.

In 1996 the Home Office laid out a three-year plan listing its main responsibilities, some of which were :

- to implement community sentences passed by the courts
- to design, provide and promote effective programmes for supervising offenders safely in the community
- to help the communities prevent crime and reduce its effects on victims.

The original idea behind the probation service was that each individual probation officer should be responsible for a certain number of offenders to whom they would offer supervision and help, often in the form of a specific treatment programme. This ethos changed somewhat in the late 1970s when the emphasis shifted to the probation service becoming involved in community-based crime prevention initiatives. The probation service was now seen as a service that should be working in high-crime communities, offering social intervention in such areas as housing and employment.

The effectiveness of any punishment is very difficult to assess and is usually done with reference to reconviction rates. Lloyd *et al.* compared these for prison, straight probation orders and community service orders. They concluded that there was little to choose between these sentencing options in terms of their impact on reoffending. Mair, commenting on this research notes that 'it may be worth emphasising that one conclusion which is certainly not sustainable is that prison is more effective than community penalties in terms of reconviction rates.'

Imprisonment
Goals of imprisonment
There are four main functions that prisons serve:
1. incapacitation
2. rehabilitation
3. punishment
4. deterrence.

The *incapacitation* of certain prisoners, especially those guilty of serious violent offences, is obviously essential in order to protect other members of the public. There are groups of criminals, however, from whom the public does not need protection, for example, those who get into debt or do not buy a television licence. Heavy reliance on imprisonment as a punishment is very expensive and liable to lead to problems of overcrowding. It also removes or seriously reduces the opportunity for criminals to find worthwhile employment both for the duration of the sentence and thereafter. Since only 8–10 percent of criminals commit around 50 percent of all crimes, it makes sense to operate a system of selective incarceration, concentrating mainly on high-rate and dangerous offenders. However, it is not always easy to predict who these will be and the selection of such people for incarceration raises problems of justice and fairness in sentencing.

The *rehabilitation* of prisoners entails the use of education, training and treatment to restore them to a useful life in the 'outside world.' The extent to which this is a desirable or practical aim is controversial. In the next section of this chapter, we will take a look at three methods of treatment and consider the extent to which they are effective. It's worth nothing that a minority think that prison should not be concerned with attempting to change prisoners and should concentrate mainly on incapacitation and deterrence.

The functions of *punishment* and *deterrence* are inextricably linked. Punishment has always been assumed to be an effective deterrent in all walks of life, no less so in prison than elsewhere. The fear and threat of punishment can act as a deterrent to offending in the first place; an example with which most of us are familiar is the sign in shops warning that 'shoplifters are always prosecuted'. Punishment is also believed to deter criminals from reoffending and to deter the public in general from embarking on a life of crime. However, the very high recidivism rates among ex-prisoners appear to suggest that they are 'schools for crime' rather than effective deterrents, but it seems reasonable to suppose that the threat of punishment does prevent a significant number of people from breaking the law in the first place.

The Psychological Effects of Imprisonment

Bartol comments that 'clinical case studies on the effects of prison life have often concluded, that, for many individuals, imprisonment can be brutal, demeaning and generally devastating.'

It is, however, very difficult to generalise about the effects that imprisonment may have on psychological functioning. Firstly, there are considerable individual differences in the way people adjust. Secondly, few controlled longitudinal studies have been conducted. Thirdly, different prisons have very different regimes so there is bound to be a wide variation in effects. Fourthly, both the different length of sentence and the reason for incarceration are likely to have an effect on individual reactions.

A common initial reaction to imprisonment is, perhaps unsurprisingly, one of depression but many offenders soon adjust. Bukshel & Kilmann report that symptoms of stress such as sleeplessness, restlessness and anxiety tend to occur at the beginning of the sentence when initial adjustments are being made and towards the end when inmates are perhaps becoming concerned about how they will cope with life outside the institution.

Some researchers report very serious effects on the mental health of prisoners, mainly those convicted of serious violent crimes. For example, Heather reported psychotic symptoms in a fifth of prisoners sentenced to life. It is not easy to ascertain whether some of these symptoms are related more to the crime than to imprisonment itself. Kruppa argues that perpetrators of serious crime may experience post-traumatic stress disorder, showing symptoms like flashbacks to the crime and severe depression.

Suicide in jail is unfortunately not uncommon and is an increasing problem; the rate doubled between 1972 and 1987 in England and Wales. Most at risk are young single men during the first 24 hours of confinement. Self-mutilation is another serious problem; Newton reports that 86 percent of a group of female delinquents in a training school cut themselves, apparently as a way of becoming part of the inmate culture.

Zamble & Porporino concluded from their study of Canadian prisoners that very few suffered permanent harm but there was little if any positive behavioural change. Many of the prisoners had led problematic and unstable lives prior

to conviction and having to adjust to loss of freedom and
other aspects of prison life was yet another hurdle with which
they had to cope. Once free, they simply returned to their old
ways of surviving.

One aspect of prison life which some inmates have to
endure and which can cause particular problems is
crowding. It can result in physical illness, socially disruptive
behaviour and emotional distress, especially in women's
prisons. Psychological studies in everyday situations have
shown that in crowded conditions it is lack of privacy and
control that are liable to produce dissatisfaction, not
necessarily the amount of space available. If you can put a
curtain around your bed to shield yourself from the gaze of
others then the psychological effects of being 'cooped up' are
not so bad. The same applies in prison. When inmates are
provided with the means of obtaining some privacy and a
place to put personal possessions then some of the negative
effects of crowding are diminished. This, of course, does not
ameliorate all of the unpleasant effects of crowding, which
include lack of control over social interaction and too much
stimulation in terms of activity, noise, smelliness and
violations of personal space.

Effectiveness of Prisons

Some research evidence indicates that for many
offenders a period of probation is likely to be as effective in
preventing reoffending as a custodial sentence. Glaser
reviewed the evidence and concluded that supervision in the
community is better for new offenders since prison often
encourages and reinforces criminal behaviour. This is
particularly true for 'low risk' offenders, especially those who
are not only in the early stages of offending but have good
job prospects and/or are in stable relationships. On the other
hand, a term of imprisonment was more effective in reducing
recidivism in habitual offenders.

With respect to the length of sentence, evidence indicates
that longer prison terms are no more effective in reducing
reconviction rates than shorter ones. However, this may again

depend on the type of prisoner. Walker & Farrington found that the length of sentence made little difference to rates of reoffending among habitual offenders, more than 85 percent of whom go on to commit further crimes. Many researchers argue that a minimum amount of intervention has the greatest effect, especially for first offenders. For example, Klein *et al.*, found that cautions were a more effective deterrent than arrests, which were in turn more effective than taking the accused to court.

Davies & Raymond, both members of the judiciary, are highly critical of imprisonment as a means of fulfilling most of the four goals discussed earlier. They do not believe that longer jail sentences deter others and that they are often imposed as a result of public demand and political expediency rather than as a means of reducing crime. Nor, they argues, does the prospect of imprisonment act as a serious deterrent to a large number of people. For example, it is unlikely to deter those who commit crimes whilst under the influence of alcohol or drugs, or who steal to obtain money to support an addiction or who commit 'crimes of passion' when they have lost emotional control. Most studies indicate that when offenders do make rational choices, they weigh up the risk of being caught rather than the sentence they may receive. Davies & Raymond argue that the evidence that imprisonment achieves any goal except punishment is so unconvincing that it should only be used as a last resort not, as it is in many countries, as an increasingly popular means of coping with crime.

Horrors Grow in Britain's Violent Jails

The teenager looked the prison governor in the eye. Jailed for a series of petty crimes, he was due to be released the following day. But he was not a reformed character. Nor was he scared of the governor.

"I get out tomorrow,' the youth calmly informed Danny McAllister, who took charge of the Brinsford Young Offenders' Institution, regarded as the most violent jail in Britain, last April. 'Before I go,' the

inmate added, 'I'm going to smash up my cell. And there's nothing you can do."

McAllister told the story last week to illustrate his extreme frustration. 'This young man went off and did just what he said he would. And he was right; there was nothing I could do.'

Last week McAllister was praised for his attempts to turn Brinsford around in an otherwise damning report from Chief Inspector of Prisons Sir David Ramsbotham. But the admits he is swimming against a tide of drug-fuelled violence and the total breakdown of respect for authority.

'We are not dealing with a cross-section of society here,' Ramsbotham said. 'This is a distillation of young men in crisis who have been failed by family, schools and the community. It is very strong stuff.'

For and Against the Use of Custodial Sentencing

+ It protect society form criminals since the opportunities of reoffend are extremely limited while in jail.
+. It acts as a deterrent to others who may be contemplating breaking the law.
+ In the better prisons, it provides opportunities for rehabilitation.
- It may simply act as a training ground for young offenders to learn more about how to commit serious crimes.
- It may have serious deleterious effects on the mental health of those who are imprisoned.
- Some members of the judiciary argue that jail sentences are often imposed to appease public opinion and that they do not act as a deterrent.

Some Therapies Used for Treatment of Offenders
Behaviour modification

The principles of learning have not only been used in the laboratory but have also been applied in many real-life settings, such as the classroom, mental hospital and prison.

The use of operant conditioning in such real-world settings is called behaviour modification, also known as behaviour therapy.

Many behaviour modification programmes rely on a technique called the *token economy,* in which desirable behaviour, such as co-operation and compliance, is reinforced by the use of tokens. These tokens have no intrinsic value but can be exchanged for primary reinforcers. When used in prisons, most of the programmes also involve the use of negative reinforcement and punishment in order to reduce undesirable behaviour such as non-compliance and aggression. Typical negative reinforcers would be removal of privileges, such as watching television or going into the exercise yard, while a typical punishment would be isolation.

Token economy programmes tend to have a direct, short-term effect on specific behaviours. For example, Hobbs & Holt recorded the effects of introducing a token economy to young delinquents across three small institutional units while the fourth unit acted as a control. Tokens were given for behaviours such as obeying rules, doing chores properly, co-operative social interactions and appropriate behaviour when queuing for meals. Extra positive reinforcers such as soft drinks, sweets, leisure activities, cigarettes and passes home were also used. The programmes showed a significant increase in the targeted behaviours compared to the group not involved in the programme. Other studies show that token reinforcement also works with adult prisoners. However, Ross & Mackay reported a deterioration in behaviour when such a programme was used delinquent girls, but such results are unusual.

Although these programmes are popular, especially in the US, not many of them have been evaluated in terms of the conduct of the offenders after release. Moyes *et al.*, reported limited success with hospitalised behaviourally disordered males and females with a criminal history. After a year they had fewer contacts with the police than a control group of similar patients, but after two years there was no difference. One long-term follow-up failed to find any benefit at all of the token economy programme.

The advantages of behaviour modification are that :

- It is successful in changing specific behaviours under controlled conditions.
- It requires little training and can be done by paraprofessionals.
- It is economical.
- It quickly controls unmanageable behaviour.
- It can be easily evaluated and researched.

However, there are several problems and limitations with its use:

- It requires a high degree of commitment from everyone who is evenly remotely involved in the programme.
- Although relatively simple to operate in controlled conditions, it is extremely difficult in an actual prison. There are many other sources of reinforcement and punishment, such as approval of other prisoners or threats by them.
- Its effects have not convincingly been shown to generalise from institutions of life in the real world.

Perhaps the most important concern with behaviour modification is its potential for violation of civil rights. Many programmes rely heavily on negative reinforcement (such as the removal of privileges until the offenders complies) rather than positive ones, with little or no emphasis on new skills. There are ethical objections to prisoners having to 'earn' basic rights, such as recreation time, by behaving compliantly.

Opinion on the use of behaviour modification is sharply divided. Some researchers argue that offenders need to feel responsible for their treatment, not have it imposed on them. Others maintain that such programmes make the whole prison environment more bearable and humane for all concerned; after all, the behaviours that are targeted for reduction are those that hurt others and make life unpleasant in the institution.

Social Skills Training

Social skills are those skills such as making eye contact, standing a certain distance from someone and turn-taking during conversation which make social interactions run smoothly. We learn them as children and take them for granted as adults. If we do not have skills or if we use them clumsily, we make others and ourselves feel extremely uncomfortable, as anyone who has tried to have a conversation with an individual who makes no eye contact or stands too close is all too well aware. Many offenders are believed to be lacking in these skills and social skills training is a technique at improving the competence of offenders in dealing with social interactions. The programmes are based on the assumptions that being deficient in these skills is associated with offending and that acquiring such skills will reduce rates of reoffending. Neither of these assumptions has gone unchallenged.

Social Skills Training (SST) is one of a number of cognitive-behavioural programmes which are all based on the principle that attitude and thoughts (cognitions) affect behaviour. There is a variety of SST programmes, all of which have certain common elements clients are first taught the skills by a combination of modelling, instruction role play and rehearsal. They then attempt to re-enact these skills themselves in various arranged situations and receive feedback on their performance, the emphasis being on the use of social reinforcement such as praise. They are also given homework assignments which aim to help them practise and consolidate the skills they have learned in various situations, including real-life ones for those who are not incarcerated.

Some programmes start by teaching certain non-verbal skills, knows as micro-skills, such as eye contact, gesture and posture and then move on to all-round skills such as how to maintain a good conversation, how to interact with members of the opposite sex or how to negotiate. The type of situation that might be practised is how to enter a room full of strangers, how to return faulty goods to a shop, how to politely decline getting involved in a drinking binge when you've already had enough, and how to say what you want to say without being embarrassed and 'tongue-tied.'

Results of SST

Feedback from social skills training programmes is mixed. Goldstein reviewed 30 studies of SST used with aggressive or delinquent teenagers and found that various skills such as the use of appropriate eye contact and how to negotiate with a probation officer had been learned. However, Goldstein *et.al.*, found that only 15–20 percent of trainees could use the skills they had learned during training in a more real-life situation. These researchers did, however, manage to increase this to 50 percent by providing additional teaching.

Some other programmes report improved self-esteem and a felling of greater control over life (a shift to a more internal locus of control). However, in this programme, individuals in a control group who received no training but spent an equal amount of time discussing their problems showed an equivalent improvement in self-esteem, so perhaps attention alone is the key to improvement. With respect to locus of control, Hollin *et al.*, (1996) found no change in individuals to whom they gave SST.

Rates of recidivism (reconviction) are a more long-term measure of effectiveness of SST. When the offending records of individuals in the Spence & Marziller programme were examined six months later the SST group did have a lower level of conviction, but when asked about offending this group reported having committed more offences. There is evidence that both the appearance of a suspect and their general demeanour (bearing and expression), including the amount of respect shown, can affect whether an adolescent is detained by the police for questioning SST. In this case, it may be that the lads trained in SST were better at talking to the police and therefore less likely to be arrested.

There have been very few studies that have investigated the effects of SST on recidivism. Hollin has made two important points in this respect. Firstly, there simply is no research to show whether or not lack of social skills is associated with offending and secondly, in some SST programmes, there has been no evidence that the participants who received it were actually lacking in the skills in the first place.

It seems reasonable to conclude that short-term changes in social behaviour can be achieved with SST, but it has yet to be shown that they are either long-lasting or that they can be generalised to real-life situations. As Blackburn suggests, it may be a useful programmes for offenders who have very serious social difficulties, but 'the available evidence does not warrant routine use of SST in correctional settings'. Hollin also comments that SST alone is unlikely to be a cure for crime but it can be a powerful means of personal change.

Anger Management

Anger management programmes are based on the idea that anger is a primary cause of violent criminal acts and once offenders can learn to control this anger, bad behaviour in prisons will decrease, as will rates of recidivism. Anger management is a cognitive-behavioural approach, which originated in North America in the mid-1970s. Its aim was to teach individuals how to apply self-control in order to reduce interpersonal anger, with the long-term goal of reducing disruptive behaviour.

There is a variety of such programmes which are run in many prisons as well as in other settings. One anger management programme used in Britain is outlined below.

The National Anger Management Package

Keen provides an example of the preparation and delivery of an anger management course within a young offender institution, conducted with young male offenders aged between 17 and 21 years. The programme, first devised in 1992 and updated in 1995, was developed by the Prison Service in England and Wales and is known as the National Anger Management Package.

The aims of the course are as follows :
- to increase course members' awareness of the process by which they become angry
- to raise course members' awareness of the need to monitor their behaviour
- to educate course members in the benefits of controlling their anger
- to improve techniques of anger management
- to allow course members to practise anger management during role plays.

The course involves eight two-hour sessions, the first seven over a 2–3 week period, with the last session a month afterwards. The details of the course are as follows.

Keen's experiences of using the course are generally positive, though there are various predictable problems with young incarcerated males, such as failure to bring the anger diary to sessions, grins and sniggers at the mention of 'bodily arousal' and a certain degree of egocentrism which can make relationships and progress in the group a little difficult at times. Overall, though, the feedback from the individuals completing the course indicates that they have increased their awareness of their anger management difficulties and have increased their capacity to exercise self-control.

Results of Anger Management Programmes

With the increasing use of anger control programmes in prisons, it is crucial to determine its effectiveness. Studies of effectiveness are few, and the results range from very limited to substantial. On the negative side, Law reported that only one individual who completed an eight-session course showed any improvement. In contrast, Hunter reported considerable improvements in certain specific areas, such as a reduction in impulsiveness, depression and interpersonal problems. The effectiveness of programmes in producing these short-term benefits in show in Research Now.

Do Anger Management Courses Work?

Aim : To assess the effectiveness of a brief group-based anger-management programme with a sample of male young offenders.

Method : A quasi-experimental design was used in which there were two comparisons made :
- pre- and post-programme scores for a 'treatment' (experimental) group
- two scores taken at the same interval for the 'awaiting treatment' (control) group.

The design : This is a quasi-experimental design because the two groups are not equivalent. In real-world research it is not possible to randomly assign individuals to each group. It would have been possible to carry research using the experimental group only, comparing pre- and post-programmes scores but the control group gives the design extra experimental rigour.

The participants : The experimental group consisted of 50 prisoners who had completed the anger management course. The control group consisted of 37 prisoners who had been assessed as suitable for the course but had not yet completed it. The two groups did not differ significantly in terms of age, offence and level of angry behaviours reported prior to completing the course.

The programme : The anger management used in this study was an adapted version of the national package which was developed in the UK by Clark (1988). It includes 12 one-hour sessions run over a three-day period.

Measures used to assess prisoners on suitability for the course : There were two measures:
1. A cognitive-behavioural interview. This consisted of various questions concerned with how often they lost their temper, what provoked this temper loss and what happened when it occurred.
2. Wing Behavioural checklist (WBC)—a checklist completed by prison officers concerning 29 different

angry behaviours with scores of 0, 1 or 2 for how often any particular prisoner had shown them in the previous week.

3. A third measure, the Anger Management Assessment questionnaire (AMA), which was a self-report questionnaire completed by the prisoners, consisted of 53 items which could indicate an anger problem.

All prisoners in the study had been deemed suitable for the course on the basis of these measures.

Pre-and post-test measures : Pre-test scores were obtained for both groups of participants two weeks before the start of the course and eight weeks later (after course completion for the experimental group and while the control group remained on the waiting list).

Results

Wing-based measures : There was a significant reduction in wing-based angry behaviours in the experimental group but no difference in the control group.

AMA: The experimental group scored significantly lower on self-reported angry behaviours after completion of the course. There was no difference for the control group.

Overall, 92 percent of the prisoners in the experimental group showed improvement on at least one measure; 48 percent showed improvement on both the AMA and WBC; 8 percent showed a deterioration on both measures after completing the course.

Conclusion : Short-term measures indicate that this programme was a success and significantly reduced the disruptive behaviour of these offenders in the prison. Future research could usefully be directed at assessing the characteristics of the 8 percent who showed no improvement. There is also a need for future research aimed at long-term evaluation of such interventions.

Evaluation of Anger Management Programmes

The effectiveness of anger management programmes to

reduce recidivism in violent offenders is called into question by several researchers. Although it may seem common sense to propose that anger is a serious problem among those convicted of violent crimes such as assault, researchers disagree about whether there is a link between anger and violent crime. For example, while Zamble & Quinsey argue in favour of such a relationship and propose that uncontrolled anger is a risk factor in predicting violence and recidivism, others dispute it.

Prominent amongst those who do not believe that anger is a primary cause of violent criminal acts are Loza & Loza-Fanous. They argue that many of the research findings linking anger with violence and rape were based on laboratory studies using students or offenders' own explanations of their violent acts. In fact they maintain that

"Unfortunately, most of the opinions supposing a link between anger and violent behaviour, rape, or recidivism are based on speculations with very little empirical support such as results of valid and reliable psychometrics."

They studied 271 Canadian male offenders, comparing a group of violent offenders with non-violent ones and a group of rapists with non-rapists. Violent offenders were those who had committed crimes such as murder, assault and robbery with violence. The non-violent offenders had a history of moderate or minor offences such as fraud or property offences. Using several psychometric measures of anger, they found no difference between violent offenders and non-violent offenders and between rapists and non-rapists on anger measures. Loza & Loza-Fanous argue that not only are anger treatment programmes ineffective with violent offenders, they have the potential to be harmful by encouraging the offender to attribute his violent actions to anger for which he cannot be blamed, rather than taking full responsibility for his actions.

Anger management programmes have, as we have seen, proved to be useful in controlling aggressive antisocial behaviour in prisons, but there needs to more research into the relationship between anger and crime before an assessment of its use and effectiveness in reducing rates of recidivism amongst violent criminals can be made.

Anger Management as an Effective Treatment for Criminal behaviour

- Some research shows that these programmes are an effective means of reducing antisocial behaviour in prisons.
- The programmes may provide criminals with greater insight into the causes of their behaviour offer alternative ways of responding to provocation.
- Some researchers that there is no link between anger and violent crime, which is often done in a cold, calculated manner.
- There is a lack of research into whether or not these programmes have any long-term benefits in preventing recidivism.

Zero Tolerance

One method by which crime has been tackled is the use of a policy known as zero tolerance. Zero tolerance policing has its roots in an approach nicknamed 'broken windows,' developed by Kelling & Wilson in 1982. They argued that if one broken window was not repaired in a building, then others would be broken and the building vandalised, followed by other buildings, then the street and the neighbourhood. The area would soon go into rapid decay and act as a breeding ground for serious crime such as drug dealing and prostitution. This would lead to a downward spiral in which respectable law-abiding citizens would leave the area and crime rates would escalate. An unrepaired window is a sign that no one cares and therefore more damage will occur.

The original idea behind broken windows was that there should more police 'on the beat,' who negotiated acceptable public behaviour and worked with the neighbourhood to maintain a decent standard of behaviour. However, since this thesis was first proposed, zero tolerance policing has become a much more punitive policy, based on cracking down on minor offences such as offensive language, loitering and begging, in the belief that this will help reduce more serious crimes as well.

The term 'zero tolerance' eventually was applied to other areas of public policy, some of which were concerned not so much with policing as with changing attitudes. One such policy was a campaign against domestic violence, sexual assault and child abuse in various countries including Britain.

We will take a look two programmes based on zero tolerance: the first one is campaign in New York to reduce the very high crime rates by a severe clampdown on all crime; the second is a community-based project designed to prevent violence against women.

Zero Tolerance in New York
The Argument in Favour

By the late 1980s and early 1990s, New York had the unenviable reputation of being one of the most crime-ridden cities in the world. William Bratton, who eventually became Police Commissioner of the City of New York, describes his experiences in arriving in New York in 1990:

"I remember driving from LaGuardia Airport down the highway into Manhattan. Graffiti, burned out cars and trash seemed to be everywhere. It looked like something out of a futuristic movie. Then as you entered Manhattan, you met the unofficial greeter for the City of New York, the Squeegee pest. Welcome to New York City. This guy had a dirty rag or squeegee and would wash your window with some dirty liquid and ask for or demand money. Proceeding down Fifth Avenue, the mile of designer stores and famous buildings, unlicensed street peddlers and beggars everywhere. Then down into the subway where every day over 200,000 fare evaders jumped over or under turnstyles while shakedown artists vandalised

*turnstyles, and demanded that paying passengers
hand over their tokens to them. Beggars were on every
train. Every platform seemed to have a cardboard city
where the homeless had taken up residence. This was
a city that had stopped caring about itself...The City
had lost control."*

Once Bratton had taken up his position in 1994, the
problems were tackled on many fronts. Seven thousand extra
police officers had been employed since 1990 and a
programmes of clear-cut goals and priorities was begun. In
addition to serious crime, particular attention was to be paid
to actions that interfere with quality of life (such as public
drinking), graffiti and other minor street crime. Crime
hotspots were to be identified to which patrol officers,
detectives and narcotics officers were assigned. Twice-weekly
meetings were held at which the Department's top executives
were called to account for the previous month's crime statistics
and asked about plans for the following month.

In three years the city's crime rate dropped by 37 percent
and the homicide rate by over 50 percent. In answer to critics
who suggested that crime rates were somehow massaged,
Bratton responded by pointing particularly to the figures for
homicide which is a crime that cannot easily be covered up or
over-reported. He believes that this approach, involving as it
does decentralisation and co-ordination, is a successful way of
policing, as borne out not only by the crime statistics but also
by the fact that New Yorkers now feel safer and the city is
slowly revitalising itself. Long-term problems still exist but the
foundations for dealing with them have been firmly laid.

The Argument Against : Short-term Fix, Long-term Liability?

Pollard, the Chief Constable of Thames Valley Police,
urges caution in the use of the policy of zero tolerance. He
argues that the crime reduction in New York is not necessarily
a direct result of this policy, since crime has fallen elsewhere
in America, including cities such as San Diego in which the
approach is very different. The success in New York, he

maintains, may be due in no small part to an extra 7,000 police officers (a huge increase), greater accountability and an enormous pressure to reduce crime such that(the rates would have fallen regardless of the particular policy adopted.

Pollard describes zero tolerance as being aggressive, uncompromising law enforcement based on ruthlessness in cracking down on low-level crime and disorderliness, including acts which are not, strictly speaking criminal, such as drinking but not being drunk, and vagrancy that involves lying on the edge of a pavement but not blocking pedestrian access. More worryingly, it may involve the harassment of the mentally disturbed who are doing nothing other than causing discomfort in others by their strange behaviour. It is interesting to note that whilst Pollard describes zero tolerance as based on heavyhanded aggressive tactics Dennis describes it as 'humane, good-natured control.'

While not disagreeing at all with the philosophy behind the 'broken windows' approach, Pollard argues that this theory was based on a solution to crime that includes a wide variety of tactics, with the police working in close co-operation with other social agencies, rather than a quick, uncompromising response to petty crime and disorder. Without this the policy creates an atmosphere of distrust between the police and public which destroy any opportunity for future effective policing. 'Going in heavy' provides a short-term fix at the expense of a long-term solution and can become positively counter-productive. As Pollard says, once this policy has been operational for sometime,

> "It may then be too late. Firstly, the police will have lost touch with the community. Confidence will have drained away. Tensions will have risen. It will then need only a spark to ignite serious disorder, as happened in Los Angles following the Rodney King case. We know about these in England too. They happened in our own inner cities in the 1980s, and we have learned hard lesson of our own."

Pollard points out that decay and disorderliness in a eighbourhood have many causes and these need to be tackled in a co-ordinated way, not just by papering over the cracks. This can only be done if the police work in close co-operation with many other agencies, such as with the refuse collection service so that the area is tidy, with the education and youth departments, with social services and the probation department, to name but a few. In this way it is not just the physical environment that is attended to but other problems as well such as lack of amenities for the young, design of buildings that encourage crime (such as those described in the next section) and the failure of public services. Such a policy tackles the root causes of crime and disorder rather than offering a superficial solution.

It is very difficult to make objective judgements on the success of any policy because each era and area is different. Comparisons between America and Britain are especially difficult not least because of the gun culture in the States which does not exist in Britain. With respect to New York, this is a unique city—Pollard himself acknowledges that Bratton was faced with a crisis that required drastic action and that he should be congratulated on his success. He does, however, urge great caution in assuming that a policy of zero tolerance would necessarily be the best policy elsewhere.

Zero Tolerance Applied to Violence Against Women

The first UK project based on zero tolerance was launched by Edinburgh City Council in November 1992 and run by the Zero Tolerance Charitable Trust (ZTCT). This ongoing campaign aims to highlight the prevalence and nature of male violence towards women and to challenge some of the attitudes that made it appear acceptable.

The need to change attitudes was revealed in research undertaken by the Trust. They interviewed over, 2,000 young people aged between 14 and 21 years in Glasgow, Fife and Manchester. The results were quite shocking. Half of the boys and a third of the girls thought there were

some circumstances in which it was acceptable to hit a
woman or force her to have sex. Over a third of boys (36
percent) thought they might use violence in future
relationships and both boys and girls thought that forced
sex was more acceptable than hitting. Over half of the
young people interviewed knew someone who had been hit
by a male partner and exactly half knew someone who
had been sexually abused. Group discussions revealed that
although hitting women was considered 'unmanly' and
'cowardly,' it was seen as okay to hit your wife if she
nagged; one young man commented that 'Some women just
need a slap to the jaw and put into the bedroom to calm
down.' It is interesting to note that the young people who
took part in these focus group discussions welcomed the
opportunity to express their opinions and discuss issues in
depth, rather than simply being told that certain types of
behaviour are wrong.

The Trust tackles the problem of male violence to women
on many fronts. It lobbies the Government, commissions,
research and develops educational intervention and training
programmes. It has initiated a three-year advertising
campaign to raise awareness and change attitudes, including
a series of television advertisements, which began in
December 2000. It also provides quality practical support for
abused women and children.

One such programme targeted at school children and
started in January 2001 in known as *Respect*. It involves the
development of primary and secondary curriculum materials,
support materials for teachers and youth workers and a
publicity campaign involving school posters and bus side
advertising. The idea is to prevent violence before it happens.
It encourages boys and girls to develop healthy relationships
based on equality and mutual respect, and emphasises that
violence against women is unacceptable in any context and
should not be tolerated.

At present it is too early to evaluate the effect of
Respect, but it appears to be a very necessary and positive
step on the road both to educating youngsters and to

encouraging a healthier, more positive and happy attitude not only to women but to relationships in general.

Environmental Crime Prevention
The Work of Jane Jacobs

In 1961 Jane Jacobs, an architectural journalist, published a book which changed the focus of criminology from a view that placed the blame on the disposition of the criminal to one that looked at the development of many urban areas as a possible cause of many of the problems involved in crime. In a swingeing attack, Jacobs blamed urban planners for 'making cities unsafe places, where vandals, robbers and other street criminals could ply their unnatural trades without fear of apprehension.' She argued that the more modern parts of many US cities, with their separate zones and physical barriers, encouraged a fortress mentality rather than community spirit. This was in contrast to the older urban quarters in which crime rates remained relatively low because, although they may be 'slum' areas, the narrow streets with lots of doorways in which to stop and talk meant that there was plenty of social interaction; streets and parks were widely and more frequently occupied as places of both work and leisure. She recommended that, in order to reduce crime.

- buildings should be orientated towards the street so that natural surveillance occurred
- there should be a clear demarcation between public and private areas so that the public ones could be protected by paid employees and the private ones valued by their owners
- semi-public outdoor space (such as lawns and play areas) should be located near areas that were easily overlooked so that they were less likely to be vandalised.

Jacobs was at pains to point out that she was not offering a universal panacea to urban crime since, in her opinion, it was essential to address the social ills that lay behind delinquency and crime; however, she did maintain that the design of cities was no small contributor to these problems. Her suggestions for crime prevention were not received by the criminal justice system. This may have been partly due to prejudice. Her ideas were revolutionary and the solutions she offered were more dependent on architects and planners than on the criminal justice system. They were also being proposed by a female 'outsider' to this justice system.

There were, however, some legitimate objections to this work, the main one being that Jacobs may have had a rather romantic notion of pre-modern urban districts as friendly, community-spirited, crime-free areas. There is evidence that rather than reduce crime, increased street activity may well result in more opportunities for it. Furthermore, her ideas were inspirational rather than based on scientific evidence.

Nevertheless, despite its limitations, Jacobs' work offered a very different and previously neglected focus on the causes and prevention of urban crimes.

The Work of Oscar Newman

Rather better received was the work of Oscar Newman who developed Jacobs' idea into his **defensible space theory.** Newman potential out that new high-rise developments went into rapid decay with high rates of residential dissatisfaction. He suggested that this was caused by the design of the housing projects because they offered little opportunity for residents to defend any secondary territory within or around buildings. Newman coined the term *defensible space* to describe the bounded or semi-private areas surrounding living quarters that residents can territorialise so that they appear to belong to someone. Newman pointed out that the design of many urban residential areas, especially those around high-rise apartment buildings, meant that there was a lack of defensible space which tended to encourage vandalism and crime because the residents had such limited opportunity for surveillance or social control and no real sense of ownership or community. Lack of surveillance was caused by several factors.

- Buildings housed large number of people with many entrances, all of which gave access to the whole building. With such frequent pedestrian traffic, residents could not be distinguished from outsiders who could, once in the building, move freely within it using the undefended staircases.
- The areas between the buildings were desolate open spaces with no territorial markings.
- The height of the buildings meant that there were 'corridors' of space between them that could not be overlooked from the windows.

Newman argued that if defensible spaces are created through design, then residents are more likely to feel ownership of them, informally keep surveillance over them and have a sense of social cohesion amongst themselves.

He advanced several recommendations to increase defensible space and thereby reduce crime. These were :

- the use of boundary markers (real or symbolic barriers, such as pathways, small walls or fences) to reduce the likelihood of intrusion so that residents had control over the outside areas adjacent to their homes and over hallways and staircases
- planning which enabled surveillance of these semi-public areas, for example by the strategic placement of windows
- a design which encouraged positive social attitudes and a sense of community such that residents felt that the area was theirs and worth looking after; such housing should not be stigmatised and should not be designed to set off from other types of housing that it was easily identified as housing for the poor
- projects should be sited in low-crime areas.

Support for Newman's theory was drawn from a study in which he looked at crime rates in 100 estates in New York and found that the greater the amount of defensible space, the lower the incidence of crime. Further support was offered by a comparison he made between two adjacent housing estates in New York City, that of Van Dyke and Brownsville. Although Brownsville was eight years older than Van Dyke, it had a far lower crime rate. The design of this development meant that it had a considerable amount of defensible space. It consisted of six X-shaped buildings with some three-story wings and entrances which, being used by a relatively small number of families, were easy to keep an eye on. Anyone approaching an entrance could be seen from any one of a large number of windows. Within the buildings the hallways and stairwells were easily monitored; children played on them and residents often left their doors ajar. This greater defensibility meant that there were strong bonds between the neighbours and a positive attitudes towards the location and the police, as well as maintenance and crime rates. Van Dyke, in contrast, consisted of mostly large 14-story buildings separated by open spaces that provided little or no defensible space. A similar projects, that of Pruitt-Igoe in St. Louis, which was designed to reduce crime and vandalism by incorporating open areas between buildings and vandal-proof fixtures, had become such a ruined wasteland that it had to be demolished.

Further support for Newman's theory comes from a project in Ohio in which a neighbourhood called Five Oaks was split from one large residential area into several small ones by the blocking of certain streets and alleys and the use of speed bumps. Once these 'mini-neighbourhoods' were established, crime rates decreased by 26 percent. However, the use of barriers to separate areas into smaller units and restrict access has been heavily criticised by some groups who see this as a means of restricting the access of poorer people to higher-income areas.

Criticism of Newman's Ideas

Newman's work has provided a commonsense and practical approach to crime prevention but it is not without its critics. The relationship between crime rates and defensible space is only correlational and therefore does not demonstrate cause and effect. Furthermore, as Repetto pointed out, we should be cautious about any theory heavily dependent on a single case study (the comparison between Brownsville and Van Dyke), especially since there were many other housing projects that could have been studied but were not. Other factors may also have neglected in the analysis of crime rates. Mawby, in a study based in Sheffield, found that while business premises based in the lower floors of residential high-rise buildings did indeed suffer from higher crime rates, this was because of greater reporting of crime rather than design features.

Taylor *et al.*, suggest that Newman's model is inadequate because it does not take sufficient account of other social factors—such as the number of families on welfare—which could have contributed to the different crime rates. They contend that sociocultural variables and social conditions, as well as design, determine the level of crime in any neighbourhood. Merry suggests that defensible space is necessary for crime prevention but it is not enough on its own. Even when the architecture of a site lends to defensible spaces these may not be defended if there is a heterogeneous ethnic mix of residents which results in them not intervening in each other's affairs.

Several studies indicate that there are certain social factors which may, at least in some cases, have a greater impact on crime than defensible space does. Wilson found that rates of vandalism are most closely correlated with the number of children living in an area : the more children, the more vandalism.

Newman himself now acknowledges that social variables, such as the percentage of families on welfare benefits, the percentage of single-parent families, the income level and the ratio of teenagers to adults, are more closely related to crime rates than are the design features of the immediate environment. However, even though defensible space may not be the best explanation for crime, it offers a very practical way of improving things.

In Britain

Like America, Britain has had considerable problems with housing projects that were at one time considered to be 'Utopian.' Jephcott & Robinson conducted a large-scale study of high-rise developments in Britain, interviewing nearly 1,000 residents of 168 multistorey blocks. There tended be an equal number of likes and dislikes, with likes being the interiors of the flats and features independent of design such as a good bus service and local amenities. The dislikes, on the other hand, were very much rooted in the design features inherent in high-rise blocks: the lifts, the loneliness and isolation, the entrances, vandalism, noise, poor maintenance and problems of refuse disposal.

Alice Coleman, a defender of Newman's theory, has extended the work on defensible space and points to various design features (namely number of storeys, number of dwellings per entrance, number of dwellings per block, overhead walkways and spatial organisation) which she believes encourage all manner of antisocial behaviour. She maintains that some design features promote child crime by undermining the normal child-rearing practices that operate when residences are separate and do not incorporate shared space. She compared housing estates with blocks of flats (apartments in terms of litter, graffiti, vandal damage, children in care, urine pollution and faecal pollution. The 3,893 houses surveyed showed far less sign of social breakdown than purpose-built flats. Litter was less common, graffiti extremely rare and excrement virtually unheard of. Like those before her, Coleman acknowledges that design is not the only factor in the promotion or prevention of social breakdown but thinks that criminology would do well not to ignore its probably considerable influence.

3
Theories of Criminal Psychology

More specifically, psychology is the study of individual
characteristics or qualities such as personality, reasoning,
thought, intelligence, learning, perception, imagination,
memory and creativity. Psychology is often separated into
two groups of theories or schools of thought: cognitive and
behavioural. Cognitive theories place the study of
psychology in the mind; they see human action as the result
of driving or compelling mental forces or to be the result of
mental reasoning and beliefs. These theories take account
of internal feelings such as anger, frustration, desire and
despair. In fact, all activity is seen as the result of internal
mental processes. In contrast, the behavioural theorists,
whilst taking account of internal factors, place them in a
social context. They see that internal mental processes can
be affected and even altered by certain factors in the
environment which either reinforce or discourage the
behaviour. Clearly there is no strong dividing line between
these two. A degree of overlap is likely, whilst some
psychological theories may not fit neatly into either school.

There are psychologists who place weight on a biological
link in the workings of the mind and link certain types of
behaviour and certain thought processes with, for example,
genetic or neurological factors (some of this research is

sometimes referred to as psychophysiology). Others place so much weight on the environmental factors that they become closer to sociological theories. Either way it is clear that psychological theories should not be studied in a void, but be assessed and balanced in the criminological arena as a whole.

This chapter is concerned with pyschological explanations for the behaviour of those who are generally seen as 'normal', in that they are not suffering from a mental defect. There will be some mention of clinical psychology, which is often thought of as the study of those suffering from mental abnormality, but is also concerned with the study of lesser psychological disturbances and, possibly more importantly, with the treatment of all these mental difficulties. For a fuller and more precise account of general psychology, see an introductory text such as those by Gleitman, Carlson and Gross.

As with the biological theories, most of the ideas in this chapter fall into the positivist school of thought. They therefore explain crime as a result of some factor—in this case mental or behavioural constructs—rather than as a result of choice or free will.

Psychoanalysis and Criminality

A number of different ideas are drawn together under psychoanalysis, but the general stand-point is that inner, dynamic forces are used to explain human behaviour. Psychoanalytical theorists perceive criminal behaviour to be the result of some mental conflict of which the criminal may be virtually unaware (i.e., the conflict arises in the subconscious or unconscious mind). Furthermore, they claim that this conflict is always present as an internal conflict between the demands of reason and conscience, and those of instinct. A 'victory' for instinct can lead to thoughts and deeds which will often be socially unacceptable. Everyone experiences this conflict, but some manage to control the instinct better than others. If the conflict is not resolved in a socially acceptable way, it may be expressed in ways which are criminal. Criminality is then seen as one of the outward signs of the disease, or of the problematic resolution of the mental conflict, just as physical deformity may be the manifestation of a physical disease.

Modern psychoanalysis began with the work of Sigmund Freud. He lived most of his life in Vienna and published most of his famous works between 1900 and 1939. His theories have had a profound effect on many aspects of modern life, on philosophy and literature, for example, and have been widely used to explain human behaviour. Frued did not write a great deal specifically about criminality, but it is possible to see how some of his behavioural theories can be used as explanations of criminality, and later theorists have expanded on these to offer slightly different explanations. Pscyhoanalysis is a complex field, and only a brief introduction to those areas of Frued's writing which are of direct interest to criminology will be offered here. Areas such as those relating to dreams or on the mechanism of transference will be largely excluded, as will suggestions for treatments. There are many detailed texts dealing with Freud's work, for example Kline.

The Constituents of the Personality

Frued split the personality into three parts—the id, the ego, and the super-ego. The id is an unconscious area of the mind; it is the most primitive portion of the personality from which the other two are derived. It is made up of all basic biological urges—to eat, drink, excrete, to be warm and comfortable and to obtain sexual pleasure. It is driven by desire; it is illogical and amoral, and seeks only absolute pleasure at whatever cost. It chracterises the unsocialised and unrestrained individual, and its drives need immediate gratification and have no conception of reality. It is the part of the personality with which one in born. It holds all the desires, even those society considered wrong or bad, and to that extent Freud says it needs to be repressed. The repression or control of the id is carried out by the ego and the super-ego.

The ego does not exist at birth, but is something the individual learns. It is largely conscious, although some of it is unconscious. It tempers the desirous longings of the id with the reality of what might happen if it is not controlled, and it also learns the reality of how best to serve the id. A baby learns that it is fed only after crying, and a child learns to say 'please' in order to obtain things. It learns that in some circumstances, giving into the id leads to punishment or unpleasantness, and so it may not follow its desires in order to avoid these consequences. For example, the child's id may desire a biscuit, but when it takes one, some form of punishment or unpleasantness ensues. The pleasure of having the biscuit is marred by this unpleasantness, and so the child may decide that taking a biscuit is not worth it. The ego has developed and learned to reason with the id about the worth of the action. Slowly, the ego develops and controls or tempers the id.

The super-ego is largely part of the unconscious personality. It may contain conscious elements, for example, moral or ethical codes, but it is basically unconscious in its operation. It is the conscience which exists in the unconscious areas of the mind. The super-ego characterises the fully socialised and conforming member of society.

Formation of the Super-Ego

Possibly the most important influences on the individual are the precepts and moral attitudes of the parents or those *in loco parentis*. These are the people most loved, most respected and most feared. They are also the people with whom a child has his or her earliest contacts and relationships. These are essential to the child. The super-ego is often seen as the internalised rules and admonitions of the parents and, through them, of society. The super-ego acts on the ego; thus when a child desires a biscuit it may not take one even if it could not be punished because the child starts to reprove itself. The super-ego may therefore praise and punish the child in the same way as the parents do and so the child slowly learns and inner set of rules or

values. If the behaviour or thoughts of the child live up to
the super-ego, it experiences the pleasant feeling of pride
but if they do not the child's own super-ego punishes it by
self-reproach and feelings of guilt.

The ego therefore has two masters, each to be obeyed
and each pushing in different directions. The id demands
pleasures; the super-ego demands control and repression. The
result is inner conflict which can never be fully resolved. Freud
argued that for the super-ego to develop, the parents scold
the child or otherwise show their displeasure, and this leads
the child to become anxious that their love will be removed.
The next time the child considered a 'bad' deed, he or she will
feel anxiety that the parents may leave. The anxiety is
unpleasant and leads to repression of the deed. As the child
does not understand the difference between thought and
action, the mental desire is also repressed in case the parents
discover it: thoughts as well as deeds become repressed.

The basis of control or repression is therefore seen as
built upon relationships with parents or those *in loco
parentis.* This analysis to an extent has been upheld by the
work of Aichhorn (1963), who found that environmental
factors alone could not account for the delinquency of the
children at the institution he supervised. The super-egos of
many of the children were underdeveloped, which he
maintained rendered them latent delinquents, psychologically
prepared for a life of crime. He postulated that the failure to
develop a super-ego was the result of the parents being
unloving or absent for much of the child's upbringing. Each
of these conditions would prevent the child from forming the
dependent, trusting and intimate relationships necessary to
the development of the super-ego. From this account, the
socialising processes had failed to work on these children
whose latent delinquency had become dominant; the children
were therefore 'dissocial.'

Aichorn treated these youths by attempting to provide
a happy and pleasant environment which might foster the
type of relationships with adults which would facilitate the
formation of the super-ego. He argued that the severe

environments offered by most homes for juvenile delinquents merely exacerbate the problem begun by the parents, or by their absence, pushing the youths towards more criminal acts and confirming their 'dissocial' state. Parental neglect was not seen as the only reason for the super-ego to be underdeveloped: over-indulgent parents, allowing the child to do anything, would have a similar effect. It was also possible for children to learn all the lessons of their parents but still end with less than fully developed super-egos because the parents' ability to teach had been imparied by diluted moral standards, often because they were criminals themselves or were not themselves fully socialised. It has to be stated, however, that Aichorn realised that not all delinquents had poorly developed super-egos and that he never claimed that the failure to develop a super-ego explained all criminality.

These ideas have been further supported by other psychoanalysts such as Healy and Bronner, who studied 105 families with two sons where one brother was a persistent criminal and the other was non-criminal. They concluded that the criminal brother had failed to develop strong emotional ties with his parents, and turned to pleasure to gratify the id. As a result they did not progress either to the reality of what will ultimately happen if desires are gratified immediately, or to the formation of a super-ego. John Bowlby, found similar results when he focused on early maternal deprivation as being the cause of criminality. His argument rested on two basic premises: firstly, that a close, unbroken and loving relationship with the mother (or permanent mother substitute) is essential to the mental health of the child, and secondly, that rejection by the mother or separation from her (or her substitute) accounts for most of the more permanent cases of delinquency. This last sweeping claim has been attacked by both psychologists and sociologists, some of whom reject his methodology while others question his findings and claims. Many do, however, recognise that strong, though not necessarily lasting, damage can be done to a child's mental development if it is rejected by or separated from its mother during the first five years of its development.

A further factor which some argue has a profound effect upon the development of the super-ego, and one of the ideas most commonly associated with Freud, is the Oedipus complex (in boys) and the Electra complex (in girls). These develop during the process of sexual growth. Each is depicted by the child, normally when about three years old, being attracted to the parent of the opposite sex whilst feeling general hostility toward the parent of the same sex. In the Oedipus complex (male) the rivalry would be between the father and son. The latter, realising the supremacy of the father, fears castration and this fear forces him to control his desire for this mother. Frued believes that it is from the resolution of this conflict that the male's super-ego, social restraint or conscience, develops, and that all this occurs before the age of about five or six years. If the conflict is not resolved in this way, then serious personality or behavioural problems may arise. If there is no formation or incomplete formation of the super-ego, then the individual may have little or no conscience and so have no reason to restrain his desires. If the super-ego is overdeveloped then it may lead to guilt feelings or to his developing a neurosis (see below).

The resolution of the equivalent Electra complex in women is more complex and, Freud believes, less complete.

Psychologists recognise that other factors such as relationships with individuals outside the family and the general social environment can also affect the formation of the super-ego. Hewitt and Jenkins categorised a group of 500 juveniles into three types:

    (a) inhibited, shy and seclusive (an overdeveloped super-ego);

    (b) unsociable and aggressive (underdeveloped super-ego); and

    (c) members of a socialised, delinquent gang (having a dual super-ego).

The gang members possess a normal super-ego with

respect to the rules of the gang, which therefore they obeyed, but they have inadequate or underdeveloped super-egos with respect to the rules of society. The behaviour of each individual gang member depends on whether or not he is with the gang. If he is, he obeys gang rules. If he is in the outsided world, he feels no compulsion to obey the ordinary, everyday rules of society. Such a pattern indicates the strong influence which the environment can extert.

Balancing the Id, Ego and Super-Ego

The balance between desire and repression is kept by the ego, and in most people the desires of the id are shaped so that they are acceptable to the super-ego whilst still satisfying the id. This is often done by sublimation or displacement. For example, the desire for aggression may be channelled into sport where it can be usefully dissipated, or destructive instincts might be channelled in childhood away from harming people or animals and towards pulling toys apart and learning how to rebuild them. The balance does not come from total repression of the id, but rather from channelling those desires into more useful activities which are acceptable to the super-ego. In this way both the id and super-ego are satisfied.

Psychoanalysts therefore argue that criminals are those who have not channelled their desires into useful, or at least harmless, pastimes. The id remains uncontrolled, and so the desires are allowed to take over and may give rise to socially unacceptable acts, some of which may be criminal. Occasionally, a criminal may be a person who has over-controlled or repressed these desires. Criminals may have a weak ego and hence be unable to balance the demands of the id and the super-ego; a weak super-ego where the conscience is insufficiently developed, making their moral standards lower than those of the rest of society; or an overly repressive ego and super-ego.

For example, guilt may be felt at the very existence of the desires (especially sexual desires), or at the performing of an act which, though not criminal, is wrong by super-

ego standards. The guilt gives rise to a need to be punished
as a form of relief or a purging of the guilt. The individual
therefore commits a crime, often a very minor crime, and
is caught and punished. The hope is that the punishment
will be enough to atone for both the original guilt and the
criminal act. Even if it does, the original desires are still
there, in the unconscious, and so the guilt reasserts itself.
On this interpretation it is understandable that further
crimes are committed: crime brings punishment;
punishment brings relief, but only for a time. A vicious
circle develops and an habitual criminal comes into
existence.

Psycoanalytical explanations are based upon the idea
that it is the inner processes and conflicts which determine
behaviour. Unresolved inner conflict and lack of emotional
ability are seen as the main causes of unacceptable behaviour;
environment plays a subsidiary role. Because some of this
inner conflict is unconscious the theory is very difficult to
test.

'Normal' Criminals

So far, most of the criminal tendencies referred to in
this section on psychoanalysis have been those of
'abnormal' criminals whose behavioural problems arise from
inner conflict (for example, individuals who suffer from a
personality problem such as neurotics). Pscyhoanalysis may
also be used to explain some 'normal' criminality. The main
trait of a 'normal' offender is that the whole personality,
including the super-ego, is criminal. As there is no conflict
between super-ego and the rest of the personality, there is
no personality problem and so they are 'normal' offenders.
This means that, presumably because of their environment
and upbringing, these people regard crime as normal and
acceptable (i.e., as natural) and they suffer no qualms
about their criminal conduct. This does not mean that the
'normal' offender is willing to commit any crime, but that
upbringing allows certain acts which are condemned by the
rest of society, whilst condemning, along with the rest of

society, many other activities considered to be criminal. This possibly suggests that society is not homogeneous but is made up of many subcultures.

Extroversion and Neuroticism

The idea that extroversion and introversion may play a part in criminality was popularised by Jung, originally a follower, but later a critic, of Fruend. In 1947 Jung said that there was a continuance from introversion to extroversion, and that everybody could be placed somewhere along the spectrum. An hysteric condition, fitful or violent emotions, are more likely to be evidence of an extrovert, whereas an anxious condition, apprehensive for obsessive, indicates introversion. These concepts are often used in criminology as an explanation for recidivism—it is said that the introvert, being more careful, is better able to learn societal norms and so easier to condition and less likely to become a recidivist. The flaw in presenting this as a general proposition is that whilst introverts may quickly learn the law-abiding behaviour taught in penal institutions, they will similarly have the capacity to relearn antisocial behaviour after being released. There are both extrovert recidivists and introvert recidivists.

The main work in this area is that of Eysenck, but see also Eysenck and Gudjonsson, whose work covers a number of disciplines and draws upon psychoanalysis and personality theories as well as learning and control theories. Eysenck's starting-point is that individuals are genetically endowed with certain learning abilities, particularly the ability to be conditioned by environmental stimuli. He also assumes that crime can be a natural and rational choice where people maximise pleasure and minimise pain. An individual learns societal rules through the development of a conscience, which is acquired through learning what happens when one takes part in certain activities: punishment for being naughty and reward for being good. Personality is then based upon a combination of these biological and social factors. Eysenck saw two main dimensions to each personality which affected

the individual's learning ability: *extroversion*, which runs
from extroversion to introversion and is often referred to as
the E scale; and *neuroticism*, which runs from neurotic or
unstable to stable and is often referred to as the N scale.
These dimensions are continuous and most people fall in the
middle range, but with some at the extremes of each.

As with Jung's idea, the extroverts are seen as more
difficult to condition, but so are the highly unstable or
neurotic personalities. Eysenck argues that there is a
hierarchy of conditionability:

(a) stable introverts (low N low E) are the easiest to
    condition;

(b) stable extroverts (low N high E) and neurotic
    introverts (high N low E) are less malleable but do
    not encounter great difficulty in social learning;

(c) neurotic extroverts (high N high E) experience most
    difficulty in social learning.

Later Eysenck introduced a third personality dimension
which he called psychoticism, which could well be referred to
a psychopathetic dimension since it is generally evidenced
by aggressive, cold and impersonal behaviour. The individual
will tend to be solitary, uncaring, cruel, will not fit in with
others and will be sensation seeking. It is lightly less well
understood than the first two and is associated with the
frontal lobe of the cortex. Eysenck associates extremes of this
dimension with criminality — the higher the P score, the
higher the level of offending. In some studies Eysenck's claims
have gained support; see particularly McGurk and
McDougall, where they found that neurotic extroverts and
neurotic psychotic extroverts were only present in the
delinquent group and stable introverts were only found in
the non-delinquent group, whereas both neurotic introverts
and stable extroverts were found in both groups.

There have, however, been many critics of Eysenck's
work. Some attack the very basis of this claims: he has argued
for a genetic basis for these traits and drawn his evidence
from studies based on twins; thus his theory suffers from the

difficulties encountered by such approaches. More fundamentally, some scholars such as Little and Hoghughi and Forrest assert that his findings are totally discredited. Little questioned whether there was any relationship between recidivism and either extroversion or introversion. For this, he drew upon research at three Borstal training institutions which purported to prove that neither release from these institutions nor recidivism rates connected to them were in any way linked to either extroversion or introversion. His research therefore questioned not only Eysenck's work but all work in this area.

The overall position is at present unclear and uncertain, especially as Eysenck himself accepted that the theory cannot explain all crime, since not all criminals will be at the extremes of these scales. However, Farrington reports that this approach seems to identify a link between offending and impulsiveness.

Psychodynamic Explanations of Crime

Psychodynamic theorists have explained crime in several ways, focusing particularly on a harsh, weak or deviant super-ego which inevitably leads to an imbalance between the id, ego and super-ego. A harsh super-ego, resulting from identification with a strict parent, can lead to strong feelings of guilt and obsession whenever the id attempts to get any satisfaction at all. People with strong super-egos will usually be law abiding, but a few such people will engage in antisocial acts and such strangely deviant behaviour as stealing women's underwear from a washing line. The unconscious desire for sex has led to such feelings of guilt that the individual unconsciously desires to be punished, and so commits a crime, and the crime is related to their problematic urges. As Jones states, 'Here, there is a reversal of the usual situation: guilt precedes crime.'

More commonly, crime arises from a weak, underdeveloped super-ego. In this case the individual is selfish and uncaring, full of uncontrolled aggression. The failure to develop a well functioning super-ego is believed

66   Criminal Psychology

by psychoanalysts to be the result of unloving or absent
parenting. This is the basis of Bowlby's theory, as considered
below.

A deviant super-ego may emerge in a boy if his father is
deviant. In this case there may be a good relationship between
father and son with the Oedipus complex fully resolved and
a super-ego which has developed normally. However, the
son's super-ego standards are those of the father, that is,
antisocial, deviant ones. Freud called this phenomenon
pseudoheredity.

Evaluating the psychodynamic approach to crime

When applied to crime, there are several problems with
the Freudian approach. As mentioned earlier, according to
this approach, females have weaker super-egos than males
have. This would lead us to expect more female than male
criminals. However, females constitute a very small
percentage of the criminal population; furthermore, some
research indicates that females show a stronger moral
orientation than males at all ages.

The theory is rather limited in the types of crimes for
which it can account; indeed, it does not claim to offer an
explanation for *all* crime. Kline suggests that many white-
collar crimes and even some aggressive crimes are carefully
and deliberately planned and executed, and are motivated
by a rational decision to profit from the proceeds of crime
rather than by irrational thought processes.

Some criminals do show neurotic conflicts but even this
does not necessarily support the psychoanalytic approach.
The validity of the techniques used to assess these conflicts
has been questioned and these conflicts may result from,
rather than cause the criminal behaviour.

Nevertheless, the psychodynamic hypothesis cannot be
summarily dismissed. It is the only theory that addresses the
importance of emotional factors in criminal behaviour. It also
offers a more plausible account than most theories for crimes
that have no obvious gain and are incomprehensible to the
logically minded, such as stealing women's underwear from

washing lines or compulsive shoplifting by the rich of items for which they have no use. The notion that unconscious processes are an important determinant of behaviour is one that is still strongly held by a significant body of pyschologists.

A Theory Based on the Psychodynamic Approach: Bowlby's Theory of Delinquency

John, Bowlby, a psychoanalyst who worked with disturbed adolescents at a clinic in London, drew on Freud's theory to explain why children who are unloved are liable themselves to become uncaring, individuals. His study of juvenile thieves is considered below in Classic Research. You can see from this that Bowlby believed that separation from the main attachment figure in early life can result in delinquent behaviour because individuals who have suffered such deprivation do not consider other people's feelings, so they do as they wish without consideration for the hurt they may cause. In psychoanalytic terms, the young child has been unable to form a strong attachment and consequently has an inadequately formed super-ego. Bowlby has been criticised for concentrating on separation as a precursor to delinquency. The important factor that determines whether an antisocial personality may be formed is the failure to form a bond with someone, whether or not this is caused by separation. It is quite possible to remain in contact with the mother (or main carer) but, if she (or he) is unloving and distant, then no proper bond will form. Some theorists argue that the hostility and apparent lack of anxiety shown by adolescents and adults who were neglected and unloved as children is an ego defence mechanism against the painful feelings of dependency and powerlessness they feel as a result of their harsh experiences.

Criticism of Psychoanlaytical Theories

Psychoanalysts profess, with good reason, that they are scientists. Their central concepts, however, are incapable of being directly observed, making their existence impossible to prove. The id, ego and super-ego are assumed to exist because of particular external manifestations which also exhibit the extent to which each part of the personality has developed. Often these external manifestations alone are not sufficient to diagnose the difficulties. They are supplemented by techniques such as dream analysis, verbal association and hypnosis, but these techniques are subjective since psychoanalysts differ over interpretation. At the very least, this makes it a very inexact science.

One of the more dubious aspects of psychoanalysis, as applied to this area, is its assumption that because a person commits a crime he has some unconscious or subconscious personality conflict. The argument is circular, in that the problem to which a solution is sought is itself used as the proof that the explanation is correct. Moreover, the link between the crime and the alleged psychoanalytical reason for it is often obscure and dependent upon tortuous reasoning. An unknown obsession with a particular type of sexual problem, or with one parent, or with a type of emotion, may give rise to acts involving symbols which represents that problem, e.g., using a gun as a power symbol and therefore as a sexual symbol. In some cases, it is asserted, a certain class of person is injured who represents the real target. For example, a particular criminal might habitually commit a crime against an older, female victim who represents his mother. The implication is that it is really his mother which the offender wishes to harm, perhaps stemming from a feeling that the mother wronged him earlier in his life. The real reason for the crime would not be admitted and may not even be known by the offender, whose motives may be hidden deep in the subconscious or the unconscious.

In such interpretations, the criminality is the outward manifestation of a disease or problem of the mind and personality, which exists in the subconscious or the unconscious. By using subjective methods on information gathered either from anecdote or methods such as dream therapy or hypnosis, the analyst follows the problem into these normally inaccessible areas of the mind and diagnoses the mental or personality problem. When asked to prove the existence of the problem, they point to the criminality. In this way the criminal act becomes both proof of the existence of the problem and the result of the problem. Proof of the worth of these theories is therefore difficult and it seems unlikely that all or even most criminality is associated with psychoanalytical problems. Nor does psychoanalysis add up to a clear understanding of crime or lead to widespread methods of preventing it — any successes have mainly been at an individual level. This does not mean that crime is not associated with the personality of the offender. In any event, psychoanalysis is not the only source of personality theories.

The Normal Criminal Personality
Introduction

Most theories using a concept of normal criminal personality assume that individuals possess definable and dominant sets of rules which determine how they will behave in virtually any situation. This is often called the central or core personality. Psychologists and psychiatrists believe that criminals tend towards certain well-defined personalities, and that their criminal tendencies can be overcome by controlling or altering those core personalities.

What is Normality?

The line between normality and abnormality is impossible to draw exactly. Normality itself is elusive and difficult to define in any positive sense. It is usually negatively described as the state of mind or personality that cannot be classified as having a mental abnormality, (i.e., which cannot be classed as mentally defective, psychopathic, neurotic, psychotic or compulsive).

The mere fact that something is numerically common does not make it normal, and similarly the bare fact that something is uncommon does not make it abnormal. An event is not made normal or healthy because it frequently occurs and will certainly re-occur. For example, there will always be murder but this does not make it a normal or socially acceptable activity. Neither does the fact that an activity is socially unacceptable mean that those who take part in it are necessarily psychologically abnormal. If it did, it would follow that all criminals are mentally abnormal, and this is patently not the case.

Although all this is true, the plain fact is that in most of the studies normality is assessed in relation to the average person or the mental standard which is portrayed by most of the population (i.e., a numerical analysis). Furthermore, most of the studies of personality are heavily based on value judgements, such as assuming that because individuals have committed crimes they should portray a different personality from the law-abiding citizen (namely, a criminal personality). The assumption here is that those who participate in socially unacceptable activities must have something which is different from what the researcher, or society generally, considers normal.

This attitude can most clearly be seen in relation to murder, especially when there appears, on the face of it, be no logical explanation for the killing. In such cases the press and public often refer to the events as motiveless crimes and term the murderer a 'monster' or a 'madman.' The activity is portrayed as something which any 'normal' person would find abhorrent and would not commit (or would like to think that they would not commit). Since most studies are tested against what society considers acceptable and normal, this is in effect the reality of the situation, and it is clear that as values in society change, so too will ideas of normality. For example, at one time homosexuality was a crime and generally considered to be a wholly unacceptable practice. It was considered to be an abnormal activity, and those taking part were deemed to be in need of medical or psychiatric treatment as well as punishment (see the Wolfenden Committee on Homosexual Offences and Prostitution). Homosexuality (between consenting adults over 18 in private) is now legal (according to the Sexual Offences Act 1967, s. 1 as amended by the Criminal Justice and Public Order Act 1994) and, although such activity is sometimes still considered biologically different or abnormal, it is less generally considered that its participants are in need of medical or psychiatric attention. From this it can be seen that the ordinary man in the street — or even the ordinary reasonable doctor, psychiatrist, psychologist, sociologist or criminologist — does not possess an absolute or constant definition of normality, personality or mental illness.

Any move away from the concept of normality may involve either together or separately at lest three aspects: psychological suffering (the affective aspect), judgmental errors (intellectual aspect), and behavioural problems (moral or social aspect). None of these is necessarily a value-free norm and so variations from the 'norm' are laden with subjective assessments. These are particularly strong in the moral or social aspect where society or the expert defines what is to be categorised as 'problem behaviour'; and as seen above, that concept may not be static.

In Britain, in relation to criminology the issue of diagnosing normality and any deviation from normality (or illness) is further complicated by the proximity of the clinical work and the criminal justice system. This renders the diagnosis particularly difficult. In Britain, the psychiatrist, psychologist or probation officer is expected to report at the pre-sentencing stage. To make an assessment of the individual at this stage blurs the role of the diagnosis. Is it meant to determine the level of punishment by assessing the responsibility of the individual for the criminal act of which he or she has been found guilty? Is it to assess whether there is a likelihood of repeat offending of a sort likely to cause much damage to victims (particularly violent or sexual attacks)? Or is it rather to be used to diagnose the individual, mentally and medically, so as to propose methods of treatment or alter the personality and enable the offender to live within the requirements or boundaries set by society? This schism causes problems: it is confusing for the professional concerned; it may provide sentences with ambiguous information; and it may relieve the offender of any feeling of responsibility.

Despite these problems in the British tradition, it has

been the psychiatric and psychological fields of criminal explanation which have generally carried more weight than the biological; they adapted more readily to the due process system of criminal trial and sentencing which is a feature of the British system. It was generally believed that any necessary treatment could be carried out while the offender was being punished in a prison or elsewhere; and the approach also fits well with a system which is rooted in controlling or altering behaviour so that it conforms to an accepted type. It is also a useful tool because the 'diagnosis' or assessment by the expert is difficult to refute.

Personality Tests

Psychologists are still searching for a general explanation of human personality. Over the years almost every aspect of human personality has been studied: the tests include self-administered questionnaires (such as the MMPI, see later), performance tests, free association tests and the Rorschach test (a test designed to show intelligence, personality and mental state, in which the subject interprets ink-blots of standard type). Despite extensive study, the human personality is still and enigma.

Many researchers have tested the difference between criminal and non-criminal personalities. Schuessler and Cressey carried out a comparison of 113 studies which used 30 different types of personality tests, all of which sought to detect a personality difference between criminals and non-criminals. They found that 42 percent of the 113 studied showed differences in favour of the non-criminal, while the remainder were indeterminate. These links were too tenuous to conclude that personality traits were consistently and systematically linked to criminality.

Seventeen years later, Waldo and Dinitz carried out a similar comparison of some 94 studies which had been undertaken during the intervening years. In 76 of the studies (81 percent) they found a difference between criminals and non-criminals. Although these tests seemed to provide evidence of a personality difference between criminals and non-criminals, Waldo and Dinitz felt that the findings were far from conclusive. Thus they too concluded that no personality traits were consistently and systematically linked to criminality. In order to comprehend this conclusion it is necessary to understand the main personality test: the MMPI.

MMPI Test

Between the 1950 and 1967 comparative studies a new, and allegedly more reliable, test become more widely operative for assessing the criminal personality. This test was called the Minnesota Multiphasic Personality Inventory, or the MMPI for short. It consists of 550 items which were developed to assist the diagnosis of adults who sought psychiatric help. The subjects decide whether the 550 statements are true or false when applied to themselves. There are a number of checks included in the questionnaire in order to catch untruthful answers. The test is split into then scales and the subject is given a score on each scale; there is no overall score. The individual's full personality is then constructed from a score profile obtained by entering the scores from each scale onto a graph. The ten scales indicate an assessment of: hypochondria; depression; conversion hysteria or disorder (where unexplained physical symptoms are assumed to be linked to psychological factors); psychopathic personality; masculinity-femininity; paranoia; neurosis; schizophrenia; hypomania (a condition marked by over-excitability); and introversion. As the MMPI is now used for the assessment of the personalities of normal individuals, the scales do not usually bear any names but are usually identified only numerically, e.g., scale 1, scale 2, scale 3, etc.

The items which the study by Waldo and Dinitz had found most often distinguished the criminal from the non-criminal lay in the Psychopathic personality (Pd) scale, or scale 4 of the test. However, they discovered that this part of the test could produce a systematic bias because it included a number of items which were most likely to be answered differently by a criminal. The most obvious was: 'I have never been in trouble with the law.' Other questions which appeared in this scale and to which the delinquent is more likely to answer differently from the non-delinquent were: 'I liked school'; 'My relatives are nearly all in sympathy with me'; 'I often was in trouble in school, although I do not understand for what reasons.' In the studies where personality differences were said to be found, this was based on the different answers given to only four questions out of 50. The small differentiation resulted in a significant difference between criminals and non-criminals in the final statistical analysis. In any event, and explanation could be found in the different environments or situations of the two groups, rather than personality differences.

It is unsurprising that the delinquent scores higher on this Pd scale, as it was designed specifically to differentiate delinquents from other groups, a factor which Waldo and Dinitz seem to have ignored. The more surprising fact is rather that the score differences on this scale were not greater. But its utility for identifying delinquents is wakened because it has been found to predict characteristics besides delinquency. For example, those who dropout of school have been found to have a higher Pd score than others, as have those who are less shy, particularly if they are more aggressive. The archetypal 'yuppie' or the hard-nosed businessman is also likely to score high on his scale. Professional actors also have high Pd scores and so do those who have 'carelessly' shot someone in a hunting accident. Used as a predictor, one would expect those who scored high on this scale to dropout of school, be outgoing, possibly more aggressive, become professional actors and the involved in hunting accidents. The practical application of such tests in criminology is thus severely limited.

One of the main reasons why these personality tests attracted so much interest was that it was hoped that they would provide predictive information on those most likely to offend in the future, raising the possibility of being able to offer special help before such persons' personalities began to cause criminally defined behavioural problems. Lundman reports on the utility of the MMPI test as a predictor of criminality. He found that three of the scales were associated

with offending: scale 4–Pd Psychopathic deviation; scale 8–
Sc Schizophrenia; and scale 9–Ma Hypomania. Of these, scale
8 was the best predictor, with 23.8 percent of those who
obtained a high score on this scale becoming officially
delinquent within four years. This still means that 76.2
percent of those with a high rating on scale 8 did not offend
within four years. A slightly better rate of prediction is
obtained when high scores on at least two out of three of the
above scales are combined: 34.5 percent of those in this
category offended within four years, but this still leaves 65.5
percent who fall within this category but who did not offend.
Crucially, the test was not able effectively to separate out
the offenders from the others: it thus gives too many false
positives to be a good predictive tool.

Interpersonal Maturity Tests

A further level of tests which came out with very similar
results was based on the social maturity levels of individuals.
These are often called 'interpersonal maturity' tests or 'I-
Level' tests. In these studies, individuals are tested for their
social and interpersonal skills and they are then placed on
one of several levels of maturity. These levels are simply given
numerical values, but each of the numerical levels is also
linked with descriptions of the person's 'core personality.' Both
Warren and Palmer discovered that most convicted
delinquents appeared in Levels 2, 3 and 4 and all were socially
immature. Level 2 personalities are asocial, aggressive and
power oriented, which is very similar to the descriptions found
in the MMPI tests. Individuals on Level 3 are characterized
by their conformity to the delinquent group, which bears
marked similarities to claims by Hewitt and Jenkins (1947),
and those on Level 4 are often called neurotic. They claimed
that 90 percent of delinquents fell into one or other of these
three levels.

Assessment of Personality Tests

The MMPI tests and the I-Level studies all suggest that
there is a link between criminality and asertiveness, hostility,

resentment of authority, dynamic personalities and psychopathy. However, while in the first two of these research studies the findings were statistically significant, their actual sizes were small. This has given rise to doubts about their reliability, and they have been questioned by later researchers. Each study compares delinquents or criminals (those who have been officially convicted) with non-delinquents or non-criminals (a group of those who have not been officially convicted but a number of whom may have committed acts which are as unacceptable or criminal). Some of the personality traits found in the criminal group could derive from their treatment by the justice system, rather than from something inherent in their characters, especially if they know of other people, possibly friends, who have committed similar crimes but not been caught. A hostile reaction would in those circumstances be understandable, as would a feeling of injustice and resentment of authority. The small personality differences found in these studies may not have been there prior to their contact with police or courts, and they might be the result of those encounters rather than the reasons for them.

Conceptually, it would be better to begin testing at a very young age and follow the children through to adulthood. Ideally, the tests should cover not only personality and official criminality, but also self-reported criminality. The researcher would then be better able to assess whether their personalities were inherent, learnt from normal socialisation, or were the result of a brush with the criminal justice system. The proposed method of assessment might also show whether these personality types actually commit more crime or whether they are just more likely to be caught. There would still be problems: the perceived personality traits may be the result of earlier conflict with figures of authority such as teachers.

In any event, it seems that the personality trait will not determine the criminal behaviour, but will only predict a certain type of behaviour, of which criminality is but one example. Some even doubt whether there is any real personality trait, claiming instead that the way each individual acts depends rather upon the situation they are in. They point out that a person who is said to have a more aggressive personality will not be generally aggressive; the trait will show only in certain situations. Thus they may be aggressive on the sports field, or whilst driving and at work, but be very gentle in their personal relationships. The argument is that it is the situation, not the individual's personality, which decides their behaviour. For example, if a police car is behind you it would not cause you to stop although it might cause you to drive with more care, but if the blue light on the police car starts flashing, you would stop. The situation of the blue light brought about the behaviour, not any personality attribute of the individual—the same behaviour would probably have occurred whether you were dominant or submissive, sociable or unsociable. But in a different situation you might not stop. If, for example, you had just committed a crime other than a driving offence, you might try to escape. This is not to deny any influence to personality, but rather to say that reactions may depend on a number of factors. For example, the behaviour of a person in a school depends partly on their position—head teacher, teacher, secretary, caretaker, prefect, pupil or parent; partly on the situation—classroom, sports field, parents' evening, disciplinary, social; and partly on the personality of the individual. It might also be affected by the pressures of a peer grouping or by the values of the community.

The Cambridge study (in which a cohort of young boys was analysed and followed until adulthood) found that the really significant links were not with personality, but between offending behaviour and impulsivity (acting without stopping to think about consequences). This in turn may be connected with low physiological arousal, especially concerning EEG and the Autonomic Nervous System. Low arousal would lead to overconfidence, sensation seeking and risk taking all of which have been linked to offending behaviour. In the Cambridge study, low heart rate (one of the measures of low arousal) was linked with violent offending; when a boy appeared to come from a high-risk background, one of the things which appeared most successfully to protect him from turning to offending was being shy, nervous or withdrawn, which Farrington suggests exhibits high arousal. This may then be one of the important causative links.

Some Comments on Treatment

The main use to which these so-called personality theories could be put is one of treatment. Some psychologists argue that drug therapy and electroconvulsive treatment is of use in disabusing and re-training delinquents and criminals, but on the whole these methods are avoided or at least do not currently form the central part of any re-training techniques. The better opinion seems to be that greater understanding of personality gives rise to the possibility of controlling actions by behaviour therapy. In this, the psychologist uses the knowledge of the offender's personality, along with general information about other people with similar personality types, in order to choose the learning theory or conditioning which is thought to be most likely to give favourable results.

Although it would be generally dangerous to use these theories to try to predict who will commit a crime, they may be useful in identifying how best to deal with criminals once they have transgressed. Many writers in this area have suggested that the criminality tends to be committed by those who possess certain personality traits such as not caring what others think, not caring about the consequences of acts when they affect others, weak or no personal ties, irresponsibility, and an out-going personality. If some of these factors do affect criminality, further criminality might be prevented by helping to alter or manage these personality traits. This may be done by, for example, making these individuals aware of the suffering they cause, making them face responsibilities, and teaching them to live in a social setting. In a few areas, some of these ideas have been tried at attendance centres which some offenders are obliged to go to as part of their probation and where some probation services provide group therapy.

In Britain, probation orders can be accompanied by a

range of conditions and are seen as a positive alternative to incarceration. Roberts reports that the probation service has worked out strategies which are focused on particular types of offenders. Raynor and Vanstone support the positive results which might be found in carefully targeted projects, particularly those built on cognitive behaviour, and Macdonald *et al.*, after examining 95 projects, report positive results in at least three quarters of them. Programmes should enhance the offenders' ability to exercise responsible choices to avoid offending, and should treat them with respect so that they come to value themselves and their rights: it is important that offenders view such programmes as positive and helpful to them rather than just for control and punishment.

Similar strategies are also tried in some prison establishments, either as part of a group therapy session or in a wider context. Inmates are made to take some responsibility for their living conditions, they are trusted with dangerous implements like scissors and metal cutlery, staff and inmates talk through problems in the units together and talk through the inmates' difficulties together. These units have taken on some of the most dangerous and uncontrollable inmates, and yet they have reported some quite surprising successes. Possibly their ideas should be used more widely in prison establishments.

Criticism of Personality Theories

Personality theories are more scientific than those put forward by the psychoanalyst, in the sense that they rely less on assessment and explanation of phenomena and draw more on mainly objective tests. They are more commonly based upon empirical research, which can be more easily assessed.

Most theories assume that each individual has a central or core personality which can explain reactions to most stimuli and will determine the likelihood of becoming criminally involved. However, different theories link different personality types to criminality, whilst the general use of empirical evidence makes it difficult to choose between them. On the other hand, there is much overlap: assertiveness and resentment of authority occur frequently as being linked to criminality.

More fundamental doubts arise from the central concept of the existence of a core personality. It assumes that a small number of characteristics can rule all an individual's actions and relationships. Many clearly believe that this core personality can be altered or controlled, otherwise their suggested treatment techniques would be rendered useless. Others assert that each individual is born with a particular core personality, or at least that it is developed at a very early age (for example Eysenck and Trasler): for them very careful and intensive treatment would be required to alter or control that inborn personality. Some researchers have claimed that the core personality can be altered naturally by environmental change, by the passing of time, or the heightened maturity of the person. Such a stance puts the whole concept of a core personality in doubt, as the concept draws its strength from the idea that it is permanent unless it is carefully treated by professionals. However, if the core personality does alter naturally over time, it might help to explain why many people who have a criminal record during their teens grow out of it in their early 20s as they mature and their personality alters. The more basic immediate point is that so wide a range of interpretation of the basic concept must undermine confidence in theories based on personality.

Despite these doubts, common sense suggests that there must be something in the idea of a core personality — we all view Batty as different from Daisy or Freda and would say possibly that one is more reliable than the other, or that one is more friendly, and so on. Similarly, we all have an idea of how a particular person is likely to react to a certain situation, and that somebody else would react different. If they do not act as expected, we would view it as 'out of character.' So we accept that although our basic idea of a person is that they portray a particular type of personality, we also accept that this can alter in small ways without losing its basic 'core.' We also accept that at certain times a person may not 'feel themselves': a normally cheery person may have an off day, but this does not alter our basic view of them. People are unique, partly because of their personalities.

To go beyond such pragmatic impressions of how criminality and personality might be related needs closer discussion of cause and effect than most of these theories provide. In almost all cases it is assumed that the relationship is direct (i.e., that criminality was a result of the personality attributes) whereas in fact the attributes may have arisen as a result of being arrested, convicted and punished, or both the criminality and the attributes may be the result of some third element. Even if the personality traits are affecting the criminality, it may not be in such a direct way as is implied. The personality traits may, for example, render the making of close relationships very difficult, which would isolate the person, who may then not feel as bound as other people are by societal norms. Alternatively, the traits may just render criminality more likely if certain other factors, for example environmental factors, are favourable to the commission of crime.

The extent to which personality attributes are accepted as a complete and reliable explanation of criminality is probably decreasing. The theories which contain a more sociological element have gained in popularity and acceptance. Despite this, personality must always play some part in the explanation of crime if only to help to understand why it is that not all people from certain social backgrounds and environments end up as criminals. Most sociologists accept this, but they would certainly question the idea of a fixed core personality and rather see personality as a continuing thread which is altered by experience and by relationships, and which of course can be affected by treatment methods.

Offender Profiling

There it was considered as a problem for the victim but what this hides is that repeat victimisation also often means that the offender is the same in each case. This is obviously the case in domestic violence; the violence is likely to be repeated at least until the relationship is ended. It is often also true of repeat property victimisation. In these instances victimisation shows a clear pattern, but there can also be a pattern to victimisation and offending in other areas. The British Crime Survey has pinpointed the types of property and persons most likely to be victimised; there are also types of people who are more likely to offend. Since the 1970s detailed analysis of crimes and crime patterns has revealed very useful information concerning offenders and has helped in a number of police investigations. Offender profiling, however, is not new: Rumbelow refers to a profile of Jack the Ripper provided, by Dr. Thomas Bond in 1888. In addition much media attention has been given to this use of psychology and they reported both high-profile successes (the apprehension and conviction of Duffy, the railway murderer, see Canter and high-profile failures, for a discussion see Britton. There have also been films such as *Silence of the Lambs* and a UK television series *Cracker,* both of which use — and sometimes misuse and misrepresent — this type of methodology. It has also led to a whole series of academic books called 'Offender Profiling Series' published by Ashgate. The approach has been used to particular effect in cases of rape, murder and arson and it is these that will be considered here, but a more modern usage is for property offences where the methodology is more statistical and less personal.

Although no two writers seem to agree on the exact nature of offender profiling, basically it consists of teasing out the characteristics of the offender from a detailed knowledge of the offence and other background information. A profiler will study the scene of the crime; the scene of the discovery of the body (if relevant and different); the surrounding neighbourhood; the last movements of the victim; the type of person the victim is or was; his or her personal appearance; statement by the victim (where it is not a case of murder); and any other information which the investigating team have. From this the profiler constructs a profile, which often covers information concerning the offender's social and physical characteristics, their behaviour and personality. Of course no profile is exact. No profile can tell the police who committed an offence; all it can do is suggest characteristics that the offender is likely to possess. Even in the most accurate profiles, such as Canter's analysis of the railway murderer, Duffy, only 13 of the 17 pointers were correct. As Jackson and Bakerian point out, the offender profile does not solve the case, it is merely 'one more tool' that the police can use, and it might help to narrow down the pool of suspects. If they have six in the frame and two do not fall within the profile, they might be sensible initially to concentrate on the four who may be closer to the profile. That should not exclude the other two: a profile neither hands the police on offender nor means that any suspect who does not match the profile can be ignored. Besides possibly helping to pinpoint an offender, a profile may also suggest ways in which he or she might be most successfully interviewed.

Much offender profiling has been attacked for its lack of scientific basis. Canter and Alison question the work of both Douglas and Olashaker and Britton on this basis. They suggest that Douglas's work (and thereby that of the FBI) is often very general, containing factors which would be common in all such offences and that Britton does not use general psychological principles to build his profiles despite having been trained in these. If these attacks are justified, they would mean that much psychological profiling is little more than intelligent intuition or guesswork. This may be unavoidable. As Smith points out, in many cases the profiler is only called in once traditional policing methods have failed or are not doing very well. At this point much of the information most important to the profiler, such as the crime scene, will have bene destroyed.

The FBI began to use profiling heavily in the 1970s and 1980s. Their methodology was to work with offenders, interviewing them to discover offender types, which could then be use to aid in building profiles. As Holmes and De Burger note they classed serial murderers into four types:

1. *Visionary Motive Type*—This serial murderer commits crimes because commanded to do so by voices or visions, e.g., Peter Sutcliffe, the 'Yorkshire Ripper.' The murder itself is usually spontaneous and disorganised.

2. *Mission-Oriented Motive Type*—This type of killer has a goal, usually to rid the world of a particular type of person. These people are not psychotic but have a strong wish to solve a particular problem, often to eliminate groups they judge 'unworthy,' such as prostitutes or tramps. Such a killer knows the action is wrong and that others condemn it. They are difficult to spot because they live otherwise normal, and often successful, lives. The victims are usually strangers, chosen because they fit into a particular category. The act is usually well planned, well organised and efficiently committed.

3. *Hedonistic Type*—These killers basically kill for pleasure. According to Holmes and De Burger, there are two main sub-categories of hedonistic serial murderers, each of which derives its pleasure from different sources. The thrill orientated killer is possibly the most difficult to understand. This type enjoys the excitement of killing and so kills for pleasure. His victims are strangers chosen at random and with no specific characteristic. They become victims purely because they are in the wrong place at the wrong time. There may be sadistic acts committed against the victims, but for this type of criminal the important thing is the act of killing. The second sub-group is the lust killer. A central part of this crime is sexual. For many of them the sexual pleasure is heightened by the amount of pain and often sexual mutilation they can inflict. They often have normal relationships and live normal lives, except that they have a problem with sexual gratification. For most lust killers the lead-up to the crime is part of the pleasure, so they fantasise about the crime and then take time in the selection of the victim, looking for specific traits, perhaps even following the victim for a period of time before the act. None the less, the victim is usually a stranger who happens to possess the desired characteristics. The act is usually planned and organised and

the sexual and killing parts of the crime are often savoured, perhaps even including the disposal of the body.

4. *Power/Control-Oriented Type*—This type of killer is very difficult to distinguish from the lust or thrill-seeking types. Many of the same traits may appear: but this criminal acts out of a desire to show absolute power over another human by taking ultimate control of life or death. In order to prove control he may commit sexual acts, but the sex is only a form of power over the victim. The victim will be a stranger who has specific characteristics, the crime will be organised and planned. The killing is often very sadistic.

Similarly they classify four types of rapist: power-reassurance; power-assertive; anger-retaliatory; and anger-excitement. One of the main aspects in their analysis is the assessment, using a number of variables, of whether the crime was organised or disorganised. Their approach has been used widely in many different countries and probably forms the basis for most offender profiling.

David Canter takes a rather different approach, one that is used alongside the FBI system by the UK Association of Chief Police Officers' Behavioural Science Investigative Support Subcommittee. It has therefore been used in a number of cases in the UK. Rather than trying to fit an offender into a rigid type Canter looks at their behaviour and assesses how this will be reflected in their normal non-offending lives. So whilst he and his associates use scientific methods such as the analysis of cases to build up a number of important criteria, they use these to assess aspects of the offender's normal behaviour and lifestyle to come up with more distinctive criteria, then are sometimes contained in the FBI profiles. Yet another system is used by another UK profiler, Britton, who analyses each case from scratch and does not use statistical analysis of previous cases to inform his judgements.

The limitations of the methodology are noted by Ormerod; it is useful only in a few cases such as rape, killing or arson; the profile only describes a possible type of person and does not identify an individual; profiles could prove prejudicial, both in the minds of the police in looking for an offender and in the minds of a jury if a case comes to court. The profile can only supplement other investigative methods, both of finding offenders and constructing cases.

Despite its prominence and the belief in offender profiling by both the public and the police its real usefulness has still to be proven. Ainsworth refers to a study conducted by Copson and Holloway where they note that it was only successful in 16 percent of the cases in which it was used and only led to the identification in 3 percent. These low figures may have much to do with the fact that the police prefer to claim to have solved the crimes by more traditional means, but even so they are very low. As Ainsworth notes, 'the fact that the suspect currently being interviewed happens to fit the profile does not "prove" that they actually committed the offence.' The authorities should be required to prove guilt by more traditional means and only use the profile as a very general aid. We must not depend too much on this relatively new investigative device.

Assessment of Dangerousness and Criminality
Defining Dangerousness

Most Western criminal justice systems include some form of assessing the danger posed by individuals who have been convicted of violent or other serious crimes. Such assessments help to decide how long those people should be removed from society, not as punishment but as protection for other members of the society. In some societies such removal is possible and occurs without any crime having been committed—in the form of civil committal to mental institutions. This is only possible where the individual's mental stability has been questioned, and it is this rather than just the dangerousness which is the deciding factor. In all these instances, someone has to decide what is dangerous and whether a particular individual fits that description. It is therefore essential that there is a definition of 'dangerousness.' On the surface, this may appear to be a very simple task. Almost everyone has an idea of what they consider to be dangerous, and for most it involves at least an element of violence or threat to personal safety. For some, however, this idea is much wider—in America, for example, the Federal Court once ruled that the writing of a bad cheque was 'dangerous' to society because the economy would collapse if everyone did it.

Some insight into the idea of dangerousness might be gained by consulting the law and discovering how it deals with the concept. In Britain there have been a number of provisions which have allowed perceived dangerousness of the criminal to play a major role in sentencing. In each case the basic concept is that of the protection of society rather than of dangerousness. The provisions are as follows :

Two interrelated provisions were introduced by the Criminal Justice Act 1991 to allow sentencing to protect the public. These are now contained in the Powers of Criminal Courts (Sentencing) Act 2000 (PCC(S) A 2000). Section 79(2) (b) allows the use of custody for a violent or sexual offence in order to protect the public and s. 80 (2) (b) allows use of a longer sentence to protect the public (still within the legal maximum). Section 161 (2) defines a sexual offence as any offence under various statutes including the Sexual Offences Act 1956 and the Sexual Offences Act 1967. Section 161(3) defines a violent offence as one which leads to or is likely to lead to the death or physical injury of a person, and includes an offence which required to be charged as arson. Section 161 (4) defines serious harm as death or injury whether physical or psychological. This means that these provisions should not be used where the person is likely to commit only minor offences. It is important to note that the Act does not say what level of risk is necessary before the provision can be used so that longer sentencing is possible even if the risk is only very slight [s. 81 (4)]. The court is permitted to consider any information about the offender when it makes its prediction of future conduct, and presumably this could include expert testimony.

In applying these provisions sentencers have relied either on the existence of a series of violent or sexual offences [see *R* v *Lyons* (1994) 11 Cr App R (S) 460] or on expert psychiatric evidence [*R* v *Bowler* (1994) 15 Cr App R (S) 78] as proof of potential serious harm. The Criminal Justice Act 1991 made it clear that most sentencing was intended to be proportional to the offence. The provisions discussed above have freed the courts to use incapacitation in selected cases in which the limiting factors are to be those necessary to protect the public, with no link to proportionality. Dingwall has suggested that the courts have been reluctant to use their extra powers. First he claims that they have interpreted violent and sexual acts fairly narrowly, secondly that they have always wanted some proof that the individual would be a danger to society if released, and finally he notes that they have introduced an element of proportionality into this extra period of incapacitation. The judge has to calculate what the offence would have got just for punishment and then the extra for incapacitation must be in proportion to what might have been necessary to punish. Possibly because of this reluctance to use their powers, Parliament has introduced minimum sentences in certain circumstances, while s. 85 of the PCC(S) A 2000 also permits a court to extend the period of licence which a sexual or violent offender must serve. Partly to prepare for this type of extended licence and partly to ensure a better community strategy for dealing with these types of offender the Criminal Justice and Court Services Act 2000 requires the police and probation services to establish arrangements for assessing and managing the risks posed by dangerous sexual and violent offenders. These are intended, together with the use of the sex offenders register, to feed into the powers already available under previously assessed legislation and furnish the courts and enforcement agencies with better and more precise information.

In addition, life sentences, both mandatory and discretionary, can be used to protect the public from dangerous offenders. Life sentence is obligatory for those, over 18 years of age, found guilty of murder. When used in this way it is largely to mark murder out as different in kind from other offences. Risk and dangerousness therefore become an issue in relation to mandatory life sentences only when such prisoners are being considered for release on licence. Under s. 109 of the PCC(S)A 2000, first enacted in the Crime (Sentences) Act 1997, there is now a second category of mandatory life sentence to be applied to persons over 18 convicted of a second serious offence. In England and Wales the Act defines a serious offence to include: an attempt, conspiracy or incitement to murder; soliciting a murder; manslaughter; wounding, or grievous bodily harm, with intent; rape or attempted rape; intercourse with a girl under 13; possession of a firearm with intent to injure; using a firearm to resist arrest; carrying a firearm with criminal intent; robbery while in possession of a firearm or an imitation firearm. In these circumstances, a judge on second conviction must impose a life sentence unless either there are exceptional circumstances relating either to the offence or to the offender which justify not passing such a sentence (these must be stated in open court), or it would be inappropriate, having regard to the circumstances of the offence or the offender. The assumption here is that past behaviour is normally sufficient to prove dangerousness in the future.

In a number of other cases life is a discretionary maximum sentence. It is most commonly used in the following cases: aggravated burglary, arson, buggery, causing an explosion with intent to endanger life or property causing bodily injury by explosions, criminal damage intended to endanger life, grievous bodily harm, incest or intercourse with a girl under 13 years of age, kidnapping, manslaughter, rape. In these cases the court is normally expected to pass a determinate sentence which indicates the severity of the offence. A court is supposed to use the life sentence only when the offence is serious enough to require a very long sentence, when the offender is unstable and likely to repeat such offences, and where if any further offences occurred they would involve serious consequences to others. These criteria appeared in *R* v *Hodgson* (1967) 52 Cr App R 113 and were confirmed in *Attorney General's Reference (No. 34 of 1992)* (1994) 15 Cr App R (S) 167. In

R v *Blackburn* (1979) 1 Cr App R (S) 205, the Court of
Appeal said that the discretionary life sentence:

... should not be imposed unless there is clear evidence
of mental instability as opposed to mental disorder which
would indicate that the persons was likely to be a danger to
the public.

Following *R* v *Pither* (1979) 1 Cr App R (S) 209,
discretionary life sentences should be for those who cannot
be appropriately dealt with under the Mental Health Act
1983, often because their mental instability or illness is not
treatable. It is the untreatability of their instability which
renders these offenders so dangerous.

The element of danger again becomes an issue at the
time when a life prisoner is being considered for release or
when a possible release date is being set. Such individuals
are released on parole licence which will last the rest of their
lives. In the case of mandatory life sentences the trial judge
is permitted to declare the minimum period he or she feels
should elapse before the offender is considered for release,
but anyway is required to make a recommendation to the
Home Secretary, through the Lord Chief Justice, informing
the Home Secretary of the conviction and giving his or her
views as to the period necessary to meet the requirement of
retribution and deterrence, the 'tariff.' The Lord Chief Justice
can comment on this information before it is passed to the
Home Secretary, or more normally one of his or her junior
Ministers, who then will decide whether the suggested 'tariff'
is appropriate or needs to be increased or decreased. Since
the decision in *R* v *Secretary of State for the Home Department,
ex part Doody* [1994] 1 AC 351, the prisoner has a right to
know the trial judge's recommendation, to make
representations to the Home Secretary and to be given the
reasons for any departure from the trial judge's
recommendations. The case will then be reviewed by the Local
Review Committee (LRC) three years before the end of the
tariff or after 17 years whichever is the sooner. If the LRC
approve release then the Home Secretary may send this to
the 'life panel' of the Parole Board. Under s. 29 of the Crime

(Sentences) Act 1997, the Parole Board can only consider a case which has been referred to them by the Secretary of State, either as a class of cases or a particular case. If the Board recommend release then the Minister consults with both the trial judge and the Lord Chief Justice. Where the Board do not recommend release the prisoner must be held, but where they recommend release the Minister then has a discretion whether or not to release. The parole dossiers, reasons for Parole Board decisions and the reasons for negative decisions by the Secretary of State are made available to the prisoner. The central issue for both of these boards and the Minister is the safety of the public, part of this must therefore be a consideration of dangerousness.

In the case of discretionary lifers or mandatory lifers under the PCC(S)A 2000, s. 109, the 'tariff' is fixed in strict accordance with the recommendations of the trial judge, and under s. 82A the sentencing court is normally required to calculate that determinate sentence would be necessary to mark the seriousness of the offence. Half that period (less any time already spent in custody or on remand) is then taken as the 'specified period' after which the offender is eligible to have his or her case sent to the Parole Board. If the offence is considered to be too serious, the court may refuse to make this calculation and the offender will not then be eligible for parole. A person must be released on licence as soon as the Parole Board so directs. Where the Board decide against release, the lifer can require reconsideration after a further two years. The prisoner is normally permitted to see reports concerning him or her and can both appear before the tribunal and have representation. He or she is entitled to a decision with reasons within seven days of the hearing. This hearing is to assess the safety of releasing the individual and therefore the assessment of dangerousness is central to its decision. Neither for mendatory nor for discretionary lifers is there a definition of dangerousness or of factors to be considered.

The Crime (Sentences) Act 1997 introduced minimum sentences for repeat offenders, now contained in the PCC(S)A 2000. When dealing with a person over 18 convicted of a class A drugs offence and who has at least two previous class A drugs convictions (at separate times) the court must pass a sentence of at least seven years. When dealing with a person over 18 convicted of a domestic burglary and who has at least two previous convictions (at separated times) for domestic burglary the court must pass a sentence of at least three years. These minimum sentences apply unless there are specific circumstance relating either to the offence or to the offender which would render the minimum unjust (these must be stated in open court). The reason given for these minima is usually that they are necessary to protect the public from a person who has been proven to be a danger to the public in the past. There is no attempt to assess whether there might be any such danger in the future, not any personal assessment. Nor is there any judicial direction which has led to severe criticism of these sentences.

There are also the provisions which allow restricted confinement of mentally disordered offenders. In the past the judiciary retained the power to decide when they would be released and did so at the time of sentencing, but in *X* v *United Kingdom* (1981) 4 EHRR 181 the European Court of Human Rights decided that such offenders should be guaranteed regular access to a tribunal to assess the lawfulness of their detention. This was later enacted and restriction orders are now available if there is a clear mental disorder recognised by the Mental Health Act 1983 and there is a special need to protect the public from serious harm (see s. 41 of that Act). It is generally used to prevent doctors discharging individuals who have committed an offence (which does not have to be serious) and where, having regard to the patient's previous record, there is a risk that further offences may occur which might lead to serious harm. Unless the restrictions are time limited the restriction lasts indefinitely and the patient can be discharged only by the Mental Health Review Tribunal or the Home Secretary. Such reviews must occur regularly. Discharge can either be conditional or unconditional; if conditional the person will be subject to recall. The fact that the authority to release is shared between the

Mental Health Review Tribunal and the Home Secretary indicates the ambiguity of the decision: the former should consider mainly the need for, and likelihood of response to, treatment; whereas the latter should be interested in the safety of the public. These will not always coincide.

Finally, in the Home Office and Department of Health (1999 and 2000) consultation document *Managing Dangerous People with Severe Personality Disorder: Proposals for Policy Development* (1999), the Dangerous People with Severe Persoanlity Disorder Bill 2000 (which was not passed) and their 2000 White Paper entitled *Reforming the Mental Health Act,* the government made clear its intention to give authorities more powers to restrain people who may be classed as dangerous. These new documents are focused on the dangerous person with a severe personality disorder. These are persons who have been thought to cause serious problems for crime control but who, because they do not suffer from any treatable mental health condition fall outside the normal powers of health care. The intent underlying these documents is to provide a wholly new framework for removing dangerous people for as long as they pose a serious risk and to attempt to deal with the effects of their disorder, even if the disorder itself cannot be cured. The Bill aimed to provide powers for the indeterminate detention of the dangerous person with a severe personality disorder in both criminal and civil proceedings. Detention would be imposed because of the risk they pose to society and would not rely on convictions. People might be sent for assessment when they have committed a sexual or violent offence, where their names appear on the Sex Offenders Register and where the authorised local authority officer deems it necessary. Restriction would then be imposed if the individual is both suffering from a recognised personality disorder and is a danger to the public. These criteria would be reviewed at least annually. Importantly there is no definition of dangerousness in the proposals nor is there any scientifically accepted idea or clear category of severe personality disorder. Severe personality disorder is often associated with the concept of psychopath, which

Cavadino suggests has no meaning except that these people are either nasty or inadequate. In partial agreement the Fallon report admits that it is not a recognised condition but suggests that it is associated with certain characteristics that can be recognised. Such substantial doubts over the class of person who might be included should perhaps make totally unacceptable the use of these very wide powers. Even with proper definitions of category and dangerousness there might be problems over the moral acceptability of detaining these people, where the detention is on top of any punishment and may even occur without a conviction. Such drastic intervention in the freedom of individuals who may have committed no offence, and may never have shown themselves to be dangerous, is itself dangerous. Even if they have committed an offence can this fact justify detaining them for periods totally outwith those needed to pay for that transgression?

It is thus evident that the contribution of the law of England and Wales to a definition of dangerousness has not been very helpful: apart from the general requirement that there be an offence committed before the assessment of dangerousness could interfere with the liberty of an individual, each of the above categories seems to cover different ideas and the last category, which does not yet (2001) have legal effect, would not even require an offence. The general presumption is that past behaviour alone predicts future behaviour.

Individuals have their own perceptions of danger and of unacceptable danger, often related to their sex, culture, social class etc., and some are deeply personal. To allow a judge unfettered powers to decide what is dangerous and remove someone's liberty on this ground would be unacceptable. Therefore certain frequently accepted boundaries are applied. For most people, any assessment of dangerousness such as to justify an individual having his or her liberty restricted would involve the individual in having already committed a serious crime, one they regard as involving danger or the potential for danger.

Unfortunately the powers being proposed seem to ignore this element. Most would agree that crimes involving personal injury are the most serious and the most dangerous, and of these crimes those involving serious injury and/or injury to more than one victim would be the most dangerous. But it is not this simple. It is true that behaviour leading to injury is generally seen as the most dangerous type of conduct, but other factors need to be taken into account in the assessment of danger. There are, for example, many people killed on the roads due to breaches of one or other of the criminal laws—driving without due care and attention; speeding; dangerous driving; driving while under the influence of drink. Despite this fact, speeding, careless and even dangerous driving are often seen as crimes of low culpability and their perpetrators are not normally locked up. Even in the case of drunken drivers, it is rare that the individual is viewed as necessarily dangerous and in need of removal from society. Dangerous or careless use of firearms would generally be viewed as far more unacceptable even if no-one was actually injured, and deprivation of liberty would be far more likely to occur.

An interesting consideration is that some of the crimes which have the worst consequences in the light of the numbers of lives lost, or levels of serious injuries as well as loss of property, are committed by corporations or those acting for corporations: pollution of the atmosphere; harmful products; breaches of health and safety regulations. The social and economic consequences of this type of crime are probably worse for society than the consequences of traditional street crime. Yet most people fear street crime more than corporate crime, and most would probably view it as more dangerous. Corporate criminals are difficult to locate and convict, but even when this is done they would usually be subject only to a fine, often a fairly small fine. In the rare cases where they are imprisoned, it would only be for as long as was necessary to punish them; they would probably not be removed to protect the public from future dangerous behaviour. From this it is clear that neither the law nor the general public seem to have any very clear view of what is dangerous.

In the US 1973 Model Sentencing Act, s. 5 states that when a court is sentencing an individual for a felony it should be permitted to commit for a term of not more than 30 years when:

The defendant is being sentenced for a felony in which he:

(a) inflicted or attempted to inflict serious bodily harm; or

(b) seriously endangered the life or safety of another and he was previously convicted of one or more felonies not related to the instant crime as a single criminal episode,

and the court finds he is suffering from a severe mental or emotional disorder indicating a propensity towards continuing dangerous criminal activity.

Whenever the court feels that an individual falls within 1a or 1b it must send the individual for assessment at a diagnostic facility.

The legal limits of this power are fairly clearly defined. It is the predictor of dangerousness that is more difficult. In other words, the legal definitions merely set limits within which the individual can be assessed and possibly incarcerated for a predicted dangerousness. The legal limits will not be accepted by everyone but are simpler to set and monitor than are many checks on the prediction of criminality. The section also illustrates that the mere fact of persistent acts of violence cannot be used to prove mental disturbance, otherwise the final part of the definition would have been unnecessary as begin tautologous.

Some have taken a very narrow view of dangerousness including only overtly extremely violent and dangerous criminal acts such as murder, grievous bodily harm, or sexual crimes such as rape, child sexual abuse etc. Many would argue that this was too limiting as it would not permit the law to intervene when a dangerous or potentially dangerous act had been committed but before it had disastrous consequences. These factors were taken into consideration by Megargee. He defined violent behaviour as: 'acts characterized by the application or overt threat of force which is likely to result in injury to people.' He uses injury to mean personal injury and so excludes all purely property crimes where there is not physical force, either actual or threatened. By including the word 'threat' it covers the instance where there is a property or other offence carried out without actual violence but with a willingness to injure, for example armed robbery. The definition also covers situations where no one is actually hurt but where there is a strong possibility of injury, for example, shooting at someone or setting an explosion where it is 'likely' that injury will result but in fact none does. It does not cover the instance where a gun is fired and no one else is present as there is no likelihood of injury. It would not cover the individual who opens a door and accidentally causes harm to someone on the other side or who crushes someone in a crowd. Most people would not view these activities as violent and it is necessary to include some element of intent even if not the intent to cause harm. Certainly such an element would be important to the usefulness of any definition in assessing dangerousness at least so far as the criminal justice system is concerned. Note this definition covers intentional acts of force which may be legal—such as killing in self-defence—as these are still violent. To exclude this behaviour one would need to define 'criminal violence'—the application or overt threat of force which is likely to result in injury to people and which is forbidden by law. Although this definition is not perfect it is one of the most useful to map out the area of behaviour in which we are interested.

Floud and Young came to a similar conclusion. They defined dangerous offenders as those who have inflicted or attempted to inflict serious bodily harm on other human beings and who are found to be suffering from a severe mental or emotional disorder indicating a propensity towards continuing dangerous criminal activity. Floud also suggested that the reason she so firmly supports longer sentences to protect the public is that it would then allow lower sentences for the run-of-the-mill offences — i.e., a lower tariff which would still mark the seriousness of the offence but exclude extra penalties for dangerousness.

Interestingly the provisions in force in England and Wales incorporate the first part of Floud and Young's definition but largely ignore the second part of the Floud recommendations — that the court should be required to inquire into whether the individual is found to be suffering from a severe mental or emotional disorder indicating a propensity towards continuing dangerous criminal activity.

Attempts to Explain and Predict Violent Crime

For many years theorists have been trying to predict who will offend and re-offend. Basically what many of these researchers do is to collect facts about convicted criminals: previous arrests and convictions; social and employment history; and, for juveniles, their school records, particularly truancy rates; drug use; family backgrounds etc. The factors which are most strongly related to recidivism are then singled out as those most likely to predict unacceptable behaviour. These factors are them tested normally in longitudinal studies no see whether the predictors stand up to the rigours of practical application. The studies do suggest a modicum of success—previous criminal records drug habits and employment histories are the most often quoted predictors, but more recently others, such as family size and the age at which the child starts school, have been included. If these were found to occur in almost all recidivists then they might be used as predictors of dangerousness and so remove the question from the intuition of the judges, but the major problem with this method is that it tends to over-predict. It does very well in picking out groups of people who fit into a high-risk category, but within this group there will be a number of 'false positives.' Many of those with the 'at risk' identifiers will not in fact be dangerous—they will not re-offend. Unfortunately the predictors have been found to be particularly inefficient at discovering those most likely to commit serious crimes, particularly violent offences which is the category we most want to incapacitate. This is partly because of the lack of research material—there are insufficient serious violent offenders around to make a reasonably sized study group from which to glean the prediction characteristics.

More effective might be more personalised psychological predictors. Most of these are related to the idea that it is a disorder of interactions and relationships. Again there are problems with prediction but as they are more an assessment of the individual rather than a group of persons they may be more accurate. Psychoanalysts have, indeed, used a number of different approaches and theories to predict violent behaviour. Several will be briefly discussed here, but for a fuller coverage see Zillman. Siann or Taylor.

Instinct Theories

Instinct theories assume there is an inner force which desires aggression and violence. Frued called it the death force or Thanatos. The life instinct, Eros, and Thanatos are in conflict and the aggression needs to be allowed to vent itself. Usually this is possible through acceptable means such as sport or competitive business, but if the force is not socially dissipated it will come out in the form of violence, either effected to others or at oneself — suicide. The work of Storr is an example of such an appraoch. But however interesting, these ideas are impossible either to prove or disprove, which limits their contribution to understanding in the particular area of criminology, and gives them little practical value.

Drive Theory

Drive theories also assume that there is an inner force which desires aggression and violence, but in drive theory the inner force is acquired through experience, and is not innate. The general argument is that each type of behaviour is motivated by a drive, and as the drive increases above its normal levels, the individual takes action to reduce it. In the case of violence the basic assertion is that when individuals are prevented from getting what they want, they become frustrated. This frustration leads to aggressive or violent behaviour, which may be aimed at the obstruction to their desire or may be used on other targets and Berkowitz. Although these theories are a little easier to verify—for example, by giving people a problem to solve and then moving them onto the next one just before they succeed, or by allowing them to watch all but the last twenty minutes of a film and watching the frustration and violence build up—they are not very useful as predictors of behaviour. It is unclear whether it is being claimed that all aggression is the result of frustration, or that whenever frustration occurs it always leads to aggression. Whichever it is, the interest of the theory is limited because it is not sufficiently precise to be useful as a predictor of dangerousness.

Personality and Violence

There are a number of different ideas under this head. The first claims that people with psychopathic tendencies, sometimes known as sociopaths or antisocial personalities, are more likely than others to commit frequent acts of violence. Sociopaths are generally viewed as those who are unsocialised; they do not hold strong values and are less capable of forming loyal relationships with other individuals or with groups, they are selfish, irresponsible impulsive, uncaring and do not tend to feel any guilt; they are easily frustrated and tend to blame others for their bad behaviour. As Checkley points out, the term psychopath or sociopath is fairly wide, and is often used to describe anyone who breaches the law, so that it becomes synonymous with criminal. He argues, however, that the true usage of the term can include businessmen, professionals, sportsmen, etc. A brasher idea of sociopathy was expounded by Guze, who said a person was a sociopath if he had been in trouble with the police (other than for traffic offences) and had at least two of the following: a history of excessive fighting; school delinquency; poor job record; a period of wanderlust; and being a runaway. For women, the fact that they had a history of prostitution could also be taken into account. He argued that sociopaths could not be treated, and therefore that they should all be locked up until middle age. This recommendation, if taken seriously, would apply to a large number of people who have never committed serious crimes and may never do so. It also confidently assumes that all sociopaths are readily identifiable without possibility of error. It promotes drastic steps with no sound proof that these would make society any safer. This is reinforced by Rafter's discussion of the evolution of the term 'psychopath' in criminology. She observes that the term is probably undefinable, being a 'misfit', 'on the borderline' between 'normality and abnormality.' For legal purposes a more precise definition would seem to be in order.

One of the most prominent explanations of violent behaviour was expounded by Megargee. He argued that violence occurs when the push towards violence, which usually arises through anger, is stronger than the individual's ability to control it. The loss of control he saw as most dangerous in two particular personality types: the under-controlled and the over-controlled. When a potentially aggressive situation arises, the under-controlled make little or no attempt to control feelings of violence. Such persons are likely to have many convictions for minor acts of violence.

On the other hand, people who are over-controlled restrain their aggression in situations where most people might be provoked but eventually reach a point where they may suddenly commit acts of extreme violence well beyond what might have been expected from the immediate provocation. The extreme level of violence which Megargee finds characteristic of this type of offender he explains by saying that most of us learn to match our level of violence to the levels of provocation by practice.

Blackburn has taken the theory further. In 1971 he carried out dour MMPI tests on 56 murderers who had been detained in mental hospitals, and claimed that they could be analysed into four groups. Two of the groups were under-controlled and two were over-controlled. The under-controlled were:

1. *Psychopathic*—poor self-control, high extroversion, hostility towards others and low anxiety;

2. *Paranoid aggressive*—poor self-control, hostility towards others and psychotic symptoms.

The over-controlled were:

1. *Controlled-repressor*—high level of self-control, low hostility and low anxiety;

2. *Depressed-inhibited*—not impulsive, high levels of introver-sion and anxiety, hostility directed inwards and high level of depression.

He found similar results when he tested violent offenders who were not hospitalised. His findings have been upheld on a number of occasions, but McGurk and McGurk discovered that non-violent criminals could also be found to have fairly large numbers of the first three categories; only the depressed-inhibited were not found in the non-violent group. Their findings have also been replicated, and this suggests that personality inventories cannot be used in this way to predict dangerousness. This finding would be upheld by the previous discussion of the MMPI test.

It is unlikely that any method used to predict dangerousness is very accurate, and this must call into question the use of this concept in the criminal justice system.

Macho Personality and Dangerousness

The final personality difference which in recent years has been closely related to violence, and therefore possibly to dangerousness, is the macho personality as measured by the Hypermasculinity Inventory. The macho personality views violence as manly, danger as intrinsically exciting, callous sexual activity aimed at women as acceptable, and interprets being tough as a form of self-control. Zaitchick and Moscher connected these personality elements with inter-male violence, callousness, violence and sexual attacks on women, gang violence and abuse of children. The utility of this test in predicting dangerousness could therefore be very strong but more scientific testing of the inventory is necessary before it can be reliably used to remove an individual's freedom.

Risk, Mental Disorder and Dangerousness

In a recent study Steadman *et al.* worked in a team of 12 people including those trained in law, psychiatry, psychology and sociology who, after reviewing empirical and clinical research, concluded that there were five central factors to an assessment of risk of dangerousness. The factors are:

(a) the level and type of social support available to the persons;
(b) how impulsive the individual is;
(c) reactions, such as anger, to provocation;
(d) the level of ability to empathise with others;
(e) nature of any delusions and hallucinations.

They designed reasonably simple and apparently accurate tests which would assess each of these factors in mentally disordered groups, recognising that these might also be valid for testing other groups. In a pilot study they had some success in these clinically assessed factors, but there were discrepancies and the team felt that these might be the result of not having taken into account the situation or context in which any acts of violence took place.

The Hare Psychopathy Checklist-Revised or PCL-R

This tries to isolate an antisocial personality disorder, or severe personality disorder, without reference to criminal behaviour. It is this type of test that is most likely to be use in the assessment under the government's new proposals if they ever become law. It purports to test for such things as 'absence of guilt or remorse', 'callous/lack of empathy', 'criminal versatility', 'cunning', 'glibness/superficial charm', 'failure to accept responsibility for actions', 'grandiose sense of self-worth', 'impulsivity', 'irresponsibility', 'juvenile delinquency', 'lack of realistic long-term goals', 'manipulative', 'many short-term marital relationships', 'need for stimulation', 'parasitic lifestyle', 'pathological lying', 'poor behavioural control', 'promiscuous.' Hare suggests that it is now quite a sophisticated measure of severe personality disorder but Hare recognises that there are some problems in administering the test and he sets out some troubling examples. The test delivers a numerical score which has an attractive simplicity, which will appeal to government given the current obsessions with league tables for everything. A major problem is that there is no precise score at which the disorder kicks in. As with all other mental problems the diagnosis is a continuum: those classed as having the disorder are simply those who fall towards one end of the continuum. Clearly there will be clinial disagreement about exactly where the line is crossed. As Taylor notes, the list of qualities tested comprises things most of us would not want in a friend, and assessments based on these criteria may have as much to do with whether the assessor likes the interviews as with any scientific analysis. People may have many unappealing characteristics but can still appear, and may be, normal in any scientific or clinical sense. Certainly they often do not feel they have a problem themselves, even if they are causing problems for those around them. What the test may be trying to uncover is in fact nastiness. Reiss *et al.* endeavoured to test its utility as a tool for clinical diagnosis on young males in Broadmoor. Its results seemed promising whilst the men were still in the hospital but on their release it failed to predict either the reoffenders or the ability to readjust to society. Taylor suggests that it may be testing not just personality disorder but also the likely response to treatment: it might then become a self-fulfilling prophesy by being used to decide on treatment.

The Q-sort and Multiple Tests

The Q-sort test was invented by Westin and Shedler and aimed to get around the subjective problems noted in the previous test. The clinician has to score a person on a scale of 1–7 for each of 200 questions on issues such as 'tendency to act impulsively.' It may prove promising in the future but there are still problems with subjective and uncomplimentary assessments.

Broadmoor uses many systems to classify illnesses in

general, and severe personality disorder in particular. Assessments are made by nurses and social workers as well as doctors and there are often a number of problems found in one patient. Thus severe personality disorder may be present with other psychotic illnesses. How they interact is unknown.

The Dangers of Prediction

As can be seen from the preceding section, the psychological prediction of dangerousness is very problematic and unreliable. In the United States, following a 1966 decision of the Supreme Court, 967 patients who had been diagnosed as dangerous were moved from hospitals for the criminally insane to ordinary mental hospitals, and in most cases this posed no problem. Only 26 individuals were returned to hospitals for the criminally insane; over 483 were later released into the community, and of these 83 percent had no further arrests. Clearly, most of them were perfectly safe. How could their detention be justified? Most countries do confine individuals to protect other members of society from harm. Can this be justified? A large part of the argument which follows is adopted from that made by Floud and Young.

In most countries the penal system is largely based upon an idea of retribution, being intended as a punishment for a crime which has been committed. Where there is some recognition of the possibility of deterrence and rehabilitation, they have generally had to be accommodated with the time period laid down for retribution. Sentences are not generally lengthened simply to enable more time for rehabilitation, and are rarely lengthened for reasons of deterrence. The exception is that most States do considerably lengthen sentences, in certain circumstances, for reason of protecting the public. Clearly, protecting the public is a function of the criminal justice system, but the removal of the liberty of people based on a judgement, difficult to prove, that they may be a danger to others raises acute problems. Of course, in most States confinement to protect others does not take place unless the individual has first committed a crime. Is this a sufficient reason for such action? Does it make it acceptable? Should all rights be removed from an individual merely because of a single, or even a series, of transgressions? Once the individual has paid the debt to society, should they not be again presumed innocent until proven guilty?

It can be argued that such questions ignore the potential harm these individuals may inflict, and abrogates the responsibility to protect the innocent who might be harmed. This argument is most forceful where the lives or the health of others are at risk. An analogy is often made with quarantine—we confine carriers of infectious disease to protect others in society from becoming contaminated and thereby harmed, and so we should be willing to protect the public from dangerous criminals. In the case of disease, we do not protect society from all contagious diseases, only those most likely to have the worst consequences for those who catch them. Similarly, most people would never argue that the public should be protected from the petty criminal. That claim is made only in the case of those whose past conduct suggests they may inflict severe harm on others, usually physical harm to the person.

It has to be noted that the analogy is far from exact. It implies that the danger from a criminal is similar to the danger of catching a disease. Whilst there is a high probability that people exposed to the disease carrier will contract the disease, people suffering from a disease are not likely intentionally to try to contaminate others; they are confined because they cannot help but contaminate someone. There are therefore two differences. Firstly, there is a very high probability, and in most diseases a certainty, that if released the individual will contaminate someone and, secondly, that the contamination will be unintentional. If a supposed dangerous criminal is released, there is no such certainty and, as was seen above, often no strong probability that he or she will re-offend. The criminal has a choice, and that choice may depend upon many factors, including the situations faced on release. For any particular case there is the possibility that the released prisoner may not re-offend, and because there is no sound way of predicting future behaviour he or she has the right to be presumed innocent until the criminal law is actually transgressed.

This is a powerful argument until there is a further victim who may well be killed or suffer serious injury. At that point it will certainly be argued that the rights of the criminal should have been forfeited before anyone else was harmed. Such a reaction has a powerful emotional appeal, but that may not be a sound basis for legal action. If individuals are to have their liberty removed on some judgement of their future behaviour, it is clear that mistakes will be made. Some perfectly safe people will be incarcerated and some very dangerous people may be released. The problem is one of discerning the dangerous from the safe, and as yet the bases for prediction are unreliable. The arguments on both sides have merits; it largely becomes as moral argument of balancing the individual right to freedom against the collective call for safety. Most States allow some use of protective confinement and accept that some will have their liberty wrongly interfered with. Equally, most States allow such protective detention only in certain, usually well defined, situations and accept that they will thereby release some dangerous people. The secret is to find the right balance of reducing mistakes whilst understanding the justice of confinement to protect others. Even if severe personality disorder can be effectively diagnosed it is still unclear whether the European Convention on Human Rights would be breached where incapacitation is not related to the seriousness of a previous offence, let alone where there is no previous offence.

Floud and Young argued that the way forward was by taking account of where the burden of risk should lie. Before individuals have committed a serious violent act, even if they fall into the dangerous group, they should retain their liberty and society should bear the risk that they may one day offend and cause some harm. But one people commit serious violent offences and also fall into the potentially dangerous group, then the burden of risk shifts to them and they should be locked up in case they do it again. Floud then argues that any detention above that necessary to mark the seriousness of the past crime should be limited to cases where the harm is severe, such as serious sexual or violent offences.

More recently there has been even more focus on risk as the central element in assessment of dangerousness. In the USA the 1991 Public Health Service report, *Healthy People 2000*, discussed the problems of violence and abusive behaviour from the health, rather than legal, perspective and focused of four main points:

(a) A move away from a legal focus towards one based solely on risk, as assessed by health professionals.

(b) Full realisation that all decision in this area are on a linear continuum and cannot be split into simple yes/no decisions. Cases rarely clearly fall into one or other category so that decisions whether or not to release should be based on where on the continuum the risk should lie.

(c) The level or risk should never be decided once and for all. A person's potential danger will alter over time and this should be recognised by allowing frequent reconsideration of treatment and release.

(d) In all decisions there needs to be a balance between the seriousness of any possible criminal behaviour and the probability of it occurring. These assessments need to be based on specific risk factors.

Clearly much of the US suggestion accepts the need for protection of the public but allows it to interfere with the liberty of an individual only where this is proved to be necessary and only for as long as is necessary. This highlights a number of problems with our present system. Under ss. 79(2)(b) and 80(2) (b) of the Powers of Criminal Courts (Sentencing) Act 2000 the judge in court will assess the amount of time necessary to punish for a particular offence and, where there is a need to protect the public (in violent or sexual cases), will also set the time necessary for such protection. This is a one-off decision which may not be assessed on any objective criteria or advice. With the exception of an immediate appeal it cannot be altered as the person changes and his or her danger to the public is either lessened or increase. In the case of life imprisonment the dangerousness of both mandatory and is cretionary lifers will be assessed only once they have served the element necessary to punish for the crime committed. Most of this assessment should be concerned with their dangerousness, but how carefully the seriousness of the possible outcome is weighed against the probability of it occurring is impossible to tell. There are certainly no specific risk factors set out which need to be considered. In relation to mandatory and minimum sentences, there is no consideration of individual risk which is assumed if certain past conduct has occurred. This Act applies the first part of Floud and Young's test, but totally ignores the second part relating to individual assent. Finally in relation to restriction orders under s. 41 of the Mental Health Act 1983, these are largely medically assessed on grounds of the need for, and utility of, treatment as well as any consideration of dangerousness. In the method of their review they probably most closely approach the US suggestions, but still no specific risk factors are set out.

One suggestion is that the assessment should take account of both past conduct, particularly very harmful criminal activity, and a personal assessment, often of the offender's mental state or personality type. The second leg of this rather assumes a measurable tendency towards criminality which, as has been indicated above, is very often questionable and thus should never, alone, be used to predict dangerousness. It should be noted that there is no necessary link between mental illness and criminality (nor more of those with mental problems commit crime than do the general population) and that psychiatrists have found it impossible to predict criminal behaviour. However, it is argued that once the first part of the assessment has been completed then the second becomes necessary. For those who have a recognised mental illness, an evaluation of whether, and to what extent, their condition could be treated and whether such treatment could occur in the community is necessary. To safeguard the freedom of the individual, a careful analysis of the mental state might indicate that appropriate care and treatment measures rather than incarceration can reasonably ensure that the offender will not be, or is very unlikely to be, dangerous in the future. In other cases past behaviour may indicate no more danger than is normal, but without some assessment this would be impossible to ascertain. Without professional assessment it will be risky for the judge to release or to incarcerate only for a short period someone who has a past history of harmful offences. The tendency would be to refuse such release even where the immediate offence does not call for lengthy incarceration, which may breach basic rights to freedom. Professional assessment does not, of course, completely remove risk, but it makes possible a more balanced judgement between the need to protect the public and the desirability of maintaining individual rights.

Assessment of dangerousness and imprisonment associated with such assessment are both fraught with problems. Three areas in particular appear to need safeguards: first procedure; secondly the factors to be considered in the assessment; and finally the type of confinement.

The procedure of permitting a judge to assess this aspect at any stage appears to be questionable. This is unlike most other judicial decisions and there are good reasons for allowing the assessment to be made by a panel of persons, possibly including a legally qualified individual but definitely including a psychiatrist or psychologist. In cases where there is an element of dangerousness the judge could still pronounce on the seriousness of the offence committed and then pass the offender over to such a panel to make a preliminary assessment of its extent. There would then need to be a separate tribunal to hear appeals and to reassess the decision at appropriate intervals. This should represent a recognition that the decision being made is different in kind and effect from the judicial decision of punishment.

Secondly, there is a need for guidelines on how to assess dangerousness, what level of proof is necessary and how to balance the possible harm to the public against the probability of occurrence. Some guidelines are necessary as this is a very grave interference with liberty which should not be taken lightly. Open public debate about where the lines should be drawn would be helpful: at present we have almost no criteria and, in some cases, no need for professional advice. The problems are legion but they need to be faced, particularly as the use of longer sentences for the protection of the public seems likely to become more common.

Lastly, there is the question of where to hold such individuals. Clearly some are mentally ill with treatable problems and are held in hospitals; others are in prison either because they are not suffering from a mental condition or because their condition is not treatable. Prisons are generally places we send individuals as punishment: should we be using them for dangerous offenders once they have served the part of their sentence necessary to punish? If they are detained to protect others rather than directly in relation to their behaviour, society should recognise this and place them in different institutions with more rights while retaining the level of security necessary to secure their removal from society. There seems to be little justice in imprisoning them in houses of punishment. However, more recently, number of researchers have been more positive about the possibility of effective treatment and suggest that this might arise in secure therapeutic surroundings, possibly separate from present mental health provisions, Quinsey *et.al.*

As was noted above Taylor has criticised the diagnosing of severe personality disorder as being too subjective and too closely linked to criminal activity. In fact the close link between disagnosis and crime has been problematic for sometime. In effect one type of past behaviour (crime) is being used to prove that the individual has a personality disorder which makes them likely to commit that same behaviour. The results are then used to incapacitate that person, imprison him or her, in order to make society safer. There are clearly problems with this approach. A different approach emerges from the work of Kohnken and Hodge *et. al.* suggesting that, for some people, crime can become addictive. Kohnken deduces

this from the observation that the best predictor of whether
someone would offend was previous offending behaviour. As
Hodge *et al.*, note it might be sensible to look at addiction
models in order to understand the crime patterns of many
who might presently be thought to have a personality disorder
or even a severe personality disorder. At least before locking
up vast numbers of people for possible future behaviour these
avenues should be explored.

4
Social Psychology of Crime

Criminal activities and the processes that sustain them are embedded in the transactions between individuals. They may therefore be seen as social psychological phenomena. Indeed, many of the social mechanisms relevant to conventional psychological explanations of behaviour are also important for understanding the actions of criminals. Yet curiously, attempts to draw upon psychological theories and methods in order to contribute to police investigations—often referred to as 'profiling'—have almost universally ignored the social dimension. The present volume fills this gap and considers the implications of social psychology for both the understanding of crime and its successful investigation.

The absence of the social psychological dimension in 'offender profiling' has largely been because 'profilers' have commonly focused on bizarre individuals, drawing upon models of individual disturbance to account for offence behaviour. We have shown in earlier volumes in this series the weaknesses of approaches that rely upon pathogenic models of immutable deviant dispositions. One failing of such models is their inability to account for the many aspects of offending that necessitate and are actually defined by socially functional behaviour.

Many aspects of offence behaviour require interpersonally 'successful' transactions. For example, the financial exchange between burglar and handler may require appropriate negotiation tactics; armed robbers may benefit from interpersonal behaviour that avoids violent transaction but nevertheless gains compliance through social manipulation; individuals who are members of a robbery team have to function effectively as a group to rob specific targets; crime syndicates rely on co-ordination between skilled individuals in order to be able to manipulate the system to their own ends. Even in some cases of rape and murder there are instances where offenders gain control over their victims through socially skilled processes of persuasion and deception.

A second and related set of issues concerns the group structures, social and cultural networks, that form the context within which many offences occur. Few offences involve a sole operator and, instead, often consist of groups or teams of individuals that, to a greater or lesser extent, have to interact to make the offence possible and for criminals to benefit from it. This is most obvious in what is known as 'organised' crime, typically dealing with the purchase and sale of illegal goods, but it is also a part of all crime that has some financial component to it from burglary to major frauds. To understand how these crimes are possible the implicit and formal organisational networks of which they are a part, have to be understood.

The recognition of the social and organisational aspects of crime offers a particular perspective for police activity. Social and organisational psychologists devote their time to considerations of how social transactions can be facilitated and how organisations can be made more effective. Yet in the criminal context the very opposite is the objective. Individuals involved in the process of investigation are attempting to incapacitate criminal networks and to weaken the social interactions of criminals. There is a sense in which such investigators need to turn organisational theory on its head, learn what factors make an organisation efficient and then see whether the same factors used 'in reverse' can render that organisation unworkable. Many examples of the possibilities for this are given in the following chapters.

The social environment is also relevant, though, even for the allegedly 'alienated' offender. Indeed as discussed by Canter the bizarre thought patterns, self images and extreme behaviours that help to distinguish offends are likely to be a product of a personal narrative of alienation, nurtured and fuelled by comparisons to the groups that the individual no longer feels part of. The increasing distance created between such offenders and these groups can only occur as a product of interacting increasingly poorly with them. Thus, to understand this alienation the social psychological process that engenders it also needs to be understood.

Learning Theory and Social Learning Theory

The learning theory view of criminal behaviour as espoused by traditional learning theories is that it is learnt in the same way as all other learning: by classical and operant conditioning. [These are discussed in detail in Jarvis *et al.*, (2000), *Angles on Psychology*]. Classical conditioning involves learning to associate one thing with another, so a child may learn to associate stealing sweets with excitement. Operant conditioning involves learning by the consequences of your actions; if you are reinforced for an action you are more likely to repeat that action in future; if you are punished, then the behaviour will decline in frequency.

When applied to the causes of criminal behaviour, the principle is quite simple and involves mainly operant conditioning—criminal behaviour is learned and maintained by the rewards it brings. For example, stealing brings obvious material rewards and may bring less obvious but equally powerful ones such as the admiration of peers, a feeling of competence, increased self-esteem and a thrill.

Bandura's Approach

Social learning theory differs in significant ways from behaviourism by considering some important *cognitive* elements to learning. Bandura postulated that their are three main influences on people's behaviour. The first is external reinforcement (as in operant conditioning); the second is vicarious reinforcement; the third is self-reinforcement. Let us explain these last two terms.

Vicarious reinforcement involves learning by watching other people, rather than by receiving rewards or punishments directly. According to Bandura, one way in which children learn is by watching other people; this learning is known as *observational learning* and is very influential. Individuals, particularly children, copy other people, especially if the behaviour is rewarded. If one child sees another snatch a toy from someone and play with it without beivg told off (without being punished), he or she may well do the same. Conversely, a child is unlikely to copy a behaviour for which the model is punished. Some people are more likely to be imitated than others, namely significant and respected models such as parents, teachers, peers and media figures.

Self-reinforcement involves the pride you feel when you do something well. Again, direct reinforcement is not necessary—if you feel good about the way you have behaved, then this motivates you to behave similarly in the future. The converse is the feeling of shame you experience if you do something that goes against your own moral standards; this puts you off repeating such behaviour.

Social learning theory, unlike traditional learning theories, does not regard people as simply passive respondents to external stimuli but argues that their behaviour is influenced by anticipation and attitudes. Based on previous experience, people have expectations about the consequences of what they do (if you are punished for walloping your brother, you expect that this may happen again if you hit him, and this may influence whether or not you repeat the action). People also create their own environments: some people don't wait for events to happen, they seek out exciting experiences, including, in some cases, criminal ones.

A lot of Bandura's work was concerned with the observational learning of aggressive behaviour. In the meantime we will look at theories of crime that are based on the principle of learning and which therefore differ significantly from the biological theories of crime.

The Theory of Differential Association: A Sociological Learning Theory

As long ago as 1939 Sutherland used social learning theory principles to advance a sociological theory of crime known as Differential Association Theory. This theory, originally written in 1939 and slightly modified in 1947, is sociological because it postulates that it is the *social organisations* in which people are socialised that determine whether or not they will participate in criminal activities. According to Sutherland, criminal behaviour, like all behaviour, is learned through social interactions. Some subcultures within society are organised so that the norms are favourable towards criminal activities whilst others are organised so that the norms are unfavourable to such law violation. Individuals come into contact with both types of attitudes or, in Sutherland's terminology, *definitions.* If they encounter more and stronger definitions in favour of law violation than against it, then they will consider crime to be an acceptable way of life. The term *differential association* reflects the ratio of favourable to non-favourable definitions of crime. This theory therefore explains why any individual may be drawn into a life of crime and why crime rates are higher in some neighbourhoods than in others.

Sutherland advanced nine principles on which the theory of differential association is based:
- Criminal behaviour is learned rather than inherited.
- The learning of criminal behaviour takes place through association with other people in a process of communication.
- Most of such learning is through association with close family and friends, that is, intimate personal groups.
- The learning involves techniques for carrying out crimes, and also criminal motives, drives, attitudes and rationalisations (such as it being all right to steal from large shops because they overcharge in order to

make excessive profits and no individual will suffer as a consequence of such minor shoplifting).

- This learning involves definitions, or norms, which may be favourable or unfavourable to breaking the law.
- If there are more definitions (attitudes) favourable to breaking the law than ones that are unfavourable then a person becomes delinquent. This is the principle of differential association.
- The learning experiences, called differential associations, will vary in frequency, intensity and importance for each individual.
- The processes by which criminal behaviour is learned are the same as those for all types of learning.
- Although criminal behaviour is an expression of general needs and values (such as the desire for material goods, the need to support one's children), the expression of these needs and values does not *explain* criminal behaviour since non-criminal behaviour is motivated by the same needs and values.

This theory, then, states that the main factors influencing behaviour are who a person associates with, for how long, how frequently and how personally meaningful the associations are. Sutherland did not propose that it was necessary to associate directly with criminals in order to learn these attitudes and methods, but that contact with people who were favourable to certain law violations or cheating was quite sufficient. For example, parents may emphasise the importance of not stealing but may falsify their tax returns or avoid buying a television licence. In this way a child may have little or no contact with deviant groups and still learn values conducive to antisocial behaviour. Sutherland, the, believed that criminal behaviour was not caused by a lack of personal fibre but by the content of what was learned. As Lilly *et al.*, appositely express it: 'Those with the good fortune of growing up in a conventional neighbourhood will learn to play baseball and to attend church services; those with the misfortune of growing up in a slum will learn to rob drunks and to roam the streets looking for mischief.' This was, for its time, a very radical theory which shifted the emphasis from individual lack of morality to problems within society.

Evaluation of Sutherland's Theory

One of the most important contributions made by Sutherland's theory was to draw attention to the fact that by no means all crimes are committed by deviant psychopathic individuals from poverty-stricken backgrounds. Sutherland coined the term 'white collar crimes' to describe the illegal activities engaged in by the middle classes in the course of their professional lives. It was his belief that in the worlds of business, politics and the professions illegal practices were accepted widely as a way of doing business. This is easily accountable within his theory but not by other theories of the day, with their emphasis on abnormality, feeblemindedness and deteriorating families living in slums.

On the negative side, this theory would find it more difficult to explain crimes of passion and other impulsive offences by people who have not been raised to have deviant values. The theory has also been criticised for being vague and untestable. One point on which it is vague is that it does not specify exactly how learning takes place: is it by classical conditioning, operant conditioning or observational learning? The difficulty in testing it arises because of the problems of measuring the number and strength of an individual's various associations and the extent of the influence they may have exerted. Yet another problem is that it says nothing about individual differences in susceptibility to the influence of other people. Nevertheless, although the theory may be incomplete, there is little to suggest, as there is with some others, that it is inaccurate and it has been used as the basis of other theories, such as the differential association-reinforcement theory of Akers.

Evaluation of Learning Theories as a Whole

Learning theories as a whole have highlighted the importance of environmental influences on criminal behaviour. However, as Nietzel points out, a major problem with them is that they try to apply simple principles to very complex and varied behaviour. Moreover, the studies used to test the theory usually involve specific learning tasks in an artificial environment and therefore lack validity since they are unlikely to reflect behaviour in an everyday setting. Learning theory, like many other theories, also finds it difficult to account for the fact that many deviant adolescents abandon their life of crime in early adulthood.

Learning Theory and Social Learning Theories of Crime

+ The theories are based on carefully conducted empirical research, which clearly demonstrates the influence of reinforcement and observation on behaviour.
+ They can help to explain why criminality does, to an extent, run in families. There is a considerable body of evidence indicating that in real-world situations, people do imitate those around them, especially family members.
+ Males and females are socialised very differently, with females encouraged not to be aggressive and to conform, while males are encouraged to 'stick up for themselves' and be independent. This may account for the considerable differences in crime rates of men and women.
– The studies on which these theories are based are conducted in laboratories or other artificial environments in carefully controlled conditions. They therefore lack validity in that they may not be sampling behaviour as it occurs in real life situations.
– The fact that criminal behaviour tends to run in families is not necessarily due to imitation but may be due to circumstances such as social deprivation, or to genetic propensity to behave in an antisocial way.
– There are biological differences between men and women, especially hormonal ones, and this, rather

than socialisation, may account for differential rates of crime between men and women.

Are Violent Criminals More Angry and Paranoid than Non-Violent Criminals?

Aim: To compare a group of violent offenders (murderers), non-violent offenders and non-offenders on measures of anger, hostility, paranoid ideation and global psychopathology. The hypothesis was that those guilty to violent crimes would, compared to the other two groups, have more anger, rage or paranoid symptoms.

This hypothesis was based on several theories of crime. The psychodynamic approach sees homicidal behaviour as stemming from unconscious conflict, an ego weakness, displaced anger or repressive coping mechanisms. From a biological interactionist viewpoint, Lewis & Pincus suggest that many extremely aggressive young men have suffered from abuse and family violence resulting in damage to their central nervous system. Psychosocial variables such as poverty, family turmoil, gain involvement, excessive alcohol intake, physical abuse, educational difficulties and exposure to violent role models either within the family or through the media have also been found to be related with adolescent aggression.

Method

Design: The method used was psychometric testing. This was an independent groups design comparing three groups of young men:
- convicted murderers
- non-violent offenders
- non-offending high school juniors and seniors.

Participants: There was a total of 77 participants, all males from Stockton in California, ranging in age from 16 to 23 with a mean age of 19. All were volunteers who were told that the purpose of the study was to assess various attitudes and beliefs in young people; they all received $5 for participating. There were 29 convicted murders; 15 non-violent offenders imprisoned for repeated robbery and similar acquisitive crimes or for violation of probation; 33 junior and senior school students from a state school, all studying psychology.

All three groups were ethnically diverse and consisted of roughly equal numbers of Caucasians, Blacks, Hispanics and Asians. The two offender groups had a somewhat larger number of Blacks and Hispanics.

The Psychometric Tests: *Three tests were used:*

- MMPI-A: a revision of the MMPI for use with adolescents. This is a personality test which measures adolescent anger, family problems, alienation and conduct problems.
- SCL-90-R: used in this study to measure hostility, paranoid ideation, interpersonal sensitivity and level of distress.
- State—Trait Anger Scale: a self-repeat measure that assesses anger in two ways: as a relatively stable personality trait (trait anger) and as a current emotional state (state anger) reflected in feelings of tension, annoyance, irritation or rage.

The participants were also asked to complete a questionnaire asking the number of times they had been arrested, the number of times they had been arrested for a violent crime, whether they had ever been a gang member and whether anyone in their family had ever been imprisoned. In order to encourage honest responses, they were asked not to put their names on the tests.

Results: The prediction that young murderers would show increased levels of anger, hostility, paranoid ideation, feelings of alienation and global psychopathology was not supported. There was no significant difference here between any of the three groups.

However, there were some difference between the groups. Compared with the school students, a significantly higher proportion of the offenders had grown up in families where at least one other family member had spent time in jail or prison.

Murderers were more likely to be gang members and more inclined to express feelings of self-consciousness, inferiority and inadequacy.

Compared with school students, young offenders expressed *less* global distress and were *less* troubled by feelings of anger and hostility; they were more likely to have been gang members or to have come from a family where antisocial behaviour was a problem.

Conclusion: There was no evidence for differences in anger, hostility and psychopathology between violent offenders, non-violent offenders and non-offenders. A history of gang membership was more likely to distinguish between the three groups. This supports a report from the US Department of Justice that sociocultural variables are the driving force behind the considerable and steady increase in the amount of juvenile crime and violence in the US.

Social and Familial Correlates of Crime

Factors of correlate with crime are those variables, such as economic deprivation, that demonstrate a relationship with the incidence of criminal behaviour. It is crucial to remember that correlations only tell us that there is a relationship between one variable and another; they do *not* tell us what is causing what. For example, there is a relationship between poor school performance and juvenile delinquency but we cannot say that low school achievement necessarily *causes* delinquency. It is equally plausible that once an individual becomes involved in delinquent behaviour, their school work suffers and exam results fall. Alternatively, there may be a third factor—perhaps the attitude of the family towards school work and offending—that causes both of the other factors. It important, though, to recognise that a relationship does have a cause and this is what researchers are trying to uncover, but we should not jump to superficial conclusions about the exact direction of the cause.

There is a myriad of individual, familial and social

correlates of crime: we will consider research on some of the more salient ones but before doing so we will take a look in Research. Now at a longitudinal study based in Cambridge which looks at many factors associated with crime. The study began in 1961–62 and was originally under the directorship of West, whose interim findings were published in 1982, so references made later to West (1982) refer to this study.

The Cambridge Study

Aim: To describe the development of delinquent and criminal behaviour in inner-city males, to investigate how far it could be predicted in advance, and to explain why juvenile delinquency began. The original study was begun in 1961–62; this is a follow-up study of 411 London boys, born mostly in 1953.

Method

Design: This is a longitudinal study based on interviews and tests conducted at various ages over, to date, 24 years.

Participants: The great majority of the sample were chosen by taking all the boys who were then 8–9 years old and on the registers of six state primary schools in one location in London. The boys were almost all white and predominantly from working-class families.

Measures used

1. Tests and interviews at school at ages 8, 10 and 14 years. Interviews in the research office at about 16, 18 and 21 and in homes at about 25 and 31. The tests in schools measured intelligence, attainment, personality and psychomotor skills. The interviews collected information concerning employment history, relationships with females, leisure activities such as drinking and fighting, and offending behaviour.
2. Interviews with the parents about once a year from when the study (when the boys were about 8) to when they were 14 or 15 years old. It was mainly the mothers who were interviewed. The parents provided

information on family size, employment history, child-rearing practices, degree of supervision and whether there had been any temporary separations.

3. Questionnaires completed by the boys' teachers when the boys were 8, 10, 12 and 14. These concerned troublesome and aggressive behaviour, attainment and truancy. Peers provided information on popularity, daring, dishonesty and troublesomeness.

4. Records from the Criminal Record Office to gain information on convictions of the boys, their parents, their siblings and, later, their wives or cohabitees. Minor offences such as common assault, traffic offences and drunkenness were not included in these statistics.

Results

Statistics on crimes committed

1. By the age of 32, 37 percent of the males had committed criminal offences. The peak age was 17. Nearly three quarters of those convicted as juveniles were reconvicted between the ages of 17 and 24 and nearly half of the juvenile offenders were reconvicted between the ages of 25 and 32.

2. Offending was very much concentrated in families. Just 4 percent of the 400 families accounted for 50 percent of all convictions of all family members.

3. The worst offenders tended to be from large-sized, multiproblem families.

4. Most juvenile and young adult offences occurred with other people, but this co-offending declined with age. Co-offending with brothers was not uncommon when the siblings were close in age co-offending with fathers (or mothers) was very rare.

5. The most common crimes in later teens were burglary, shoplifting, theft of and from vehicles, and vandalism. All of these declined in the twenties, but theft from work increased.

6. Self reports showed that 96 percent of the males had

Criminal Psychology

committed at least one crime that might have led to conviction, so criminal behaviour was not deviant.

Predictors of crime at age 8–10

1. Antisocial child behaviour including troublesomeness, dishonesty and aggression.
2. Hyperactivity-impulsivity-attention deficit.
3. Low intelligence and poor school attainment.
4. Family criminality.
5. Family poverty, including low family income, large family size and poor housing.
6. Poor parental child-rearing techniques, poor supervision, parental conflict and separation from parents.

Conclusion: Any one these factors independently predicts offending and the following suggestions are made as to the reasons for this. Children from poorer families are more likely to offend because, due to poor school attainment and an inability to manipulate abstract concepts, they are less able to achieve their goals legally, Impulsive children cannot see the consequences of their actions and desire immediate gratification. Children who are exposed to poor child-rearing practices, conflict or separation do not build up inhibitions against antisocial behaviour. Lastly, children from criminal families and those with delinquent friends develop anti-establishment attitudes and the belief that it is justifiable to offends. This research demonstrates that problem children grow into problem adults who in turn produce problem children. Sooner or later serious measures must be taken to break this cycle.

Poverty

Crime has often been perceived as more common amongst the poor than among the more affluent but the evidence is equivocal. Ehrlich found a positive correlation between rates of property crime in America and the percentage of homes receiving half the average income. In the Cambridge study low family income was found to be related to later delinquency, regardless of other factors. Several studies have also demonstrated a link between dependence on welfare and delinquency. However, no such relationship was found by Jacobs when looking at levels of burglary, robbery and theft.

It is necessary to use several measures of poverty, rather than simply income, in order to gain a more complete picture. Messner used 'structural poverty' as a measure, that is an assessment based on income, one-parent families, poor education and high infant mortality, and found a stronger relationship between these measures and crime rates.

Poverty due to unemployment has also been implicated in the incidence of crime. Benyan reviewed a number of studies of offenders and concluded that unemployment was one of the principal causes of crime and disorder in Britain. Similarly, Wells commented, with reference to Britain, that a society that had such large numbers of children in poverty ran a high risk of widespread delinquency. However, unemployment has a large number of effects other than poverty, including a loss of status and self-esteem, boredom and alienation, and it would therefore be misleading to imply that it is the poverty resulting from unemployment that is implicated in criminal behaviour. Given that the relationship between unemployment and crime is fairly clear, society cannot afford to be complacent about the social consequences of unemployment.

Sociologists draw our attention to the importance of economic inequality rather than poverty as an important influence on much social behaviour, including crime. Economic inequality entails a comparison of the levels of material wealth between different groups within society. Goodman *et al.*, in an analysis for the Institute for Fiscal Studies, reported that the level of economic inequality has risen massively in the last 20 years: the combined income of the top 10 percent of earners was equal to that of the bottom 50 percent of all earners. It has been suggested by several theorists that there is a relationship between crime and inequality. From an analysis of 16 studies of crime and economic inequality between 1974 and 1985, Box (1987) found that eleven showed a positive correlation between economic inequality and crime and he hypothesised that this inequality was responsible for the rise in crime during periods of recession, especially amongst the poorest—the young, women, and ethnic minorities. From an analysis of the situation in the US, Hagan suggested that the increasing inability of the poorest citizens to attain any upward social mobility is likely to lead to increasing competition and violence in the underworld of vice and racketeering. Ironically, this is liable to give the wealthier more opportunity to exploit the poor, both by legal and illegal means.

In conclusion, it would be misleading to equate crime with absolute poverty. The great majority of poor people are law-abiding citizens and the poor do no steal solely because they lack food or clothing. There is more evidence for a relationship between economic inequality and crime. Nevertheless it is important to recognise the possibility that the poor are more likely than the wealthy to be apprehended. It is widely recognised that some of the wealthiest people in society engage in all manner of acquisitive illegal acts such as tax evasion and fraud, and they get away with it.

Family Background

Certain patterns of family life have consistently been shown to be related to crime, as evidenced by the finding that a small minority of families accounts for a large proportion of offences. For example, in the Cambridge study 4.6 percent of families accounted for 48 percent of all convictions. There is an abundant amount of folk wisdom as to what aspects of the family environment are conductive to criminal or delinquent behaviour, with the blame at various times being placed on parental irresponsibility, physical abuse, broken homes and lack of affectionate parenting, to name but a few. We will take a look at research which has investigated some of these variables.

Many studies indicate that delinquents are more likely to come from broken rather than intact homes. As we saw earlier in Classic Research, Bowlby's research supports this idea. This has often led to statements by politicians and other high profile groups that divorce and separation are directly responsible for delinquency. This superficial conclusion has been repeatedly questioned by those who analyse data in greater depth. There are many variables that are associated with the broken home and may therefore have an influence on the child. For example, the divorced are more likely to belong to the lower socioeconomic groups. It is quite possible that factors associated with socioeconomic status, such as poverty and poor educational opportunities, are more closely correlated with delinquency than the number of parents raising the children. Another factor that may be influential is the amount of conflict in the home. There is evidence that children from broken but harmonious homes are less likely to be delinquent than those brought up in intact but conflict-ridden families.

Certain styles of parental discipline are also related to delinquency. Harsh physical punishment is more likely to result in more delinquency than reasoning with the child. This is especially true if the corporal punishment is inconsistent and dependent more on the mood of the parent than on the transgression of the child. Other forms of abuse such as neglect or emotional abuse (for example, screaming, constantly criticising and frequently insulting a child) may also play their part in later delinquency; indeed some researchers suggest that this can be more devastating than physical punishment.

Large family size is also related to delinquency. Farrington found in the Cambridge study that delinquents were more likely to come from families with four or more children. Recidivists, that is criminals who relapse into crime, also come from larger families. Again, explanations are complicated by the presence of other variables: larger families tend to be poorer and live in more overcrowded accommodation, so stress may be a causal factor. However, when large families are matched with smaller ones on family income and socioeconomic status the difference in delinquency rates still persists, so it is possible that lack of attention, difficulties with discipline and/or lack of parental supervision have an effect.

Any single one of the aforementioned family variables (with perhaps the exception of harsh physical punishment) is unlikely to be a strong predictor of delinquency, but the more of such factors that are present in family, the stronger the relationship. In the Cambridge study, 73 percent of boys reared in homes showing three or more of these factors had convinctions by the age of 32 compared with just over 30 percent of the remainder. However, a very important rider is necessary here. Both in the Cambridge study and in others, a large percentage of the offenders (more than two-thirds) had not been reared in deprived families. We need, therefore, to be very careful about the contribution that family variables make to delinquency and to remember that correlation is not causation. Poor parenting and conflict in the home may well be the result of poverty and poor housing which may be more of a direct influence on delinquency.

School and Peer Group

Children who become delinquent do not do well in the school system. Some sociologists maintain that the educational system, with its emphasis on middle-class values, alienates some working-class children and eventually drives them towards delinquency. An alternative explanation is that the problem lies not so much with the educational system but with the individuals whose intellectual ability is so limited that they fail and become alienated, or who lack the necessary skills to cope with the demands of the classroom and playground. Most analyses of educational establishments seem to assume that all schools are the same but, as pointed out by Blackburn, schools vary in their educational philosophies and social organisation which in turn may influence whether they inhibit or facilitate antisocial behaviour.

A major predictor of delinquency among adolescents is the deliquency of close friends; few youngsters engage in solitary offending, most work in groups of two or three.

Hargreaves argues that 'status deprivation' of those who fail in the school system leads to both negative attitudes towards education and the motivation to join delinquent groups. Gold, however, argues that different processes are acting in the two situations. School failure results in lowered self-esteem whilst antisocial behaviour amongst peers helps to present an attitude of defiance which is rewarded by peer admiration. When boys are unloved and maltreated at home and have been made to feel a failure at school, it is not surprising that they turn to a group who provides friendship, admiration and a sense of belonging, as well as excitement and some material rewards.

There is disagreement amongst theorists about the extent to which certain adolescents are passively recruited into delinquent groups and how much they seek out those who they perceive as similar to themselves. It would appear that unsocialised youths tend to seek out similar partners for friendship and that once these alliances are formed, the associates tend to become more alike over time, suggesting that they influence each other. This is consistent with research on interpersonal attraction showing that people form relationships with those who share their attitudes and that stable friendships are maintained by mutual influence.

Others argue that the peer group is a relatively unimportant influence in deliquency and occurs only after early life experiences in the family and school have led the adolescent towards a life of delinquency. Finding friends with whom to commit crimes is incidental to this process. However Hirschi, who originally espoused this view, later acknowledged that association with delinquents could influence even those boys who had strong family ties. The strength of peer group influence is as yet still not established. The evidence does suggest that whilst the peer group may facilitate criminal behaviour, a propensity for delinquency is already present in individuals who join such groups.

Finally, we need to note that not all delinquents work in gangs or are influenced by peer group pressure. A considerable number make solitary rational choices to engage in criminal behaviour for financial gain or as a means of venting their anger and seeking revenge.

Ethnicity

In Britain and the USA the proportion of certain ethnic minority groups convicted of offences is much larger than their proportion in the population as a whole. This applies particularly to people of Afro-Caribbean and black African origin. For example, in June 1998, the rate of incarceration in Britain per 100,000 of the general population was 1,245 for black people, 185 for whites and 168 for Asian. There has been huge high-profile media coverage of this issue, often very emotive in tone. The argument centres on the extent to which these statistics reflect discrimination within the criminal justice system or are a true reflection of the rates of crime among these groups.

It is extremely difficult to ascertain whether black youths do offend to a greater extent than their white counterparts but, if this so, it is probably a reflection of the factors already considered, that is, alienation and economic deprivation. Black people are also significantly more likely than whites to be the victims of crime.

Certainly there is evidence that discrimination does exist in the criminal justice system. Crawford explored the effects of race on over 1,100 habitual female offenders in Florida and found that African-American women were given harsher sentences than their white counterparts. Similarly, when crime seriousness, crime type and prior record are controlled for, black males receive harsher sentences than white males do.

The Macpherson Report, commissioned to address concerns about police recism in Britain, identified unequal treatment of the black community at the hands of the police and a report by the Howard League for Penal Reform similarly identified discrimination against ethnic minorities, ranging from the disproportionately high rates at which the notorious 'stop-and-search' is applied to young blacks right through to the sentencing procedures and even beyond. Dodd, a reporter, writes that

*"Every key stage of the criminal justice system is riddled
with racism, leaving black people with a greater prospect
of being arrested and jailed than whites, according to a
study by a penal reform group.*
*British Afro-Caribbean people are seven times more
likely to be in jail despite being no more likely to commit
crimes, says the Howard League."*

The British Crime Survey, asks people about crimes they
have experienced in the last year and about their contacts
with the police. Bucke, reflecting BCS findings of 1994 and
1996, reported that Afro-Caribbeans were more likely to be
stopped by the police while on foot or in a car and were also
more likely to experience multiple stops. The rate for Asians
was no greater than that for whites. Afro-Caribbeans were
also more than twice as likely as whites to be searched when
stopped and four times more likely to be arrested.

Racial discrimination is, of course, not confined to the
criminal justice system but extends across the whole of society.
This limits the educational and employment opportunities of
ethnic minority groups and, as we have seen, increases the
likelihood that they will participate in crime. These wider
issues, as well as the specific problems within the justice
system, need to be addressed if any real justice is to be
achieved.

Gender

Women are, on the whole, a law-abiding lot: they are
consistently convicted of crimes to a far lesser extent that
men and this pattern seems to hold true across the world.
Despite the fact that this difference is far larger than any
other, it is only since the 1970s that criminologists have paid
it much attention at all. Studies from a variety of countries
show that approximately 80 percent of crimes are committed
by men. In Britain, around 1 in 3 men will have a conviction
for a serious offence by the age of 31 (a staggering statistic),
while this applies to only 1 in 13 women. Moreover, women
are usually convicted of less serious offences than men (UN
statistic, 1975–1985; 1996 Criminal Statistics for England

and Wales). The general pattern is that although men and women commit similar crimes, they do so at very different rates; for example, women are far less likely to commit robbery, sexual offences or murder. Some criminologists argue that women are under-represented in crime statistics but others argue that they may even be over-represented since they seldom have the opportunity to be involved in organised and corporate crime of which many men are guilty but not convicted.

Traditionally the explanation for the relative infrequency of female criminality is that girls are socialised to be more conforming, are more strictly supervised by parents and are shown greater disapproval for breaking society's rules than are boys. In a study of high school children in Toronto, these researchers found that girls were subject to more control within the family than boys were. The effects of early socialisation are carried through life. It has also been suggested that because most adult women have part-time and low-level jobs they are reluctant to risk them by engaging in criminal activity. They are also controlled by the threat of violence on the street which makes them more likely to stay out of harm's way.

These are some of the reasons why women do not get involved in crime. Looking at the other side of the coin, various theories have been advanced to account for why some women do get involved in criminal activity. Lambroso believed that women were evolutionarily inferior to men, a lower form of life. Having, as we saw earlier in the chapter, hypothesised that the criminal male was an evolutionary throwback, his ideas about women made it difficult for him to account for their relative lack of offending. He suggested that the 'natural' female criminal was so physically unattractive that natural selection had operated to make her unlikely to breed. Those who remained were among the few not 'neutralised by maternity' and were likely to be even more horrific and monstrous than their male counterparts.

Freud offered an explanation of female crime. He

believed that women, who universally are not able to fully resolve the Oedipus complex, have a great deal of need for the approval of men, so as a rule they do not risk upsetting them by committing crimes. The exceptional female who does offend is seen as suffering from extreme penis envy and, in a desire .to be a man, takes an aggressive, non-conforming attitude that may result in criminal behaviour. As Jones comments, 'If anything, this explanation of female crime is likely to induce more ridicule and mirth than that of Lombroso.'

Box explains female crime in terms of poverty and unemployment. Women's usual response to lack of opportunity and school failure, he argues, is to blame themselves rather than society so they are less likely to turn to crime. When they do, it is as a desperate attempt to escape from poverty rather than, as in the case of many men, an aggressive response to the social situation. Carlen conducted in-depth interviews with criminal women and concluded that many crimes were an attempt to escape financial hardship.

A rather different approach to the issue of gender and crime is taken by Messerschmidt who argues that it is society's concept of masculinity that leads to criminal behaviour in boys and men. To be masculine means, he argues, to assert authority and control over others, to be individualistic, aggressive and independent. If legitimate male outlets are unavailable, the only way to assert one's masculinity is to turn to crime. This is very different from the biological view that because 'boys will be boys' a certain level of violence and antisocial behaviour is inevitable. Messerschmidt has considered in detail how masculinity is asserted by different groups but he has not provided a detailed analysis of why some men assert their masculinity by behaving in a deviant fashion whilst others use alternatives such as sport.

Although a start has been made on investigating the relationship between gender and crime, there is a long way to go. Most research on female crime has focused on minor offences, such as under-age drinking and truancy, carried

out by young girls. The study of older women convicted of
serious crimes has received little attention so as yet we know
little about it. If society has a commitment to reducing crime
rates, then taking a serious look at the processes that result
in so few women offending may be very productive, for, as
Wotton commented '.... if men behaved like women, the courts
would be idle and the prisons empty.'

Cultural Theories and Criminal Networks

Mars provides a particularly helpful framework for
examining the social psychology of crime by drawing on
cultural theory that has its roots in anthropological
consideration. Mars empahsises two underlying dimensions
that help to distinguish between the various criminal cultures
that exist. One dimension is the extent to which a culture
imposes rules and classifications on its members. The other is
the strength of the group of which a person is a members
and how much of the person's life is tied into that group.
Combinations of these distinctions help of draw attention to
important differences in the social context of which a criminal
may be a part.

For example; Chinese *triads,* a group that is suggested
to have a high degree of classification, and clearly defined
ranks, requires the person to be strongly committed to that
group whilst providing for all aspects of his life. Such a group
is thought to be less vulnerable to police informants than
and *ad hoc* gang of armed robbers who only come together to
carry out one particular crime. It follows that one task for a
police investigator is to determine where on these dimensions
any criminal network actually resides. From such
examinations the vulnerabilities of those networks can be
revealed.

McAndrew describe in detail the mathematical
possibilities that now exist for describing criminal networks.
In doing this he shows that some of the central concepts for
describing groups can be very ambiguous unless given
mathematical precision. Such precision then allows sensible
consideration of crucial investigative questions. For instance,

where the vulnerabilities really are in any networks or if the criminal organisation really will be fatally wounded if its apparent leader is removed. These analyses also facilitate the monitoring of changes in communication networks and the revelation of just how fluid they are and how difficult it may be to specify their structure. Likewise, Johnston uses particular analyses to draw out the structural details of football hooligan networks and the relationship between a person's position and their individual background.

The importance of considering the social transactions and parallels between the investigative team and the groups that they are dealing with is nowhere more important than in hostage negotiation situations where the subtleties of the dynamics between hostages, terrorists and the negotiation team must be observed to avoid potential catastrophe. Wilson and Smith emphasise that these processes, even though they occur in high stress situations, follows surprisingly conventional social roles and rules.

As Donald and Canter have previously shown in their work on behaviour in fires, though potentially high stress situations may lead us to believe in more chaotic behaviour being a product of traumatic conditions, actually contextual features result in surprisingly rule bound behaviours. This, as Wilson and Smith argue, is primarily a function of the social dynamics that evolve between the parties involved in the hostage situation. Negotiation strategies appear to follow processes similar to normal equity situations with totally unreasonable demands rarely being made and even the most extreme agendas being flexible enough occasionally to result in compromise.

Wilson and Smith point out that both parties often make concessions. Holding to absolute values, i.e., no concessions, can be very dangerous for government policy and particularly unfruitful for the terrorists. Thus, whilst undoubtedly there are occasions where the behaviour of terrorists groups appear irrational, uncompromising and brutal, such occasions are rare. Perhaps this is because terrorists do not see themselves as deviant or as offenders. Their actions may be more likely to conform to what they see as their own ideology, seeking justice, equity and freedom. They often see themselves as acting out an historic episode that gives meaning to their actions. Living a narrative that assigns them heroic roles.

Inner Narratives of Crime

In order to understand the actions of many criminals it is useful to consider the self-created narratives that help to give shape and significance to their actions. It seems plausible that it is not only terrorists who structure their lives around key episodes and particular patterns of transaction with others. This process of embedding the view of the self in an unfolding personal story, called by Canter an "inner narrative," helps to explain many aspect of criminal activity. It is especially helpful in explaining those crimes that are not of obvious financial benefit or are extremely high risk. The white-collar criminal may see himself as obtaining redress for earlier slights; an unwilling victim rather than a manipulative villain. The member of a criminal gang may view himself as a dashing leader or professional 'hard-man' rather than the dishonest bully that others may recognise.

The roles that are drawn on to give meaning to offenders' lives are embedded in a social matrix. They are supported and refined in the contacts the criminal has with other criminals. They also connect with the notions of antagonist and protagonist that are present in the larger culture of which the criminal partakes. This enables the criminal to legitimise, in his own eyes and those of his associates, the acts he performs and to neutralise in his mind their destructive consequences.

Criminal Identity and Socialisation

Maruna argues that a true understanding of criminal behaviour can only come through indepth analysis of such narratives, and connecting those narratives to roles and behaviours. The criminal narratives to which offenders subscribe may lead them to consider their actions as acceptable and not 'criminal.' Or they may revel in being part of an 'outlaw' group that lives by rules that break conventions. Thus these narratives of offending can be seen as a product of social processes. This 'evolution of identity' accords with social constructionist perspectives:

> "*Identity is formed by social processes. Once crystallised, it is maintained, modified, or even reshaped by social relations. The social processes involved in both the formation and maintenance of identity are determined by the social structure. Conversely, the identities produced by the interplay of organism, individual consciousness and social structure react upon the given social structure, maintaining it, modifying it, or even reshaping it.*"
>
> —Berger and Luckmann

Vygotsky noted that mental functioning is shaped by and situated within social life. This socio-cultural approach to mind emphasises how interpersonal contact shapes individual and mental processes. This can also be seen as a natural psychological consequence of the Sutherland's seminal argument that criminality emerges out of differential association. To the psychologist Sutherland's criminology implies that it is not just the actions of the criminal that are shaped by his social network but the whole way in which the criminal sees his world and makes sense of himself. Like all cognition, criminal cognition is socially situated. The social context of any criminal therefore has a profound relevance for the way in which that criminal's self identity is determined. The organisational structure of criminal groups may therefore be examined to reveal the varieties of roles available to offenders and the implications they carry for any offender's identification with criminal activity.

Studies of the organisational structure of criminal groups show the many levels of and varieties of involvement in offending that are available. For example, Johnston's examination of the structure of football hooligan groups shows there are differences in levels of 'commitment' to offending depending on the extent to which the individuals identify with the hooligan group. This is manifest in such differences

as, for example, the extent to which individuals are prepared
to travel to organised fights. The more committed members
travel further. So strong are these group processes that
fighting is often dictated by the extent to which the individuals
feel a part of the 'in' or 'out' group. As Johnston points out,
two groups that have recently fought one another may form
into a larger group to fight against a jointly perceived more
dissimilar, and therefore 'threat' group. Thus persistence and
the severity of offending appears to be a product of subtle
social processes.

Criminal 'Careers'

The organisational processes that Johnston indicates can
be seen in many other forms of offending and have been
explored at least since the early ethnographic studies of the
20s and 30s. Many of those studies and more recent
explorations, such as Marsh *et al.*, have demonstrated the
existence of role differentiation and consequent
organisational structure within gangs and teams of offenders.
Donald and Wilson's study of ram raiders shows that the
different roles within a team are derived partly on the basis
of the different skills available to and necessary for the
purpose of carrying out ram raids. In fact the authors argue
that the offence requires such a level of skill that it can only
be effectively carried out if it is considered and planned as a
professional activity. Donald and Wilson see no need to draw
upon diagnostic or pathological models to explain behaviour
but instead develop an argument for group processes as
evolving from principles of organisational and social
psychology. They draw heavily upon Guzzo's research on
work groups. These are defined by the existence of social
entities within a larger social system, where tasks are
performed as a product of the group not by discrete
individuals. Moreover, they note that in ram raiding there
are specified roles that the offenders appear to be well aware
of.

Indeed McCluskey and Wardle reveal from interviews
with members of armed robbery teams that these criminals

have a clear conception of roles amongst their members and they appear to enjoy these self descriptions. Katz has pointed out the value in examining the 'seductive' qualities of the image that certain criminal lifestyles promote. Thus, in denying a belonging to the conventional, non-criminal group, some offenders define themselves as members of an 'out group.'

If such roles can be found in groups of criminals, and those roles relate to the offence histories of the offenders, then the question arises as to what paths lead criminals into these different positions in criminal organisations. Are there any parallels here to the 'careers' that people follow in legal organisations?

The idea of a criminal career, in which offenders take on different roles in an illegal enterprise and possibly move through those roles over time, is rather different from the notion that, for example, Blumstein et al., offer. They merely consider the temporal progress of serial criminals in order to establish if there are any defining consistencies to that progress. From a social psychological perspective a career implies changing relationships to the other people with whom the person is working. Therefore understanding where an offender is on his career path can assist in understanding his current actions and criminal history, both matters of great significance to police investigations.

This development in a criminal's involvement in crime, as Johnston has illustrated for football hooligans, may involve more commitment to the 'job' being carried out. For an offender this would imply that they identify with the life of crime, becoming a 'career criminal.' They can come to see significant aspects of themselves as defined by the 'job' they do, namely committing crimes.

Maruna develops the implications of this social construction of criminality of stage further. He contends that proposals for the existence of criminal 'genes', neuro-physiological damage, traits or any other pathogenic explanation of criminal behaviour must deal with the fact that the overwhelming majority of individuals stop offending.

He emphasises that there is nothing stable about most criminals' careers.

The fact that so many individuals desist from crime presents a serious problem for the stable trait theory. Instead, Maruna asserts that a narrative perspective, which is a social process model, helps to explicate the changing dynamic features of the individual's life – the way in which identity is formed as a product of each individual's 'story-line.' This internalised autobiographic narrative is continually evolving to help promote coherence and meaning in individuals' lives. These processes of 'self-telling' have the capacity to shape events and therefore result in a dialectic process between the individual and his social environment. This joint construction of identity, as shaped by the social environment, clearly does not involve pathological diagnostic criteria though the routes through which individuals develop their identities may be deviant and destructive. Criminogenic socialisation processes therefore are not, as Maruna puts it, "created in a vacuum" but are shaped by the opportunities of each individual's social world. Such developments have implications for our understanding of the development of these life stories and the social context from which they evolved.

Social Psychology Police Investigations

There has been little direct application of social psychological concepts and findings to police investigations. As a consequence, the ways in which the results reported in the present volume can be utilised by police investigators have still to be explored in practice. However, various possibilities for making police investigations more effective are indicated in the following chapters. Four main aspects will be summarised here of the social psychology of crime that have broad ranging implications for police investigations.

The Criminal's View of Himself is Socially Constructed

It is often assumed that a criminal's view of himself can only be determined by asking him directly. The social psychological perspective emphasises how much that view is influenced by the contacts the offender has with many other people. So, although the evidential constraints on hearsay are very important, for investigative purposes there is much to be gained by building up a picture of known offenders from interviewing their close associates and relatives. This can provide important information for lines of enquiry as well as insights that can help when interviewing a suspect.

If the community of which an offender is part does not see certain actions as especially criminal then it is very likely that the offender views the actions in the same way. Indeed the perpetrator may measure his own personal worth in terms of the way he contributes to criminal endeavours. This could be revealed through discussions with other members of that criminal community.

The search for 'motives' can also be seen as rather unproductive in many investigations if the actions being investigated are recognised activities within that social group. If those actions, whether it be unprovoked violence or casual theft, for instance are 'what people do' in certain situations. It may be no easier to establish 'motivations' for those crimes than to establish motivations for why some people are altruistic, for example, and help others when there is no benefit to themselves.

Moreover the social psychological perspective helps to dispel the belief that horrific acts of brutality are simply the produce of 'evil' minds, with the consequent investigative implication of searching for a person who is recognisably evil. Often, even the most macabre acts of sadism have logic to them. That is, they need not have evolved as a product of a chaotic, unpredictable and disordered mind but instead have an unfolding personal logic that draws upon accepted practices within particular subgroups within society.

It would be useful for investigators to bear in mind the possibility that even the most deviant acts can be understood through a thorough examination of the social processes that have contributed to the behaviour. For investigative psychologists the routes through which these behaviours evolve must be understood. The challenge is to reveal these latent paths and establish lawful relations between sets of events and actions of offenders. This will only occur through the systematic evaluation and empirical analysis of the personal learning histories of offenders and the manifestations of offence actions.

Most of the features of these learning paths are likely to connect very closely with the ways in which interpersonal relations have developed over the life span. For example, an individual who is used to controlling others or gaining influence through threats or acts of violence is more likely to be violent in a robbery than one who has learnt to control others by planning and determination. The means by which offenders control their victims may be revealing about their personal histories. In order to explore such issues, greater attention must be paid to the social landscape within which offence behaviour occurs.

Criminal Groups will have Varying Degrees of Group Structure, which carry Implications, Relating to Specialism in their Roles and to the Predictability of their Actions

From the labile networks that burglars exploit to sell stolen goods to the organised hierarchies within professional robbery teams, the notion of role and the contextual features that surround it carry many implications for criminal behaviour. Roles may be socially rule bound and occur within more or less strict contextual parameters. Moreover, more explicit rules may be employed in more overtly 'managed' groups in order to guide behaviour. In all cases, however, knowledge of the social process that shapes these behaviours may prove invaluable to investigators. It may help guide both the enquiry team's social structure as well as impose frameworks within which to examine and narrow down particular behavioural 'paths' of offending. This may even be useful for the prediction of certain forms of criminal behaviour.

Investigations into criminal teams and networks do need to identify the cliques and groups that offenders move within. Tightly bound cliques will create their own internal pressures on individuals to perform in certain ways, whereas more labile structures take on their own momentum. The issue is then that the genesis of much behaviour lies within the different structural properties of groups rather than 'inside' the criminal mind. The studies that are presented here demonstrate that a clear understanding of the ways in which groups influence individual behaviours has great relevance for the way in which crime might be investigated. The identification of structural properties of the group may lead the investigator to make reliable assumptions about the likely characteristics of offenders within that network. It will also help the investigator to understand the likely consequences of isolating any individual from his criminal network.

At a Larger Scale the Organisation of Criminal Networks will take on Many Forms, but often they will not Reflect Legal Organisations as Readily as is Sometimes Assumed

Investigators should not assume that the organisational processes within criminal networks, groups or teams reflect perfectly the types of legitimate institutions upon which they may be distortedly modelled. Although the present volume points to the many overlaps between legal organisations and criminal activity, there are many levels and qualitative variants of organisation that, although conforming to generalisable social processes, do not necessarily depend upon the structural properties within conventional organisations. As one might intuitively anticipate, many features of criminal activities reflect a weaker allegiance to an organisational structure than do non-criminal activities. They sometimes more readily reflect expressions of anarchy.

If investigators can identify central figures in the criminal network and establish if there are any cliques that support these central figures then the investigation has a firm basis for planned actions to weaken that network. The further identification of peripheral but potentially knowledgeable members of the networks could also open routes to informants or forms of access for undercover agents.

It is also worth noting that there may be particular forms

of social behaviour that are peculiar to the realm of offending. Thus, although it is unlikely that criminals operate within entirely alien social systems that bear no relationship to legal society, there remains the possibility that we still do not have a clear understanding of the peculiarities of criminal social behaviour. The identification of its unique features is best discovered by relying on the careful collection of intelligence, guided by hypothesis testing based upon current knowledge. Through a number of iterations, these processes may reveal those particular features and, in turn, have a significant application to investigations. This volume is just one example of how researchers can work with material that reveals these patterns.

One further point is the impact of the overall culture in which crime occurs on the criminal culture itself. Leyton, for example, looks at the way in which the nature of murder can be understood as a product of the cultural processes within which it occus. He suggests that murder rates and the subsequent responses to murder by the murderers themselves may be understood as a product of the overall societal perspective on murder. Leyton's view that murder manifests itself in different ways according to cultural parameters is rarely considered in the criminology literature. But Cooke's studies of psycholpathy indicate that the trans-cultural perspective can have significant implications for understanding the actions of individual criminals. Cooke has argued that UK psychopaths reveal the features of their disorder in markedly different ways to American psychopaths. In essence, Cooke reports that UK psychopaths reveal more muted versions of processes of manipulation and selfishness than do the more 'florid' and blatant strategies of the American psychopaths. If substantiated this claim would have major implications for the investigation of crime as well as its treatment and punishment. In particular any readiness to adopt American practices in the investigation and treatment of psychopathy would have to be cautiously considered.

Thus in terms of understanding criminals we should raise questions about how much of the explanation should be sought within the individual and how much is the product of what people absorb from their culture. However, there has been little systematic analysis of criminal social roles. For example what is expected of a leader in a gang may vary considerably according to the role structure of the gang and the general cultural attitude to leadership. There is even likely to be variation in the extent to which labelling of that role occurs; with some groups studiously avoiding such labels.

Many of the social networks of criminal activity extend beyond the boundaries of the specific individuals involved in the immediate features of the offence itself. For example, 'handlers' who purchase stolen goods are not necessarily involved in the details of the offence but are, for example, concerned with the products of a burglary. McAndrew points out that investigators have long been aware of the importance of the links that are external to the crime scene. They are, increasingly, developing systems to help identify relative positions, roles, subgroups and communication methods within the criminal network. McAndrew illustrates how social network analysis has been employed to examine relational and position features of such networks, outlining how various patterns and structures impact upon the means and methods of engaging in crime.

As a developing area of criminal intelligence, a wide range of systems are being created to handle a whole variety of information across different modes of constant—from analysis of surveillance observations to the documentation of phone calls amongst offenders. However, as with all statistical summaries, care has to be taken to avoid the assumption that an organised group necessarily exists as a distinct sub-set of the population just because an intelligence analyst can produce a striking diagram indicating links between the individuals concerned. At both the individual and group level it is clear that the social boundaries are far less clear than many of these structural diagrams may suggest. Future research does need to explore the relationship between representations of criminal group structure and coherence and the actual experience of being members of those hypothesised groups.

The Future

With the increasing capacity of communication systems and with the breakdown of geopolitical barriers, many and varied contacts between criminals are more feasible than ever. Changes in the national and international market places have made old types of crime more global and more part of world wide communication systems. This widespread communi-cation network also opens up many opportunities for new types of crime. For example, fraud is more possible now with international markets. Academics and investigators are likely to find themselves concentrating more closely on the social processes that afford opportunities for offending. In turn, they must develop improvements in their own processes of networking and acting as teams to work effectively in understanding the processes of criminal behaviour.

On direct investigate implication is that the police may have to develop structures that mirror those they are studying and see if loose networks of crime are better examined through a more loosely coherent investigative team. There may be many disadvantages to the military model of policing— particularly in relation to certain types of offending. These problems may be overcome by examining differently structured investigative teams for different types of problem. Attempts to develop different combinations are likely to be merely a process of trial and error unless based on studies of the ways in which behaviour is affected as a product of context. For investigators this is true both in terms of the group that they are studying as well as the groups of which they, themselves, are a part. Increasing knowledge of these social processes is therefore the first step in tackling many forms of present day crime as well as being in a position to deal with new forms of crime in the future. The examination of criminality as a product of the transactions between people is likely to be far more productive for investigators than delving ever further into the supposed 'internal chaos' of individual criminals.

This examination of criminals in what is, in effect, an organisational context opens up the possibility of a rather new form of organisational psychology. In a concluding chapter, written as a sort of Epilogue to the present volume, Canter has called this "Destructive Organisational Psychology." He offers the prospect of utilising what is known about the vulnerabilities of organisations to seek out the weakness in criminal groups, teams and networks. These weaknesses can then be the target of police activities. He points out, though, that one of the greatest potential weaknesses is that members of criminal organisations may not get the benefits from them that they desire. If these dissatisfactions can be encouraged the whole basis of the criminal network is thereby challenged.

The social psychological perspective on crime thus does take account of what may loosely be referred to as the 'motivations' for crime within the individual, but looks for the support of those motivations within the social, organisational context of which the criminal is a part. A fuller understanding of how criminal groups, teams and networks operate will therefore offenders that keeps them criminality active. It also provides new possibilities for the reduction of crime.

5

Physical and Biological Factors and Crime

Physical Environment

For many generations, some scholars have attempted to discover and demonstrate physical determinants of criminal behaviour. They have reported that crimes against property are more frequent in winter months and crimes against the person are more frequent in summer months; and, analogous to this, that crimes against property increase and crimes against the person decrease with the distance from the equator. It has been reported also that crime rates vary with changes in barometric pressures and with direction of the wind. Other scholars have reported that crimes are frequent in mountainous areas and infrequent in plains areas, or are frequent near the coast, and infrequent in the interior.

These reports and claims may be appraised in two propositions. First, the association between crime rates and these physical conditions at best is slight; in some cases not even a slight association has been demonstrated. In general, many exceptions can be found, such as the fact that infant murders are highest in the winter, although most other crimes against the person are highest in the summer. Second, these physical conditions provide the habitat for human life and consequently may facilitate or impede contacts among human beings and perhaps in that sense be related to opportunities for criminal behaviour. For example, the greater frequency of crimes against the person in summer months is presumably due to the greater frequency of contact among human beings in those months. Schmid reported that in Seattle homicides reach the maximum in the winter and explained that this was due to the influx of migratory labourers in the late autumn. It has not been demonstrated that changes in physical conditions change the attitudes and values which are conducive to criminal behaviour.

Heredity

In the early part of the present century the discussion of causes of crime was concentrated on the controversy between heredity and environment and this controversy continues , with decreasing attention, in the present generation. Five methods have been used in the effort to reach conclusions on the question of whether criminality is hereditary: comparison of criminals with the "savage," family trees, Mendelian ratios in family trees, statistical associations between crimes of parents and of offspring, and comparison of identical and fraternal twins.

Lombroso and his followers used comparisons of criminals and "savages" as their method of studying inheritance of criminality. They considered that the typical criminal was a born criminal and attributed this to atavism, or "throw-back" to lower animal and savage life. Their principal evidence that criminality was atavistic was the resemblance of the criminal subjects to the savage, but the characteristics of the savage were assumed, not determined by reliable methods. The result was that Lombroso had no significant proof or explanation of the inheritance of criminality.

Family trees have been used extensively by certain scholars in the effort to prove that criminality is inherited. Perhaps the most famous of these is the study of the Jukes family by Dugdale and Estabrook, who reported that of about 1200 members of this family, 140 were criminals; seven were convicted of murder, 60 of theft, and 50 of prostitution. Often compared with the Jukes family were the descendants of Jonathan Edwards, a famous preacher in the colonial period; none of this descendants were found to be criminals, while many were presidents of the United States, governors of states, members of the Supreme Court and of other high courts, and famous writers, preachers, teachers. The specific difficulty about this comparison is that some of Jonathan Edwards' ancestors did have criminal records; his maternal grandmother was divorced on the ground of adultery, his grand aunt murdered her son, his grand uncle murdered his own sister. If criminality be inherited, Jonathan Edwards and many of his descendants should have been criminals. The more general argument against a conclusion from the study of family trees is that it shows only that a trait appears in successive generations; this does not prove that the trait is inherited. The use of the fork in eating has been a trait of many families for several generations, but this does not prove that a tendency to use a fork is inherited. Every child in the Jukes family has been subject to the influences of environment as well as of heredity, and the environment in this family was customarily conductive to crime. Dahlström has shown that in a family of criminals whose records for four generations were known, six children removed from the family before the age of seven became respectable members of society and two removed after the age of seven became criminals.

At least one person has attempted to demonstrate that criminality not only appears in successive generations but also that it appears in accordance with the expected Mendelian ratios. Carl Rath, in a study of family histories of 98 inmates of a penal institution in Sieburg, Germany, concluded that the offspring in these families were criminal in a ratio which was fairly close to Mendelian expectations. The criminality in the families investigated by Dugdale, Estabrook, and others showed no resemblance to the Mendelian ratios. The fallacy in Rath's analysis is that, since criminality is assumed to be a recessive trait, the trait of an ancestor (duplex, simplex, nullipex) can be determined only by assumption; the criminality of the offspring is used to determine the nature of the parent and then the nature of the parent is used to explain the criminality of the offspring. There is a necessary defect in studies of this kind, for it is not possible to control the breeding of human beings for a sufficient period of time to determine whether a particular individual is "pure," as can be done for plants and insects.

Goring attempted to prove by elaborate correlations that the criminal diathesis or criminalistic tendency is inherited and that environment conditions are of slight importance to criminality. He found that criminality, measured by imprisonment, of fathers and sons was correlated by a coefficient of +.60, which is very nearly the same as the coefficient for stature, span, length of forearm, eye colour, diathesis of tuberculosis, insane diathesis, and hereditary deafness; and that brothers had a coefficient of correlation for criminality of +.45, which is approximately the same as for physical traits. Goring realized that such correlations might be the result of either heredity or environment or both, and he attempted to eliminate the factor of environment on the hypothesis that if the influence of environmental factors is found to be very low, heredity will, by elimination, be the explanation. In order to do this, he divided environmental factors into contagion and force of circumstances, and his argument regarding them is as follows: (a) The resemblance of fathers and sons regarding criminality is not due to contagion, first, because the coefficient of correlation is no higher in crimes of stealing, in which fathers are examples for their sons, than in sex crimes, which fathers ordinarily attempt to conceal from their sons and in which therefore they are not examples; second, because children taken away from the influence of parents at an early age, by imprisonment, become confirmed criminals to a greater extent than those taken at a later age. (b) This resemblance is not due to the force of circumstances, such as poverty, standard of living, or ignorance, because, after the influence of defective intelligence is eliminated by the use of partial correlations, the correlation between criminality and force of circumstances is negligible.

The argument and methods that Goring used are open to criticism at a great many points, but, without multiplying criticisms, the following essential defects are found in his argument : (a) He attempted to determine the importance of heredity by eliminating the factor of environment. In order to do this accurately it is necessary to measure completely the influence of environment, but Goring considered only eight environmental factors, which are a relatively small part of the total environment. (b) He assumed that mental ability is not at all affected by environment, and by thus under-rating the environment he over-rated heredity. (c) His comparison of stealing and sex offenses is based on an assumption that parental contagion is restricted entirely to techniques of crimes, while as a matter of fact the transmission of more general values is more important. (d) The removal of a child from the home to prison at an early age does not remove the child from a criminalistic to a non-criminalistic environment, as Goring assumed. (e) He restricted his study to male criminals, although he mentions the fact that the ratio of sisters to brothers in respect to imprisonment is 6 to 102. If criminal diathesis is inherited to the same extent that colour of the eyes is inherited, it must affect females to the same extent as males unless it is sex-linked; since, according to Goring, the diathesis consists entirely of physical and mental inferiority, sex-linkage is not plausible. These defects in Goring's arguments undermine his conclusion so that it carries no weight as a demonstration of the inheritance of criminality.

The fifth method of measuring the relation of heredity to criminality is the comparison of identical twins, which are the product of a single egg, with fraternal twins, which are the product of two eggs fertilized by two sperms. Heredity is assumed to be indentical in the former and different in the latter. Lange made a study of thirty pairs of adult male twins; thirteen of the pairs were identical twins and seventeen fraternal twins. One member of each pair was a criminal, and whenever the twin was also criminal the pair was termed "concordant." The problem was to determine whether concordance would be more frequent among the group of identical twins than among the group of fraternal twins. He found that 77 percent of the pairs of identical twins and only 12 percent of the pairs of fraternal twins were concordant, that is, both criminal. The similarity of identical twins with reference to criminality was thus 6.4 times as great as the similarity of fraternal twins. This greater similarity was assumed to be a measure of the inheritance of criminality, but it is subject to scepticism on two points. First, the number of cases of each type is very small, and a shift of one or two cases from one category to the other would produce a significant difference in the conclusion. Second, the classification of a particular pair of twins as identical or fraternal must be doubtful in many cases, since evidence as to the birth process is seldom available.

Lange's work was hailed by many people as a final and indubitable proof of the inheritance of criminality. However, later work by the same methods has certainly reduced by a large amount the significance to be attributed to heredity, and careful analysis of the methods and logical should reduce this significance to zero. Three later studies of twins in European countries by methods similar to those of Lange show for all the cases in the three studies that the frequency of similarity in criminal behaviour among identical twins was only 1.4 times as great as the frequency among fraternal twins. One of the most extensive studies of the criminality of twins was made by Rosanoff and others on adult criminality, juvenile delinquency, and child behaviour problems. This study showed for all types of cases combined approximately three times as much concordance among identical twins as fraternal twins. The procedures in this study, however, are so inaccurate that the conclusions are worthless. This may be illustrated with reference to the juvenile delinquents in the study. A juvenile delinquent was defined as a child under eighteen years of age brought before the juvenile court on a delinquency petition and either placed on probation or committed to a correctional institution. According to the brief descriptions given in the Rosanoff report, all of the juvenile delinquents of the fraternal type conform to this definition, while 9 of the 29 male juvenile delinquents of the identical-twin type fail to conform to the definition, and consequently should not be included as concordant cases. If correction be made for those cases which do not conform to the definition, concordance appears among identical twins only 1.1 times as frequently as it appears among fraternal twins. This difference is not sufficiently great to create a presumption of inheritance.

Even if the difference between the two types of twins in reference to concordance in criminality be accepted, the conclusion that criminality is inherited does not necessarily follow. The difference between the two types of twins may be explained in whole or in part by two other conditions. First, as compared to the homes of the fraternal twins, the homes of the identical twins seemed to be more frequently characterized by economic distress, illegitimacy, drunkenness, feeble-mindedness, and psychoses; in such homes, regardless of the nature of twinship, both members of the pairs of twins are more frequently delinquent than in homes reported to be on a higher social level. This observation is based upon descriptions given in the report, but no explanation for this relationship between identical twins and poor homes is available. Second, the environments of identical twins are more nearly alike from the point of view of social psychology than the environments of fraternal twins. Because of the difficulty of distinguishing one of the identical twins from the other, the reactions of other persons toward identical twins will be more nearly alike than the reactions of others toward fraternal twins. These reactions of others are the most important part of the social environment. In general, therefore, the study of twins has failed as completely as other procedures to demonstrate the inheritance of criminality.

Two positive propositions and one negative proposition can be stated as conclusions regarding the relation of heredity to crime. First, criminals are human beings, and all human beings have some inherited traits which make it possible for them to behave like human beings. This proposition, however, does not aid in explaining why some human beings commit crimes and others do not. Second, some inherited characteristics may be significantly related to criminal behaviour by virtue of the fact that members of a society have learned to react to them in a certain way; the colour of the skin of the Negro is reacted to in a certain way in the United States, and the crime rate is high among Negroes. But neither does this proposition aid in understanding criminal behaviour, for traits which are not inherited may be reacted to in a significant way and may likewise be associated with criminal behaviour. The third proposition is that except in the two senses previously stated, heredity has not been demonstrated to have any connection whatever with criminal behaviour. It is obviously impossible for criminality to be inherited as such, for crime is defined by acts of legislatures and these vary independently of the biological inheritance of the violators of the laws. If persons with certain inherited traits are more likely to commit crimes than persons with other inherited traits, these traits have not been identified and their connection with criminal behaviour has not been demonstrated. Anyone who speaks of the direct or indirect inheritance of criminality except in the senses stated in the first two propositions in this paragraph is speaking from his preconceptions and assumptions and not from factual evidence.

Anatomical Conditions

Lombroso insisted that criminals differed from non-criminal with reference to certain physical traits which he called "stigmata of degeneracy." He found these physical deviations in all parts of the anatomy but placed particular emphasis on deviations in the shape of the cranium. Goring, an English physician, made careful measurements of several thousand prisoners in comparison with the general population and reached the conclusion that prisoners

158

Criminal Psychology

differed anatomically from the general population only in being slightly shorter in stature and slightly lighter in weight. Goring's work is generally accepted as having demolished the early Lombrosian view that criminals are characterized by certain stigmata and constitute an inferior biological type. However, in the late 1930's Hooton, an American anthropologist, attempt to revive the Lombrosian theory. At great cost he made elaborate measurements of thousands of prisoners and of a few non-prisoners. He found a few slight differences between the two classes and concluded that "the primary cause of crime is biological inferiority." Three principal criticisms of Hooton's procedures and conclusions have been made. First, his control groups are so small and so selected that they are worthless as a sample of the non-criminal population, and consequently he has no means of showing that criminals differ from non-criminals. He used 29 Italian-Americans as a sample of the Italian-American non-criminal population, and about 150 Nashville firemen and 150 Boston outpatients, militiamen, and patrons of a bathhouse as a sample of the native-white-parentage, non-criminal population of the United States. The Nashville firemen differed from the Boston control group in more respects than either of these control groups differed from the prisoners. Second, he found few significant differences between criminals and non-criminals and used a surprisingly large number of measurements which were practically identical. Consequently his data given practically no basis for his conclusions. Third, he has no criterion of biological inferiority. He apparently assumed that persons who were imprisoned were inferior; by this logic males should be appraised as biologically inferior to females since a larger proportion of males are imprisoned, and because of this inferiority the males should be weeded out of the population. It has been pointed out by Merton and Montagu that the criminals differed from the anthropoid apes in more respects than did the control groups; if similarity to anthropoid apes be accepted as a criterion of inferiority, the non-criminals are the inferior group and the criminals the superior group.

Other studies in the last generation have generally reached the conclusion that criminals are not significantly different in physical traits from non-criminals. For example, a study by the Institute for Juvenile Research of approximately 4,000 school boys between the ages of six and sixteen in two delinquency areas in Chicago concluded that on the average delinquents had fewer "stigmata of degeneracy" than non-delinquents. Red hair was classified by Lombroso as one of the stigmata in degeneracy, and interest in this trait was revived by von Hentig, who presented some evidence to the effect that American outlaws were red haired to an unusual extent. This was vigorously denied by Rasch, and the relation of red hair to criminality has certainly not been demonstrated.

The general body-build or somatotype also has received considerable attention as a possible explanation of criminal behaviour. Kretschmer developed a classification of somatotypes in relation to psychoses and general personality. Attempts have been made to use Kretschmer's classification in the study of criminals but thus far no relationship has been found between his body types and criminal behaviour.

Sheldon has recently made another attempt to differentiate criminals from non-criminals in respect to somatotype. He finds three somatotypes—the endomorphic which is round and soft, the mesomorphic which is round and hard, and the ectomorphic which is thin and fragile—and claims that three temperamental types and three psychiatric types are closely related with their somatotypes. In a study of 200 young adults in a Boston welfare agency, whom he describes as "more or less delinquent," he concludes that delinquents are different from non-delinquents in their somatotypes and in their related temperamental and psychiatric types. Also he assumes that these differences are in the direction for inferiority and that the inferiority is inherited. His data, in fact, do not justify any of these conclusions, either that the delinquents are different from the non-delinquents in general, or that the difference if it exists indicates inferiority, or that the inferiority if it exists is

inherited. On the contrary, he finds that body types of these
delinquents are much like those of business and military
leaders and of psychiatrists ; he has no criterion of inferiority
and the only evidence of inheritance he has is that sons
resemble their parents, and this similarity obviously may be
due to social experience rather than heredity. The Gluecks
have used the logic of Kretschmer and Sheldon in a study of
juvenile delinquents. Like Sheldon, they have adopted a
system characterized by a noted physical anthropologist as a
"new Phrenology in which the bumps of the buttocks take
the place of the bumps on the skull."

Physical and Physiological Defects

Physical defects such as blindness, deafness, and
lameness are sometimes regarded as important in relation to
criminality. These physical defects may be due to heredity, to
antenatal conditions, to difficulties in the birth process, and
to postnatal conditions. Regardless of their origin, their
frequency in the criminal population in comparison with the
non-criminal population is not known. The Massachusetts
Census of 1905 reported that blind persons were not over-
represented in the delinquent and criminal population, but
there was a considerable excess of lameness and deafness
among the offenders. The definitions of these defects,
however, were not standardized and the difference shown in
this census is not clearly reliable. No other statistical material
in the United States or European countries carry any greater
confidence. Optometrists have reported wide differences
between the delinquents and school children in respect to
defective vision, and offer the explanation that children with
defective vision are more likely to become delinquent because
of the physical irritation caused by defective vision and
because of the difficulty in reading, which drives them into
truancy and gag activities. It has been reported, also, that 55
percent of a criminal group had "flap ears" as compared with
23 percent of a non-criminal group. This difference was
explained as due to the ignorance or neglect of parents :
children who are neglected are permitted to sleep with one ear

twisted under the head. They become delinquent for the same reason that they develop "flap ears," namely, the ignorance and neglect of the parents.

Though these defects have not been shown to be significant from the statistical point of view they are unquestionably significant in some cases, and this significance depends largely on the reactions of other persons toward the defects. The child with enlarged tonsils who consistently holds his mouth open, the child with crossed eyes, and the child who stutters or lisps meet ridicule and suffer loss of social status. Both the persons with the physical defects and other persons are likely to find the defects irritating, and for the person with the defect the sequence of irritation, retardation in work, dissatisfaction with school or work, truancy, association with delinquents, and a general view of one's self as an outcast may result. A former convict presented a different explanation of the assumed excess of these defects among criminals, as follows :

> I have wondered a great deal about the connection between crime and physical ugliness or deformity. That there is such a connection I have no faintest doubt. The physically unattractive man is naturally handicapped in the competition for women and sexual satisfaction. To compensate for this he desires money with which to bribe or impress the women he desires. Unable to get it quickly enough by legitimate means, he steals it. If this is true of the thief, how much more so is it true of the raper and the murderer.

Sexual frustration is certainly too narrow an interpretation of the social difficulties of the deformed, as if the general frustration-aggression hypothesis.

Undernourishment, disease, and poor health are sometimes reported to be found among criminals in excessive proportions, while in other investigations no significant difference is found between criminals and non-criminals. In some studies recidivists are reported to be in better health than first offenders. While there is no reason to minimize the importance of good health, it is apparent that the connection between crime and physical ailments is not close or necessary. Many criminals are quite healthy; many non-criminals have physical ailments. Even if a difference could be shown, the criminality would not be demonstrated to be a direct product of the poor health rather than of the conditions which produced the poor health.

Other physiological abnormalities which are less evident have also been regarded as important by some writers. During the decade of the twenties popular and semi-popular writers placed much emphasis on the endocrine glands as determiners of personality and of criminal behaviour. Endocrinologists in general have been much more cautious than these popular writers, and they generally state that no conclusion has been reached regarding the relation between the endocrine glands and criminal behaviour.

Age Ratios in Crime

Age appears to have an important effect, directly or indirectly, on the frequency and type of crime committed. However, the statistics on the incidence of crime among various groups are generally in the form of records of arrests or convictions. Such statistics are probably somewhat biased and tend to exaggerate the crime rates of young adults. Children are less likely than adults to be arrested or fingerprinted for the same overt offense.

After allowing for the bias of the statistics, the following nine conclusions regarding the age ratios in crime can be drawn : (1) The age of maximum general criminality is probably during or shortly before adolescence. English statistics show that the age of maximum convictions for indictable crimes is twelve or thirteen for males and sixteen or seventeen for females. While American statistics place this age higher, ranging from eighteen to twenty-four, these statistics are based on finger-prints submitted by local police departments to the Federal Bureau of Investigation and American police departments seldom take finger-prints of young people. (2) The age of maximum criminality varies with the type of crime. For example, males aged 15–19 have higher arrest rates for auto theft and burglary than does any other group of males. In 1957, however, the two sexes were approximately equal in regard to the proportion of arrests for crimes committed during the years of young adulthood—about 30 percent of the males arrested in 1,473 United States cities were under twenty-five, 19 percent were under twenty-one, and 8 percent were under eighteen; the comparable percentages for females were 31, 20 and 7. (4) The age of concentration of the more violent types of crimes, such as burglary and robbery, has remained relatively constant for several centuries. Reports show that the burglars and robbers in England in the fifteen century were young adults. Of all persons charged with serious offenses in England in 1835, 72 percent were 30 years of age or younger; 24 percent were under 21. (5) The age at first delinquency appears from a small number of special research studies to be lower in areas with high delinquency rates than in areas with low delinquency rates. The type of crime committed at a specific age also varies from area to area. It is reported, for instance, that boys of twelve commit buglaries and robberies in certain delinquent areas in Chicago, while boys of the same age in less delinquent areas steal from fruit stands and vending machines. (6) Juveniles who are oversize for their chronological age appear from a few special studies to have higher delinquency rates than those who are normal or undersize. (7) The crime rate decreases regularly and steadily from the age of maximum criminality until the end of life. The conclusion is derived from the general statistics of many nations, although Pollak has found some conflicting statistics in a study of criminals in Pennsylvania. Several studies have reached the conclusion that the number of first offenders per 10,000 of the same age decreases regularly from the age 15–18 to the last recorded age for both males and females. Although it has been asserted that older men are more disposed to sex offenses than men in middle age, the evidence is conflicting but generally negative. The evidence is fairly conclusive, however, that sex offenses do not decrease in old age as much as does larceny. (8) The crime rates at the several ages vary decidely from time to time. In England the crime rate for persons over sixty decreased more between 1911 and 1928 than did the crime rate for any other age group, and this was explained as probably due to the system of old age pensions. On the other hand, the juvenile delinquency rate in England has increased enormously during the last twenty years in proportion to the crime rates at older ages. (9) Juvenile delinquency is probably related in some manner to adult criminal behaviour, but it is not correct to say that the juvenile delinquent of today is the adult criminal of tomorrow, as has frequently been stated. The error is due to the fact that practically all juveniles commit delinquencies, but not all of them develop into adult criminals. Moreover, many persons acquire their first formal record of crime after passing the juvenile age. Frum found that the criminal histories of 46 percent of the 319 recidivists in the Indiana Reformatory and State Prison officially started prior to age eighteen. There is evidence, also, that after about age 25 the percentage of criminals who are first offenders increases with increasing age. (10) The younger a person is when he is first convicted of a crime, the greater the likelihood that he will be convicted again and that he will continue to commit crimes over a long period. (11) The younger a person is, the shorter will be the interval between his first and subsequent crimes.

One of the theories presented as an explanation of the age ratios in crime is that they are due directly to biological traits such as physical strength and vigor: crimes are committed frequently by persons who are strong and active and infrequently by persons who are weak and passive. Another biological theory is that crimes are concentrated in three periods, ages three to six, fourteen to sixteen, and forty-two to forty-five, and that these periods are products of libidinal tides due to changes in the instincts of sex and aggression and to changes in the ago strength. A third biological theory is that inheritance is the direct cause; Goring stated that persons predisposed by heredity to crime commit cirme at a very young age, while those with a weaker tendency delay longer.

These biological theories obviously provide no explanation of many of the variations in the age ratios in crime; indeed, it may be said that they do not explain even one of the facts outlined above when that fact is considered in its ramifications. On the other hand, all of these facts are consistent with the general theory that crime and criminality are products of social experiences and social interaction. It must be agreed, however, that the sociological theories of crime causation have not been sufficiently demonstrated as to any of these facts.

Sex Ratios in Crime

Statistical studies indicate that delinquency and crime are very closely associated with sex status. The male sex has a great excess of crimes in all nations, all communities within a nation, all age groups, all periods in history for which organized statistics are available and all types of crimes except those which are somewhat intimately related to the female sex, such as abortion and infanticide. In the United States at present, approximately ten times as many males as females are arrested, fourteen times as many committed to all types of correctional institutions, and twenty times as many committed to state and federal prisons and reformatories. Approximately 85 percent of the delinquency cases in juvenile courts are boys. While these statistics certainly reflect a bias in favour of females, they are supported by statistics from sources other than the police and the courts. Death certificates indicated that males committed 88 percent of the 821 homicides occurring in ten North Carolina counties in one eleven-year period; 83 percent of the males and 71 percent of the females killed males. A questionnaire study of two thousand school children resulted in the conclusion that girls have a stronger sense of honour than boys. Even if correction could be made for the statistical bias in favour of females, the male crime rate probably would still greatly exceed that of females.

Some scholars have claimed that the higher rate of delinquency of the male sex is due to the biological

characteristic of the male. This conclusion has no more
justification that the conclusion that a death rate of males by
lightning six times as high as of females is due to the biological
differences between the sexes. The variations in the sex ratios
in crime are so great that they can be explained only by
differences in the social positions and traditions of the two
sexes. *First,* the sex ratio in crime varies widely from one
nation to another; male criminals are 342 times as numerous
as females in Belgium and 2,744 times as numerous in Algiers
and Tunis in proportion to the populations of the several
groups. In Ceylon, 98 percent of the delinquents placed on
probation in 1946–1956 were male. The female crime rate
shows some tendency to approach closest to the male in
countries in which females have the greatest freedom and
equality with males, such as Western Europe, Australia, and
the United States, and to vary most from the male rate in
countries in which females are closely supervised, such as
Japan and Algiers. If countries existed in which females were
politically and socially dominant, the female rate, according
to this trend, should exceed the male rate. *Second,* the sex
ratio in crime varies within any nation in relation to variations
in the social positions of the sexes. In the United States the
ratio is nearest to equality in the Southern states, where the
Negro females show a close resemblance to Negro males in
social positions. Radzinowicz found in an intensive analysis
of Polish statistics that the sex ratio in crime ranged from
176 to 1163 in 42 groups which were based on age, civil status,
provinces, rural-urban composition, and religion. *Third,* the
crime rate of females is closer to that of males in American
cities than in small towns, and this presumably reflects an
approach to equality in the cities. The ratio of male arrests to
female arrests for crimes against the person in Massachusetts
in 1957 was 5 to 1 in "towns," most of which have less than
12,000 population, and 17 to 1 in cities above 12,000; for
offenses against property the ratio was 36 to 1 in towns and
11 to 1 in cities. *Fourth,* the ratio of girl delinquents to boy
delinquents varies from one section of a city to another. While
areas with high delinquency rates in general show a larger

proportion of girl delinquents than the areas with low delinquency rates, some of the high delinquency areas show very small proportions of girl delinquents. *Fifth*, some evidence that girls and boys are tending to approach equality in delinquency rates is available. The percentage of girl arraignments to all arraignments in the Children's Court of New York City increased from 12.7 in 1907–1914 to 27.1 in 1923–1930. In 1938, females were 5 percent of the persons under age 18 whose arrests were reported to the FBI; in 1947 females were 10 percent, and in 1957 they were 12.7 percent. On the other hand, Hacker's study of the Canton of Zürich for the period 1834–1936 showed many variations but no unified trend for adult females; the percentage of female delinquents to all delinquents decreased generally from 1855 to 1875, increased generally from 1875 to 1915, and then decreased from 1915 to 1936. *Sixth*, the female crime rate increases in war years, when women take over the occupations of men and in other ways approach social equality in men. Women in Germany and Austria had a conviction rate for theft during the First World War which was higher than the conviction rate of men for theft in the same countries in prewar years, and during World War II female crime rates increased tremendously in the United States, Sweden, England and Denmark. *Seventh*, the comparative crime rates of males and females vary in different age-periods. The English statistics of convections for indictable crimes in 1958 show a sex ratio 772 for all ages; however, for the ages under 17 the ratio is 1266, for the years 17–21 it is 850, and for the ages 21 and over it is 589. In earlier years, these data were compiled for all age groups, and they indicated that after age 10 the two sexes became progressively more alike with advancing age until the age of 40, with little change thereafter. Hacker's statistics of convictions in eight European nations show the greatest difference between the sexes in the young-adult ages with smaller differences after 40 or 45 and with early childhood in two cases intermediate between the young-adults and the older ages. On the other hand, Dahlberg reports that in Sweden the sexes differ least in the rate of first convictions in the age period 20–25, when males have six times as many first convictions as females, that the difference becomes steadily greater with increasing age to the age 40–45, when males have 24 times as many first convictions, and that the ratio is irregular after the age of 45, perhaps because of the small number of cases at those later ages. In the United States, the commitments to state prisons and reformatories are more nearly the same for the two sexes in early age and become progressively different with advancing age; thirteen times as many males as females are committed at ages 15–17, and twenty-six times as many in the ages 60–64. Since these variations are not the same from one nation to another, they obviously cannot be explained by biological differences in the sexes. *Eighth*, according to a small number of special studies, the ratio of males to females is lower among delinquents from broken homes than among delinquents from homes which are intact. That is, more delinquent girls than delinquent boys come from broken homes. It appears that boys are less dependent on the home for regulation of conduct than are girls and that the break in the homes removes an impediment to delinquency which is greater for girls than for boys. *Ninth*, girls with siblings who are all males have a higher rate of delinquency than girls with siblings who are all females or siblings who are mixed as to sex.

Few, if any, other traits have as great statistical importance as does sex in differentiating criminals from non-criminal. Feeble-mindedness, psychopathies, and other personal traits are much less significant. But no one feels that he has an explanation of criminality when he learns that the criminal is male. It is obvious from the variations in the sex ratio in crime which have been described that maleness is not significant in the causation of crime in itself but only as it indicates social position, supervision, and other social relations. Moreover, since boys and girls live in the same homes, in equal poverty, and with equally ignorant parents, and have the same neighbourhoods which are equally lacking in facilities for organized recreation, these gross factors in the social environment cannot be considered as causes of delinquency. The significant difference is in the social positions of the girls and women as compared with the boys and men, and the difference in social positions either determines the frequency and intensity of the delinquency and anti-delinquency patterns which impinge upon them or determines the frequency of opportunities for crimes which are available to them. Probably the most important difference is that the girls are supervised more carefully and behave in accordance with anti-criminal behaviour patterns taught to them with greater care and consistency than in the case of boys. From infancy, girls are taught that they must be nice, while boys are taught that they must be rough and tough; a boy who approaches the behaviour of girls is regarded as a "sissy." This difference in care and supervision presumably rested originally on the fact that the female sex is the one which becomes pregnant. The personal and familial consequences of illicit pregnancy leads to special protection of the girl not only in respect to sex behaviour but also in respect to social codes in general. Grosser has shown that stealing has a different functional significance for boys and girls; it can be integrated with and can express features of the masculine adolescent role, but it cannot do so for the basic features of the feminine role.

Eysenck's Theory of Personality and Crime

Eysenck's theory of criminal behaviour is not as biologically deterministic as the previous two: it postulates that it is the interaction of personality (which is biologically based) and the environment that produces antisocial behaviour. This theory is not intended as a theory of criminal behaviour in general but is one that seeks to explain why certain individuals fail to comply with rules. Indeed, Eysenck himself suggests that his theory applies only to certain crimes, namely 'victimful' crimes and that sociological theories are particularly relevant in relation to victimless crime.

Eysenck argues that personality is determined by an individual's biological constitution which is, in turn, determined by their genes. Certain personality traits are more likely to lend themselves to antisocial behaviour and if someone inherits these traits *and* is brought up in an environment that nurtures crime, then they are liable to engage in criminal acts. As Eysenck & Gudjonsson (1989) comment: 'What is inherited are certain peculiarities of the brain and nervous system that interact with certain environmental factors and thereby increase the likelihood that a given person will act in a particular antisocial manner in a given situation.'

According to Eysenck's basic theory of personality, an individual's temperament can be measured on three dimensions:

- extraversion–introversion (E)
- neuroticism–stability (N)
- psychoticism–normality(P).

Most of the research on crime and personality has confused on extraversion and neuroticism—stability, so it is on these dimensions that we will concentrate.

Extraversion-introversion

Extraverts have a high need for excitement and for a varied, changing environment. They enjoy company lively parties and are impulsive and optimistic. They are inclined easily to lose their temper and to be aggressive and unreliable. Introverts, on the other hand, are reserved, cautious and dislike change and noisy gatherings. They tend to keep themselves to themselves, are reliable, unaggressive and place great value on ethical standards.

Biologically, Eysenck contends the dimension of extraversion–introversion is based on the nature of the reticular activating system (RAS), a part of the brain responsible for arousal levels. Everyone has an optimum level of arousal which they strive to achieve. In extraverts, the RAS strongly inhibits incoming sensations, resulting in the need to seek stimulation. By contrast, in introverts the RAS amplifies sensory input, hence they seek far less stimulation. Another important difference between introverts and extraverts is that the latter are much harder to condition, and therefore far more likely not to do as they are told when young or care about societal disapproval when older.

In contrast to an introvert, an extravert's need for constant stimulation and new and dangerous experiences is liable to bring them into conflict with the law, and they are more likely to engage in criminal activities, especially those such as joy riding, which bring excitement. In short, according to this theory, most criminals are extraverts.

Neuroticism–stability

The dimension of neuroticism–stability is controlled by the level of reactivity of the autonomic nervous system (ANS), that part of the nervous system which, by releasing the hormone adrenalin into your bloodstream, makes you 'jump' when something frightening happens. People who score highly on neuroticism have a more reactive ANS than those who score at the stable end of the continuum: they tend to be nervous, jumpy and anxious, and find it difficult to cope with stress. They are moody, easily upset by others and prone to physical ailments such as headaches and stomach upsets. Those at the stable end of the continuum are emotionally stable, calm, even-tempered and not easily upset by other people. They are unlikely to panic when confronted by extreme stress but keep their wits about them and respond to emergencies in a productive manner.

Eysenck assume that people who score highly on the neuroticism scale, those whom he labelled as high on emotionality, are more likely to behave in a criminal manner than those low on nueroticism or emotionality. This is because emotionality acts as a drive and those high in emotionality are liable to repeat behaviours until they become habitual. If these habits are antisocial ones, then this may lead to criminality.

Since the two dimensions of extraversion–introversion and stability–neuroticism are independent, it is possible for individuals to be neurotic introverts, stable introverts, stable extraverts or neurotic extraverts. It follows from the theory of personality that it is the latter group, the neurotic extraverts, who are most likely to engage in criminal behaviour.

Psychoticism

Only a limited amount of research has been conducted on the dimension of psychoticism in relation to crime but Eysenck has suggested that this is likely to be a characteristic shown by a large proportion of the criminal population, especially hardcore, habitual, violent offenders. Psychoticism within this theory means a hostile and uncaring attitude to others, cold cruelty and a lack of empathy. (It is important to note however, that this use is not the same as the clinical term 'psychotic' as used to describe someone who is out of touch with reality).

Evaluating Eysenck's Theory

In evaluating Eysenck's theory, it is useful to look separately at the theory itself, and then at the research done on it.

Evaluation of the theory

There are numerous problems with the theory. Firstly, there is no evidence that there are consistent differences in EEG measures (which are used to ascertain cortical arousal) between introverts and extraverts. Secondly, some studies indicate that sensation seeking is not necessarily related to extraversion. Indeed some theorists argue that boredom arises from *increased* rather than decreased arousal. Smith *et al.*, have carried out research which indicates that sensation seekers have an excitable central nervous system, being more aroused and arousable. This seriously compromises Eysenck's proposal that criminal behaviour is the result of stimulus seeking by extraverts attempting to achieve an optimum level of stimulation. Thirdly, several researchers have discovered personality traits other than ones identified by Eysenck which are related to criminal behaviour.

Evaluation of the research

Having considered problems with the theory, let us turn out attention to the research on which it is based. In support, some studies that have compared prisoners with non-criminals have found that the criminals score more highly on the scales of extraversion, neuroticism and psychoticism as measured by the Eysenck Personality Ques-tionnaire (EPQ). However, Passingham drew attention to some methodological flaws in these studies, namely that the control group of non-criminals was not matched with the criminals on relevant variables such as socioeconomic class, cultural background and intelligence.

Many other studies have not been supportive. Bartol *et al.*, compared EPQ scores of 398 inmates of maximum security jail in New York with a control group of 187 male job seekers in the same city who were, like the prisoners, mainly African-American and Hispanic and were matched in terms of age, race, socioeconomic class and employment record. The criminals were categorised into six groups according to their criminal history. Although, as a predicted by the theory, sex offenders were the least extravert and robbers the most extravert of the criminals, *all* six groups of offenders were *less* extravert than the control group. Bartol *et al.*, suggest that the main reason for this may be because their study was conducted on a completely different cultural group than that studied by Eysenck, whose sample was predominantly European White criminals guilty of property crimes. A theory that claims to be universal but cannot be generalised to other populations is not valid. Many other research studies have been, in various ways, equally unsupportive. Farrignton *et al.*, in a review of such research, concluded that neither the theory or the personality scales were useful in explaining the origins of delinquency.

Nevertheless, on the positive side, this theory does recognise that both biology and the environment may be important determinants of criminality and, even if the specific mechanisms suggested are inaccurate, it draws attention to the possible importance of genetics in influencing behaviour.

As Bartol comments, 'Criminology cannot afford to discount the existence of biological factors in antisocial behaviour, even if these factors account for the behaviour of only a small percentage of the population.'

Evaluating Biological Theories

In considering biological theories as a whole, it is unlikely that they alone can offer a convincing explanation for criminal behaviour. Even if some individuals' physiology predisposes them to be impulsive, aggressive and erratic, these characteristics can be channelled into legal activities. Any link between physiology and criminal behaviour is inevitable indirect and mediated by social factors, which will be considered later in this chapter. In humans, biology never imprisons us entirely.

Biological Theories of Crime

+ They draw attention to the importance of biology, particularly genetics, in influencing behviour.
+ They take account of personality differences that might exist from birth, such as impulsiveness and a desire for excitement.
+ They help us understand how genetic potential can lead to such problems as poor achievement in school and inadequate socialisation, which in turn may result in criminality.
− They are simplistic theories, taking account of only one factor (biology). It is very unlikely that criminal behaviour can be reduced to a biological explanation alone.
− They ignore or underestimate the social causes of crime such as antisocial role models and emotionally deprived childhood.

6
Criminal Psychology of the Stranger

Research on the psychology of crime has concentrated on distinguishing the specific personality traits of offenders. Since, by definition, traits are largely constant over time and social context, this emphasis implies that the "criminal personality" is a stable and permanent "thing" to be measured. In fact, considerable longitudinal and ethnographic research on crime over the life course indicates that "criminal careers" are sporadic, short-lived and largely shaped by social and developmental contexts. Therefore, criminologists need to use a richer, more dynamic framework for understanding the personalities of those involved in crime. Narrative psychology offers an ideal theoretical backdrop for understanding socially contingent and developmentally contextual behaviour over time. Self-narratives are shaped by experience, and then reflected in behaviour. An understanding of why individuals commit crimes requires an analysis and understanding of these internal stories.

Dating back to the origins of the discipline, criminology has had a rather uncomfortable relationship with personality psychology. Though many criminologists have tried to isolate the psychological factors that differentiate offenders from non-offenders, the notion of a "criminal personality" or a "psychology of crime" has been ardently debated by criminologists with sociological backgrounds. Nonetheless, over the last 20 years, personality variables have ascended to the foreground of popular and professional criminological though. This would be in large measure thanks to their acceptance by influential criminologists outside of the field of psychology like James Q. Wilson and Travis Hirschi.

The vast majority of this research on criminal personalities involves the study of stable dispositional traits. For instance, in the influential *Crime and Personality,* Eysenck defines criminality as a "continuous trait of the same kind as intelligence, or height or weight" that is innate in a small minority of individuals. A short list of the traits that have been proposed as correlates to criminal behaviour includes: aggressiveness, assertiveness, dependency, ego-centricity, emotional instability, extroversion, fearlessness, hostility, impulsiveness, insecurity, irresponsibility, low arousal, low empathy, low intelligence, obsession, pessimism, recklessness, unconventionality and weak socialisation. Various combinations or constellations of these traits have been described as an "antisocial" or "criminal" personality. Criminologists have even formally operationalised "criminality" with a stable personality profile on the Minnesota Multiphasic Personality Inventory (MMPI), characterized by high scores in psychopathic deviation, schizophrenia and hypomania.

According to Allport the personality trait is "a neuropsychic structure having the capacity to render many stimuli functionally equivalent, and to initiate and guide...behaviour." William James suggested that such traits are "set like plaster" after one reaches thirty years of age, and in fact, the relative stability of trait scores over the life course is one of the most robust findings in personality psychology. Costa and McCrae argue not only that traits remain consistent over the life course, but that they are also transcontextual. Using the framework for understanding personality, criminologists commonly view criminality from an ontogenetic framework, and the development into delinquency is viewed as an unchanging course of "maturational unfolding" set in one's early childhood years. In fact, Loeber suggests that a "consensus" has been reached in favour of the "stability hypothesis" of criminal behaviour, and Sampson and Laub call the continuity of criminal traits over time "an impressive generalisation that is rare in the social sciences."

Nonetheless, criminal trait theory has a serious problem to overcome. Though it is true that most adult criminals showed signs of being 'delinquent' children, the majority of juvenile offenders *do not* become adult criminals. By age 28, nearly 85 percent of former delinquently desists from offending, with only a tiny fraction of delinquents progressing on to life-long "criminal careers." In fact, in the same article in which they suggest that there is "stability of offending over the life course," Gottfredson and Hirschi report that criminal behaviour "declines precipitously and continuously throughout life." One of the perplexing paradoxes of criminology, therefore, is the simultaneous finding of *stability* in "criminal personality" or "criminality" over time and the marked *instability* of criminal *behaviour* as recorded by official criminal justice data and surveys.

Following McAdams in *Can Personality Change?* I will argue that one way to provide insight into this apparent paradox might be to move beyond dispositional traits and view personality as a multilayered process. Temperamental traits provide only what McAdams calls the "psychology of the stranger," or precisely the types of attributes one knows about a person she knows little about. McAdams describes a broader, three-level approach for understanding the "whole person," involving not only dispositional traits, but also strategies or motives, and the narrative identity or self-concept. According to this theory, though dispositional traits like aggressiveness or low self-control may be stable over the life course, individuals can still 'change'—the change simply understanding the person, a central component of what is being called 'narrative psychology,' can have important ramifications in criminology, investigative psychology.

A Brief Review of Trait Criminology

Criminal trait theories can fall under the rubric of either 'nature' or 'nurture,' and range from sociological explanations about 'delinquent subcultures,' to genetic theories of the 'born criminal.' Historically, these trait theories can be broken down into three general and overlapping 'eras.'

1860–1950 : The Search for the 'Born Criminal'

At the turn of the century, trait theories comprised the most influential strain of criminological thinking. According to the social Darwinism-influenced theories of Lombroso and Garofalo, offenders tend to lack the intelligence, maturity, self-control and sensitivity of non-offenders. Foucault describes this early era of positivist criminology as involving the creation of a "new type of dangerous individual"— the criminal without a crime, who exhibits delinquent "tendencies" and "signs" but may not have broken any laws. This "psychiatrization" of criminality shifted the focus of crime studies "from the crime to the criminal; from the act as it was actually committed to the danger potentially inherent in the individual; from the modulated punishment of the guilty party to the absolute protection of others." These early trait theories frequently either deny or question the possibility "rehabilitation." Lombroso writes, "Atavism shows us the inefficacy of punishment for *born criminals* and why it is the *they inevitable have periodic relapses into crime.*" (emphasis mine).

Lange, Hooton, and Sheldon *et al.*, further developed this understanding of the biological determination of criminal behaviour, but the most scientifically sophisticated early research into criminal personality was the work of Sheldon and Eleanor Glueck. Glueck and Glueck provide a comprehensive biosocial theory involving everything from physical and temperamental traits of delinquents to the emotional, disciplinary, and intellectual character of their families. Family environments, in which parents are either hostile or indifferent to children they argue, frequently produce children who score highly on measures of traits like hostility, narcissism and extroversion.

1930—1975 : Environmental Traits

Beginning with the early Chicago School of sociology, these individualist theories of crime—especially those based in genetic and eugenic concepts—began to lose ground to sociological theories. Matza writes, criminologists began to "relocate pathology...from the personal to the social plane." Moreover, several sociological criminologists began to systematically criticise earlier studies of the criminal personality during this time. In their review of 113 studies of criminal psychology, for instance, Schuessler and Cressey conclude that most of the early personality studies lacked methodological rigour and failed to conclusively illustrate a link between crime and personality. Waldo and Dinitz review 94 studies of offender personality between 1950 and 1965, and reach similar conclusions.

Nonetheless, sociologists of this era did not abandon the notion of a criminal personality altogether. In fact, subsequent reviews have suggested that sociological criminologists merely 'disguised' the similarities between their social explanations and more psychological ones. In many ways, concepts like the 'culture of poverty' and 'culture of violence' became trait-like substitutes for the stability of genetic explanations of behavioural differences. Foucault (1988) writes, though "The age of criminal anthropology with its radical naivete's seems to have disappeared with the 19th Century, ...a much more subtle psycho-sociology of delinquency has taken up the fight."

Banfield, for example, traces the crime and unemployment of impoverished communities to the inheritance of a 'present-time orientation' and a lack of an internalised work ethic among ghetto children. Rooted in the functionalist notion of 'cultural lag,' this subcultural theory represented an explicit departure from most environmental theories of behaviour. The 'nurture' side of the nature/nurture debate traditionally represented the Enlightenment principle of human plasticity and adaptation. Yet, like nature itself, this new 'culture' produces bounded traits that are nearly as self-reproducing and resistant to changed as genetic traits. For example, Lewis writes, "By the time slum children are age six or seven, they...are not psychologically geared to take full advantage of changing conditions or increased opportunities which may occur in their lifetime."

1965–Present : Criminal Inventories

Aided by the development of reliable personality inventories like the MMPI, research on the personality characteristics of offenders was revitalised in the 1960s. These true-and-false questionnaires are designed to gauge the degree to which a person exhibits traits such as neuroticism relative to others. A majority of studies between 1966 and 1975 found a positive correlation between various traits and criminal behaviour. Gough, for instance, reports on a large-scale, international study using a socialisation scale of the California Psychological Inventory, modelled after the MMPI. He found that the scores of criminal offenders have differed substantially from those of non-offenders across ten countries, and that offenders in every country scored in same general range.

Eysenck focused primarily on extroversion, neuroticism, and psychoticism, and their roots in biology and genetics. According to Eysenck, an under-aroused cerebral cortex causes extroverts to seek out stimulation from the environment and makes these individuals more difficult to socialise than introverts. When this extroversion is mixed with an autonomic nervous system characterized by either neurotic or psychotic tendencies, the individual is even more likely to be difficult to condition and control. Eysenck's theory has received mixed empirical support, but increasing attention over the last 20 years.

Still, offender personality studies gained the most ground when the authors of two of criminology's most well known texts developed new arguments suggesting that personal traits were essential for understanding why some

persons commit crimes and others do not. Both Wilson and
Herrnstein and Gottfredson and Hirschi posit that
'impulsivity' or 'low self-control' differentiates those persons
likely to commit crimes from those who are not. Gottfredson
and Hirschi write, "People who lack self-control will tend to
be impulsive, insensitive, physical (as opposed to mental),
risk-taking, shortsighted and non-verbal, and they will tend
therefore to engage in criminal and analogous acts."

Like the Gluecks, these authors suggest that young
people with low self-control and generally raised in homes in
which parents do not know "how to punish." Delinquent
behaviour, they argue, is the product of families who punish
irregularly, sporadically and often unjustly. Again, though
this is an environmental cause, these researchers suggest
that the psychological effects of this parenting are highly
intractable. Gottfredson and Hirschi write, "Enhancing the
level of self-control appears possible in early childhood, but
the record suggests that successful efforts to change the level
later in life are exceedingly rare, if not non-existent." These
trait theories have received empirical support, and have
inspired several personality researchers to develop more
refined and integrative theories of "criminality" over the last
decade.

The Challenge of Desistance

The study of personality traits has helped criminologists
understand why two persons with similar backgrounds and
environments can have very different criminal histories. Still,
many critiques have been made of this 'reductionist' emphasis
on individual psychology over situational or macro-social
causes of crime, and the empirical evidence has also been
criticised.

Few critiques have had the effect of David Matza's
argument in *Delinquency and Drift*, though Matza faults
trait theories for their tendency to vastly overpredict criminal
behaviour, which he calls an "embarrassment of riches."
Though it is true that most adult criminals showed signs of
being "delinquent" children, he argues, the majority of

juvenile offenders *do not* become adult criminals. Matza suggests that most trait theories, from biological to sociological, fall apart when this notion of impermanence is introduced. For instance, if delinquency is the product of the behavioural norms of the ghetto, then why do forty year-olds seem to be so immune to these pressures? Or why do impulsive seventeen year-olds commit so many more crimes then impulsive thirty year-olds? Matza says, few positivist criminological theories can provide a coherent answer.

This critique remains highly salient today. Almost no one disputes the relationship between age and crime. Loeber, Caspi and Moffitt, and others have identified a small percentage of "life-course persistent" delinquents, who seem to continue to engage in criminal behaviour throughout adulthood. Yet, the typical delinquent *does* change his behaviour in early adulthood. Moffitt writes, "In contrast with the rare life-course-persistent type, adolescence-limited delinquency is ubiquitous."

Though the exact figures differ for various offences, criminal behaviour generally rise through adolescence, peak in the late teens and early twenties, then drop sharply throughout adulthood. This pattern emerges in studies using various methods of measuring offending and has remained "virtually unchanged for about 150 years." As far back as 1913, Goring called this age-crime relationship a "law of nature"—the young simply commit the most crimes, and older persons desist from such behaviour. Similarly, many contemporary scholars, like Gottfredson and Hirschi argue that "the age effect is invariant across social and cultural conditions." Though such claims are controversial, almost everyone agrees that some sort of reform or desistance process does seem to take place during early adulthood in contemporary Western society.

Yet, desistance remains an "unexplained process." In fact, in one of the most thorough analyses of the topic, Rand suggests, "The phenomenon of desistance has received no specific theoretical or empirical attention." Though this is overstated, studies of desistance do tend to be difficult to locate

and seem to exist in relative isolation from one another. Wilson
and Herrnstein conclude that the linkage of age and crime
"resists explanation," and Shover writes, "Although it is
conventional wisdom that most offenders eventually desist
from criminal behaviour, criminology textbooks have little
on nothing to say about this process."

Moffitt calls the "mysterious" relationship between age
and crime "at once the most robust and least understood
empirical observation in the field of criminology." Gove
argues, "All of (the major) theoretical perspectives either
explicitly or implicitly suggest that deviant behaviour is an
amplifying process that leads to further and more serious
deviance" in *direct contradiction* to the "empirical facts about
the enormous amount of desistance from crime that happens
soon *after* adolescence." Mulvey and LaRosa conclude, "In
short, we know that many youth "grow out" of delinquent
activity, but we know very little about why."

Maturational Reform and its Critics

One of the first criminologists to address the question of
reform was Adolphe Quetelet. Like other students of crime in
this period, Quetelet takes a biological approach to
delinquency. He argues that the penchant for crime "Seems
to develop by reason of the intensity of man's physical vitality
and passions." Criminality peaks when physical development
has "almost been completed," then "diminishes still later due
to the enfeeblement of physical vitality and the passions."
Sheldon and Eleanor Glueck develop this into their theory of
'maturational reform', in which they argue that criminality
naturally declines after the age of 25. Glueck and Glueck
suggest that with the "sheer passage of time" juvenile
delinquents "grow out" of this transitory phase and change
their life goals. They find that "ageing is the only factor which
emerges as significant in the reformative process." Young
adults "burn out" physiologically and can no longer maintain
the type of energy and aggressiveness needed in delinquency.

Though the Gluecks explicitly urge future researchers
to "dissect maturation into its components," Shover and others

assert that criminology's "explanatory efforts have not progressed appreciably beyond (the Gluecks') work." Maturational reform continues almost by default, to be one of the most influential theories of desistance in criminology. For instance, using data collected by Rowe and Tittle, Wilson and Herrnstein argue that none of the possible correlates of age, such as employment, peers of family circumstances, explain crime as well as the variable of age itself. "That is to say, an older person is likely to have a lower propensity for crime than a younger person, even after they have been matched in demographic variables," they write. Similarly, Gottfredson and Hirschi, write, "We are left with the conclusion that (desistance) is due to the inexorable ageing of the organism" rather than any social variables.

According to each theory, ageing 'causes' desistance. Yet, as Sutton suggests, "To say that age influences everything is to say nothing." Importantly, developmental psychologists have deemed biological age an "ambiguous" and "irrelevant" variable, with little meaning except that which is socially attached to in. Few criminologists would be satisfied with the assessment : "Criminal behaviour peaks at age seventeen, therefore, crime is caused by turning seventeen." Yet, ageing is seen as an adequate explanation for desistance.

Though age is certainly a very strong correlate of desistance, criminolgogists have generally failed to "unpack" the "meaning" of age. Some efforts have been made to use normative pattern of adult development to explain desistance as a "natural" process of human development, borrowing from the theories of Levinson and Erikson. Yet, much of this research also commits what Dannefer refers to as the "ontogenetic fallacy," by accepting the changes in behaviour reflect the natural and universal "properties of the aging organism" rather than changes in social or institutional conditions. Like theories of "burnout" or "maturation," developmental theories of desistance generally re-name the age-crime relationship, but do little to increase or understanding of how this change takes place. As Matza argues, a simple notion like 'burning out,' "merely reiterates the occurrence of maturational reform. It hardly explains it."

Personality, Policy and Change

One reason for this lack of an explanation may be the dominant paradigm for understanding the psychology of crime. Criminology needs an understanding of criminal behaviour and personality that will allow for this sort of plasticity and change, while still acknowledging the role of individual difference in cognition and identity. Since personality traits are almost inherently static, trait theories cannot easily answer this challenge. Like Matza Moffitt writes :

> (Psychological) theories typically rely on the stability of individual differences in traits such as impulsivity, neuroticism, autonomic nervous system reactivity, or low intelligence. Psychological theories cannot explain the onset and desistance of adolescent delinquency without positing compelling reasons for a sudden and dramatic population shift in criminogenic traits followed by return to baseline a few years later (694).

By definiton, if personality traits changed radically over time, they would not be traits, but rather temporary states or phases, and would lose their predictive and theoretical value.

Consequently the *policy implications* of many trait studies also contrast sharply with the promising recent studies on offender rehabilitation and reintegration. If persons are nothing but the sum of their stable dispositional traits, they why waste money trying to rehabilitate such populations? In fact, dating back to the tradition's historic link to eugenics, criminal trait research leads almost inevitably to the pessimistic attitude of "lock 'em up" currently dominating the crime policy agenda. Lilly, *et al.*, similarly argue that trait theories generally "lend credence to the idea that offenders are largely beyond reform and in need of punitive control."

To be sure, the conclusion the offenders are characterized by unchangeable bodily or psychological characteristics leads logically to the conclusion that offenders should be either eliminated, caged indefinitely (incapacitation), or altered physically through intrusive measures).

In order to understand desistance, and design innovative new programmes for ex-offender reintegration, criminology must go beyond psychological traits in efforts to understand criminal behaviour.

Beyond Traits

McAdams might suggest that one reason for the difficulty in understanding desistance is that the majority of criminological work dwells solely within the "psychology of the stranger." This involves the sort of simple, typological and comparative ways one "sizes up" someone he or she has met, but really does not "understand." One might say, for instance, "That woman seemed so shy and depressed, I wish I knew what she was *really* about," or "I wish I could get to *know* her." Her traits only give us the *beginning* of the "whole" personality, McAdams would argue.

Though some psychologists argue that personality is made up entirely of dispositional traits, research by Bromley and Thorne indicates that when most people talk about "who they are" they generally conceive of something very different than simple temperamental characteristics. Moreover, many of the most important theories of personality—including those of Adler, Erikson, Fromm, Jung, McClelland and Tomkins—cannot be broken down into the language of traits. Erikson and Jung saw the life span as involving a continual process of possible change. Similarly, according to developmental, social learning and interactionist perspectives, personal behaviour is guided by changing social expectations and norms as well as personal contexts and social environments.

McAdams argues that to fully understand personality, we must move beyond stable traits to the "flesh-and-blood, in-the-world doer, striving to accomplish things, expressing himself or herself" through plans, tactics, self-understanding and life stories. Statistical differences on the "simple, comparative and only vaguely conditional" measures of extroversion or impulsiveness can be helpful "first reads" into personality, but they do not constitute the "whole person." Though individual differences in traits might be relatively stable over time, therefore, there is more to personality than what can be measured on a series of linear continua.

This argument has considerable support from critics of criminology as well. Toch, for instance, has argued that :

> Positivist approaches to classification help to produce explanatory theories, which in turn help us to 'understand crime.' These theories, however, do not permit us to 'understand criminals,' because they are segmental views rather than full-blooded portraits. ...These must be supplemented with portraits of offender perspective, and with a review of unique personal histories.

Citing Magnusson and Bergman, Sampson and Laub suggest that criminology research should shift from a purely "variable-orientation" to include a "person-orientation" as well. And, Cairns argues that personal transitions in the life course are one of the "phenomena lost" by over reliance on large-scale quantitative research.

Essentially, what seems to be missing from most criminology research is "the person"—the wholeness and agentic subjectivity of the individual. Sartre argues that trying to explain behaviour, and individual change in particular, by relying on "the great idols of our epoch— heredity, education, environment, physiological constitution" allows us to "understand nothing." He writes:

> The transitions, the becomings, the transformations, have been carefully veiled from us, and we have been limited to putting order into the succession by invoking empirically established but literally unintelligible sequences.

Sartre makes the same point as an expanding group of researchers in cognitive and personality psychology : we need a literally *intelligible* sequence, or a coherent "story" of the

188188   188   **Criminal Psychology**

individual if we want to understand changes in behaviour such as desistance.

This growing new perspective, occasionally referred to as "narrative psychology" has been called "a viable alternative to the positivist paradigm." Kotre even argues that there is a "quiet revolution taking place in psychology" that is putting narrative ways of knowing and thinking at the foreground of the understanding of personality and cognition. According to this view, in order to achieve a contingent, temporally structured and contextualized understanding of human behaviour (Toch's "full-blooded portraits"), one needs to look at the self-narratives or subjective self-concepts of individuals. In his narrative theory of psychological development, McAdams argues that personality should be seen as a three-level process, involving traits, personal strategies, and identity narratives or self stories. Though traits are relatively stable over the life course, the second two, more contextualized domains leaves open the possibility of substantial personality change in adulthood.

Motives and Strategies

McAdams' second level of personality is the level that criminal investigators are typically trained to concentrate upon: the person's central motives. What does the person want? What plans or goals is she trying to accomplish?

Psychological research on this second level of personality has concentrated on the observation and assessment of constructs such as tasks, projects, strivings, and life scripts. Individuals are aware of the reasons for many of their actions and such "self-knowledge" is viewed by many as the "richest of all data." Brown and Canter write, "Recourse to ordinary explanations of experiences is often made with the admission that people have a rich and elaborate conceptual understanding of what, and why, they do what they do." Linked to attitudes and group norms, these goal articulations are explicitly contextualized and change with situational and development demands. This information can be studied through qualitative analysis of interview and life history data, but does not necessarily appear on true-false tests of temperamental traits.

Narrative Identity and the Self-Concept

McAdams' third level of personality in the internalised and evolving narrative individuals construct to integrate their pasts, presents and perceived futures into a sort of sustaining identity. Essentially, understanding the person means understanding the person's "story." Overwhelmed with the choices and possibilities of modern society, modern individuals internalise this autobiographical narrative in order to provide a sense of coherence and predictability to the chaos of their lives. According to Giddens, in modern society, "a person's identity is not to be found in behaviour, nor-important though this is—in the reactions of others, but in the capacity to keep a particular narrative going." Bruner writes:

> The heart of my argument is this : eventually the culturally shaped cognitive and linguistic processes that guide the self-telling of life narratives achieve the power to structure perceptual experience, to organise memory, to segment and purpose–build the very "events" or a life. In the end, we become the autobiographical narratives by which we "tell about" our lives.

The storied identity can be seen as an active "information-processing structure," a "cognitive schema" or a "construct system" that is both shaped by and later mediates social interaction. Giddens writes, "Each of us not only 'has,' but lives a biography," while Denzin suggests we are "attached to the world through a circuit of selfness'. People tell stories about what they do and why they did it. These narratives explain their actions in a sequence of events connect up to explanatory goals, motivations, and feelings. Moreover, these self-narratives then act to shape and guide future behaviour, as persons act in ways that accord to the stories we have created about ourselves.

These narratives have an "internal logic" and are used

to make life understandable and predictable. While our life goals and strategies give us a direction in which to act and our traits give us our behavioural styles; out individual *identities* provide the shape and coherence of our lives. Epstein and Erskine use this "need to maintain a coherent, integrated conceptual system" or "theory of reality" to explain "behaviour that either is manifestly self-destructive or is maintained in the absence of reinforcement." Human subjects, unlike their counterparts in the hard sciences, react differently to stimuli based on how events and constructs are "perceived and interpreted...in line with pre-existing and emerging goals."

Importantly, these "structured self-images" are not created in a vacuum. Identity theorists like Erikson and Giddens argue that identity is very much shaped within the constraints and opportunity structure of the social world in which people live. Rather than stripping individuals of community and macro-historical context, therefore, narrative analysis can inform our understandings by illustrating how the person sees and experiences the world around her. Katz calls this the merging of "phenomenal foreground" with "social background," and theorists like Groves and Lynch would argue that the two are intricately intertwined. Narratives are also excellent data for the analysis of the underlying socio-stuctural relations of a population.

Moreover, whereas personality traits are supposed to be both stable and transcontextual, the narrative identity "has to be routinely created and sustained in the reflexive activities of the individual." Unlike stage theorists, McAdams argues that a life-long project that individuals continuously restructure in light of new experiences and information. Individuals change their personality and behaviour by rewriting and restructuring their understandings of their pasts and their theories of reality.

Identity narratives can be analysed to discern the "themes" and roles that guide an individual's behaviour. Verbal and written life histories are not the identity myths themselves, but they "hold the outlines" of these internal narratives. The precise methodology of this thematic analysis varies, yet some of the most innovative studies have borrowed constructs from the work of semiotics, linguistics, hermeneutics and psychobiography. Importantly, the accounts and explanations themselves (not the "facts" they contain) are the primary "data" of these studies. These stories represent personal outlooks and *theories* of reality, not reality. Rouse suggests, our autobiographical tales are "much embellished but truthful even so, for truth is not simply what happened but how we felt about it when it was happening, and how we feel about it now."

Narrative Applications to Criminological Research

Criminal behaviour is a multidimensional phenomena that requires multiple tools if we are to understand it. Astute critics like Rafter warn of the "growing insularity" of criminology and point out the need to share and "swap" ideas with those in different disciplines lest we create an (ivory) "tower of Babel." I am proposing that criminologists swap the notion of the self-concept or narrative identity process from our colleagues in social and personality psychology.

Criminologists have widely abandoned the notion of understanding identity or personal subjectivity along with other "humanist" and existential concepts in favour of more quantifiable and empirically testable concepts such as reinforced learning. Yet, new psychological conceptions of the "self" and recent developments in social science (particularly in postmodernist and symbolic interactionist research) have mounted a challenge to conventional views of the self-interested individual that should not go unnoticed by criminology. As Groves and Lynch write:

Criminology should take subjective orientations seriously *because people have them.* Experience exists. Hopes, fears, and memories exist. ...If these feelings and experiences are beyond the grasp of some particularistic vision of criminology, so much the worse for criminology.

A narrative perspective can be particularly useful in research concerning developing "criminal careers," and as

Canter has shown, the narrative perspective can also inform the field of investigative psychology.

Applications to Understanding Crime

Criminology has had a long tradition of using life history data, especially in the Chicago School of sociology during the first part of the century. Discussing life histories like *The Jack-Roller,* for instance, Shaw writes, "So far as we have been able to determine as yet, the best way to investigate the inner world of the person is through a study of himself through a life-history." Scott and Lyman even argue that stories are intimately connected to behaviour such as crime that is outside of socially approved boundaries. "Since it is with respect to deviant behaviour that we call for accounts, the study of deviance and the study of accounts are intrinsically related, and a clarification of accounts will constitute a clarification of deviant phenomena."

Nonetheless, the marriage of oral histories and criminology has been rocky, and the method has been all but abandoned by criminologists today. Lewis and Maruna (in press) argue that this is largely because criminologists have traditionally viewed these documents as purely sociological rather than psychosocial data. Bennett writes that despite the numerous oral histories collected by criminologists over the last century, delinquent narratives have never been explicitly analysed as explorations of "somatic, psychiatric and psychological regions" of human identity. He argues that the small amount of non-sociological commentary that was included in the life story research in this time was merely "inserted to placate and psychologists who headed the institute for Juvenile Research." Finestone similarly points out, "Shaw made no attempt to pursue the implications of the Jack-Roller's idiosyncratic point of view for an understanding of his involvement in delinquent conduct."

Precisely by drawing attention to these subjective aspects of first-person accounts, narrative psychology can provide a methodological and theoretical framework for exploring many of the concepts and constructs thought to be related to criminal behaviour. As far back as 1926, Bolitho argued that criminal offenders were driven by "personal myths." The "definitions," "attitudes" and "norms" of Sutherland's differential association theory also could be investigated from a narrative framework, as could Kaplan and Reckless "self-factors," or Yochelson and Samenow's "errors in thinking." Loeber and LeBlanc point out that labelling theory represents one of the few inherently developmental/longitudinal theories of crime. The labelling process is also, to a large degree, about identity and ("looking glass") self-concept, and could be explored further from a narrative perspective.

The most developed strain of criminology interested in self-perceptions, the study of offender accounts, attributions and rationalisations, may benefit the most from a narrative framework. Sykes and Matza describe the various "techniques of neutalisation" delinquents use to absolve themselves from experiencing guilt for their crimes. These include the denial of responsibility, denial of injury, denial of the victim, and condemnation of the condemners. In the framework of narrative psychology, these "accounts" or neutralisations have implications for the way that a person views the world around him and his control over that world.

Addressing the Stability/Change Paradox

For many of the issues and concerns of criminological inquiry, there is little need to undergo the considerable work involved in collecting and analysing narrative data. Yet, traits alone cannot explain "the social and cognitive processes" and the "complex interplay between objective contingencies" that lead to desistance from crime. Only by looking at the "whole person" can we begin to understand this type of change.

Narrative psychologists have started to lay the fundamental groundwork for this study of personal change, and the study of desistance would be an ideal area in which to continue this research. Most identity researchers agree that a person's self-understanding can change over time, through the change needs to "make sense" or be internally consistent Epstein and Erskine compare personal identity change to paradigm shifts in the sciences, where past information is reorganised and understood in a new light. Individuals interpret and assimilate every emotionally salient experience into this evolving and cohesive narrative. When information is processed that does not fit into one's story, the person can either change her story to accommodate the new facts or distort the information to fit her story.

Erikson and Elkind argue that people first begin to shape individual identities during adolescence. Consequently, teenagers go through a "psychosocial moratorium" where they "try on" various possible selves "for size." Identity theorists would argue, therefore, that it is no coincidence that these "disorganised" early narratives correspond with high rates of criminal behaviour. Canter writes, "Many acts of violence seem to erupt at a time when the perpetrator is searching for identity and personal meaning."

To test this, identity stories could be collected for individuals over time, comparing versions of the same incidents constructed at different times in the life course or "criminal career." Cross-sectional designs comparing stories of "unchanged" individuals to another "changed" group have also been designed. Theorists like Giddens and Rotenberg even argue that a person's autobiographic identity can be "reconstructed" in order to act as a "corrective intervention" into the past that can change the course for a person's future.

To date, however, only a few empirical studies have addressed the issue of narrative identity and desistance from crime and delinquency. Greenberg and Moffitt offer extremely potent and testable theories of desistance that centre around adolescent self-concept and identity, yet neither has been qualitatively tested. In retrospective interviews with ex-offenders, Graham and Bowling Irwin, Maruna, Mulvey and LaRosa and Shover have all found indications that a change in identity and self-concept is critical to the process of reform. Similar results have been found in research on the cessation of addictive behaviours such as drug use.

Nonetheless, prospective longitudinal research is also needed in order to "dissect maturation into its components" as Glueck and Glueck suggest. Moffitt, in fact, calls desistance research and delinquency studies in general "woefully ill-informed about the phenomenology of modern teenagers from their own perspective." If policy makers hope to reduce crime rates, it would benefit them to begin to know and understand the young people who commit crimes as well as those who are able to change their behaviours.

Applications to Investigative Psychology

Canter has been instrumental in outlining how the field of investigative psychology can benefit from this narrative perspective as well. He argues, in fact, that the analysis of self-narratives should be "at the heart of offender profiling." Canter views crime as an interpersonal transaction that involves characteristic and psychologically entrenched ways of dealing with other people. By understanding the stories offenders live by, he argues, investigators can better predict offender behaviour.

Conventional criminological research on offender traits, on the other hand, gives investigators little information about the individuality and uniqueness of specific offenders. As Canter writes. "The criminology literature is remarkably quiet about variations between criminals, usually preferring to treat them all as one particular kind of person." Narrative psychology, based in research on the "whole person," is more individual-based and provides a more comprehensive understanding of a person's unique personality than do trait-based profiles. Alison and Parkinson write :

The advantage that the narrative approach has over 'modus operandi' is that in the latter the investigator can only make limited and static inferences about the offender's background. ...In the former the investigator may gain insight into the whole psychological pattern that identifies that individual.

Self-narratives, after all, are shaped by experience, and then reflected in behaviour. Therefore, the specific themes and patterns in and unknown person's past *behaviour* can provide important insight into the person's self story. Once reconstructed, this self-story can be used both to predict *future* behaviour as well as other characteristics. Canter has referred to this as the Actions to Characteristics (A to C) canonical equation. Whereas in most prediction studies in criminology, the characteristics of individuals are used to predict future actions or outcomes, in criminal investigations, the reverse of this process is also necessary. Police investigators try to hypothesise the characteristics of likely offenders based solely on the actions (e.g., styles of burglary or murder) of an unknown offender.

Research in investigative psychology has involved looking for correlations between the themes that an offender exhibits in his transactional styles and the themes and patterns of his non-criminal lifestyle. As this approach grows in profiling, clusters or "categories" on narratives may arise that can improve upon the FBI differentiation between "organised" and "disorganised" offenders. Narrative typologies could also benefit the classification schemes of treatment providers and aid the development of social policy geared toward high-risk populations (Lewis and Maruna, in Press).

Nonetheless, identity is an on-going process, not a tangible or permanent quality of an individual. Any narrative typology needs to be based on the understanding that individuals develop and adapt their stories constantly over time. Though various categories of self-*stories* may be identified, narrative psychology does not seek to divide *persons* into "types" in the way that offender categories based on trait scores might. Canter characterises such a misuse of narrative psychology as being based on a "cafeteria view" of life stories, whereby a narrative identity is understood as a permanent "thing" that can be quickly identified and labelled :

> The cafeteria view of life stories pulls the framework back into the realms of static characteristics. Instead of having distinguishing ear lobes, criminals can be recognised by the particular heroes they endorse. Life

is not that simple. Narratives are moving targets that change their shape in response to life circumstances.

Efforts to predict future criminal behaviour based on psychological traits and background variables have had mixed results, and the "high false-positive" problem of these past efforts becomes even more critical when the stakes involve criminal investigation and possible prosecution. Though Canter is right that narrative theory offers a richer method for profiling offenders, he also warns that any application of psychological theory to the investigative process should proceed with extreme caution. Narrative theory is best used as a means of understanding specific individuals in full social and developmental context.

7

Feminist Perspectives on Criminal Psychology

In both these areas, until the last twenty years, the lack of literature on female criminality is often astounding. One reason given for this lack of interest is that females have traditionally been seen as being intrinsically law-abiding. It is certainly true that, from the statistics available, crime appears to be a largely male, and young male, activity. Although sex crime ratios (the proportion of men and women offending) differ depending on what crimes one is considering, men are generally represented more frequently than women. Even in shoplifting, a crime which is traditionally linked with women, there are more males than females convicted. In Britain of those convicted of serious crimes 80 percent are male, and women make up only about 3 percent of the prison population, suggesting that their offences tend to be less serious. The figures of sex ratios in the United States are similar to those for Britain. Indeed, these sorts of figures are fairly global, indicating the law-abiding behaviour of most females, making gender possibly the easiest predictor or criminality. If one were put into a room with twenty people chosen at random, half male and half female, and were told that ten of them were convicted criminals, the best single predictor would be sex.

It could be that female crime remains undetected vastly more frequently than male crime. This seems unlikely, as the two largest areas of hidden crime are white-collar and corporate crimes, which women have less opportunity to commit, and domestic crimes such as spouse battering and child physical and sexual abuse, both of which are more commonly carried out by men than by women. It is true, however, that when women do commit crimes of violence these are often committed in the home.

The different involvement in crime of men and women is one of the most striking and consistent criminological truths, and it is therefore surprising that it has not been more widely studied in order to ascertain what causes this difference. As we shall see in this chapter, the female is generally overlooked in the explanation of criminality, and even in the explanation of conformity—where one would expect women to be the central consideration—they are often marginalised in favour of discussion from a purely male perspective.

Biological, Hormonal and Psychological Theories
Introduction

Physiological and psychological theories subsume a number of explanations which basically attribute female criminality to individual characteristics (physiological, hormonal or psychological) which are either unchanged or only marginally affected by economic, social or political forces. These theories often conclude that criminality is due to the inherent nature of particular 'abnormal' women who are bad and begin their life with a propensity for criminality; that is, in everyday language, they are considered to be 'born criminals.'

Because these theories are centred upon the individual, they all suggest a 'cure' based upon adjustments to the individual. These 'cures' range from sterilization in order to prevent crime in future generations through to psychoanalysis. Little, if any, consideration is given to the role, status or socio-economic position of women in society. The neglect of social factors has an immediate attraction for

anyone wishing to retain the *status quo* in society, helping
to explain the popularity of these theories amongst the better-
off sections of the community. Such an approach also lent
support to the idea that the penal system should 'reform'
prisoners whilst in custody. Criminals were thought of as
persons who suffered from something which could be 'cured.'
It takes time to 'cure' or to 'help' people, and so it is necessary
to incarcerate them for long enough to have the desired effect.
In this way, these theories also influenced the lengths of
prison sentences.

   None the less, it is important to bear in mind that at
the time they were written they represented novel and
innovative thinking. For our purposes, they study of female
criminality will begin with the work of Lombroso, whose
writing on this topic started in 1895. At that time, little had
been done to study the criminal individual, whether male
or female, and merely to begin such work was innovative.
His theories were topical, as they could be seen to have
their basis in the then relatively new and still controversial
arguments of Darwinism. It is therefore not surprisingly
that they became popular and widely accepted. With
hindsight it is now all too easy to point out flaws in his
rather simplistic arguments, but it is not possible wholly to
discount his ideas on physiological reasons for female
criminality. After Lombroso, a selection of the work of other
writers illustrates the way in which physical and
psychological explanations of female crime have progressed
to the present day.

Lombroso

   Although Lombroso's work on female criminality is now
largely discredited in its pure form, its relevance continues
because several influential later writers base their ideas upon
his work. Lombroso is also a good starting-point because he
states explicitly what is only implied by later theorists.

   His basic idea is that all crime is the result of atavistic
throwbacks, that is, a reversion to a more primitive form of
human life or a survival of 'primitive' traits in individuals.

Although Lombroso wrongly includes in 'atavism' such non-hereditary factors as tattooing, his use of the term is generally correct. He argues that the most advanced forms of human are white males, and the most primitive are non-white females. He studied the physiology of both criminal and non-criminal females (this is one of the few occasions on which he studied a control group). Any traits found more commonly in the criminal group he described as atavistic: large hand size; low voice pitch, having moles; being short; having dark hair; being fat, and so on. All his tests were carried out in Italy, and some of the so-called characteristics can be seen to be particularly prevalent in certain areas, most markedly in Sicily. He gave little consideration to the fact that within Italy Sicilians were generally poorer than other groups and that their social conditions rather than their physical appearance may have led to their criminality. In later writings he did compromise by admitting that the 'born criminal' accounted for only 35 percent of criminals, and that some crime was committed by pseudo-criminals who might be pushed into crime by adverse environment, passion or criminal associations. But his main arguments explaining persistent criminals were based on atavistic traits.

On this basis, women portraying certain 'atavistic' characteristics would become more criminal than others. However, if crime was to be explained merely by primitive traits, female crime would be greater than made crime because, according to Lombroso, all females, are less advanced than males. Lombroso's theory therefore seems to point towards a higher female than male crime rate, whereas the female rate was, and is, according to the statistics, lower. He explains this apparent anomaly partly by maintaining that prostitution was the female substitute for crime and partly by attributing the lower female crime rate to women's proximity to lower life forms. He claimed that women had a smaller cerebral cortex which rendered them both less intelligent and less capable of abstract reasoning. This, he argued, led to a greater likelihood of psychological disturbance and was also more likely to lead to sexual anomalies than

crime. He further maintained that because females are more
simplistic than males, women, like lower animal life, are more
adaptable and more capable of surviving in unpleasant
surroundings. This might explain why he largely ignore the
poverty of the environment in which criminal women often
lived. In his view, with this ability to adapt, they can survive
male manipulation and male control and, in this respect, are
seen as a stronger though less well-developed sex. This ability
to survive evidences and inability to feel pain and a contempt
of death, making them insensitive to the pain and suffering
of other people. However, in most women the coldness is
controlled or neutralized by pity, weakness, maternity, and,
he argues, most importantly by underdeveloped intelligence
and lack of passion. On the other hand, criminal women,
and all men, possess passion and intelligence. So criminal
women have a cranium closer in size to that of men, and
have more body hair and other masculine physical traits
which are not signs of development in women. Rather they
represent anomalies, being unnaturally masculine and
showing signs of atavism. He argues that passion and any
over-activity in women must be a deviation from normal, as
their nature is normally passive. The more passive a woman,
the more highly developed she is, and the further from being
a 'born criminal.'

Lombroso was not himself consciously race- and class-
biased, but the whole idea of a passive female gives rise to
criticism to his theory being prejudicial. A racist criticism arises
because Lombroso's atavistic traits are necessarily more
prevalent in certain races, particularly the non-whites (traits
such as large cranium, square jaw and dark hair). Such traits
necessarily appear more commonly in certain races and
although five characteristics had to be portrayed before a
person was labelled a born criminal, the possession of one of
these traits by a whole race puts every member of that race
closer to the category of 'born criminal.' This has led to his
theories being criticised as racist, although they were probably
not written with this intention nor seen in that light at the
time they were written. His approach can also be said to be

rooted in class because in order to have a wholly passive female, devoted only to family and home, it is necessary to have a society in which someone works in order to support these women. Of course, when Lombroso wrote, this was the way society was structured, and was seen as normal, acceptable and just. Both the racist and class bias can be illustrated by looking at the application of his traits to Italy. There was a distinct prevalence of 'atavism' amongst the Sicilians, who were both darker skinned and poor labourers.

Lombroso's ideas re-appear as threads in theories right up to the present day. Partly this is because he and his followers provided the basis of the positive school of criminology, but Lombroso also influenced at least two main areas of criminological thought, namely, the notions that crime can be explained by reference to biological and inherited characteristics; and that crime is caused by a pathological or chemical abnormality which needs to be treated. Latter writings based on Lombroso tend not to express these ideas quite so directly, but they often make similar assumptions.

Recent Biological Factors

In seeking to explain differences between male and female criminality most writers in the physiological or psychological arena have remarked on the passivity and basic lack of aggression on the part of females, asserting that this explains their lack of criminality. In a more specifically biological approach it has been suggested, that the genetic passivity of females is related to the different brains of men and women and the difference in hormones between men and women. Clearly, it is difficult to experiment on hormonal change in humans, so all tests have been done on animals, mainly rats. Soon after birth a rat's brain becomes either male or female. If there is a predominance of female hormones (oestrogens), the brain becomes female; if a predominance of male hormones (androgens), the brain becomes male. If, early in life, a female is injected with androgens, she becomes aggressive and indistinguishable from a male, and an early castrated male will be more passive later in life. It has been claimed that these tests, and some rather more complex ones involving monkeys, show that the same may well be true for humans.

The extrapolation of any finding from rats or monkeys to humans is necessarily very risky. It remains unclear what, if any, the effects are of hormones, particularly in early life. Behaviourists such as Marsh try to claim that differences between the sexes are purely a result of socialisation. It could be argued that upbringing over many generations has actually over-emphasised what was originally a negligible difference between the sexes. It is very difficult to ascertain which, if either, of the social or the genetic has had the greater effect.

'Generative Phases' of Women

This biological theory is based on changes connected with the menstrual cycle. The argument is that at times of menstruation women are reminded that they can never become men, and the distress to which this gives rise makes them increasingly prone to delinquent acts. The best known proponent of this idea is Pollak, who also suggests that the hormonal disturbance resulting from pregnancy and the menopause may be a cause of female crime, but his claims have never been proven. If he is correct, most women could spend much of their adult lives in a hormonal state which predisposes them to criminality. In 1961, Dalton believed she had proven the thesis when she discovered that 59.8 percent of imprisoned women studied committed their crimes in the 16-day period covering pre- and post-menstrual hormone imbalance. This, of course, means that 40.2 percent (almost half) of women committed their crimes at other times (during the other 12 days). Since simple arithmetic shows that 16 out of ?8 days is 57 percent it is questionable whether these figures prove anything, but if they do, it could merely mean that women are more likely to be caught committing crimes at these times. Results are therefore inconclusive.

Although it is unclear whether women generally suffer a higher incidence of criminality during their generative phase, it is clear that the law takes account of these elements in deciding some cases. Menstruation has been used as a partial defence plea, and both menstruation and menopause have been accepted as factors which should reduce sentences. Here the case of menstruation will be considered, but similar factors apply to menopause. Although both these 'generative phases' have been commonly used in such relatively minor cases as shoplifting, more serious cases will be considered here. Susan Edwards notes that in the nineteenth century pre-menstrual tension (PMT) was frequently discussed as being an important element of a defence in cases of violence, killing, arson and theft. Both she and Luckhaus refer to cases in the early eighties where PMT was successfully pleaded. In one of these, the woman faced a murder charge which was reduced to manslaughter due to diminished responsibility attributed to PMT, and had received a probationary sentence with a proviso that she undergo hormone treatment. Only a few months after the first offence, the same woman was charged with threatening to kill a police officer of possessing an offensive weapon. Although convicted, PMT acted as a factor to reduce sentence and she was again placed on probation and required to undergo an increased hormone dose. In another case a woman, charged with murder, was convicted only of manslaughter due to diminished responsibility; there was no custodial sentence, not even the requirement of hormonal treatment . Clearly, in the cases of these women the law accepted that PMT, although not amounting to a full defence, was the most important reason for the behaviour. PMT was accepted as a partial excuse and as a reason for lenient sentencing; the total effect was the acceptance of the controversial idea that PMT amounted to a causative explanation. This is an interesting acceptance in the light of the fact that medical evidence is divided about the existence of such a syndrome and its effects. If there are effects, they appear to be mainly psychological, such as tension, irritability, depression tiredness, mood swings and feelings of loneliness, although Dalton has included some relevant physical effects such as epilepsy, fainting and even hypoglycaemia. Rose would wish to see women receiving treatment at an early stage to avoid both the later criminal behaviour and the need to admit this type of evidence in ·court.

In the case of post-natal depression there is, of course, the special case of infanticide. Again, in this instance the law accepts as a partial excuse the fact that a woman's mind and behaviour are affected by the hormonal changes in her body. If a mother kills her child within its first year as a result of post-natal depression or lactation, she would have a partial defence to murder which would render it infanticide. This is clearly only a defence open to women, and is the only sex-specific defence recognised in the criminal law. Some of these killings may possibly be the results of exhaustion through caring for the child, guilt through not feeling affection for it, or the effect of other social pressures, all of which could equally well be suffered by a man if he was the person primarily in charge of the care of the child. The Law Commission's Draft Criminal Code suggested (clause 64(1) that these social reasons for infanticide be recognised but only in the case of women. But a man cannot rely upon the same defence and would have to argue that his mind was unbalanced in some other way in order to plead diminished responsibility.

Certainly when one looks at the figures there appears to be an unfairness, Marks and Kumar show that the rates of killing of children under one have remained constant since 1957 at about 45 per million per year. This is higher then for any other age group and represents about 30 killings a year. They further discovered that women who kill such children are dealt with much more leniently (more are subject to probation) than are men (who are frequently imprisoned), even when the level of violence used by the women is greater. The leniency could arise because the charge of infanticide is available for women. Dell, has shown that in cases of manslaughter the sentencing has been steadily becoming more and more severe, but Maier-Katkin and Ogle, suggest that even when women are convicted of manslaughter they are treated leniently (often with probation) which suggests that it is not so much to do with a special defence being available but is connected with greater compassion for these women. Whatever the reason the men suffer much more serious sentencing for relatively similar cases. It is questionable whether such imbalances is just. The solution should not be to remove the defence of infanticide which recognises the severe pressures of new motherhood and reduces the stigma and the punishment. Perhaps there is scope for extending this defence; in the case of women to include 'circumstances consequent on the birth' as suggested by the Law Commission in the draft Criminal Code Bill; and in the case of men for severe stress caused by the birth and care of a child. In some of the most severe cases there may even be worth in pleading insanity and obtaining a finding of not guilty by reason of insanity.

The hormonal imbalances suffered by men do not normally affect either their conviction or their sentence. Women, however, can successfully plead such imbalances even in the most serious cases where they take the life of another person. For the individual women involved, this is probably an advantage as they will either elude an unpleasant label or an unpleasant sentence, or both. For women in general, its effects are not so positive. It allows the continuation of the idea that women are incapable of controlling themselves and that their actions can be explained through medical reasoning—they are mentally or physically sick, or both. Widely used, the implication of this reasoning would be that women should be treated for this 'sickness' rather than punished. It removes from women the idea that they may choose the criminality, that it might be a rational decision arising out of a social economic or political situation. As PMT is such a medically controversial area, and it is not possible to give it an exact diagnosis or definition, its use is even more problematic. If it were relegated to a plea in mitigation, to be taken into account in sentencing, it would be much less threatening. In most cases, this is how it would be seen. In the case of a murder

charge there is no discretion in sentencing, and therefore
to allow the judge any discretion PMT must be used to
reduce the charge to manslaughter.

Thomas

The work of Thomas acts as a stepping-stone between
physical and psychological explanation. In his early work he
reiterates much of Lombroso's theory concerning the passivity
of females and the abounding energy and creativity of males.
He argues that this divergent development can be seen best
in civilized white races where human selectivity is more
refined. Again, like Lombroso, this assumes the white 'upper
class' definition of femininity; it is arguable whether such an
assumption, in 1907, sprang from a conscious class or race
bias. For Thomas, it was a biological fact that certain types of
women are more criminal than others and, if nothing else,
these must be severely punished in order to protect society.
In the later work (1967, first published 1923) he argues for a
form of rehabilitation by controlling the mind rather than
just deterring by punishment, sterilization or other physical
preventive measures.

Thomas moves away from Lombroso's idea of female
criminality being due to masculine tendencies towards saying
that, for civilized cultures, female criminality is an
unacceptable use of female traits. Female criminals are
considered to be amoral, that is, without morality, not immoral,
which implies loss of morality. They are described as being
cold, calculating people who have not learned to treat others
with pity and concern. They use the less developed and colder
sides of their natures in order to gain something for themselves
through sexual promiscuity, soliciting, prostitution, or other
'unacceptable' and sometimes illegal means.

For Thomas, there are four basic wishes which drive
every individual: the desire for new experience (for example,
hunting or dangerous sports); for security (the fear of death);
for response (maternal and sexual love); and for recognition
(dominance within the group). Thomas argues that for
females generally, it is the response wish which is most

marked. In 'normal' law-abiding women, this wish for
response is fed by retaining her chastity as a good way of
obtaining a devoted husband who can give her security and
a family to love. For 'amoral' women the need for love drives
her to commit any act in order to gain affection; her own
sexual and other feelings take a minor role. Female criminality
is thus largely seen as being based on sexuality, leading
Thomas to emphasises prostitution and soliciting to explain
all unacceptable and criminal behaviour. If the 'amoral' and
generally lower-class female was controlled and taught the
same standard as her 'normal' middle- and upper-class
counterpart, she would be law-abiding. Social conditions are
ignored: if women adhered to their model role in society, there
would be no female crime. Re-educating those who failed to
come up to the conventional role was the change advocated
by him. These ideas were common to the time and were
extensively used in the control of women by the authorities.
Women were channelied, both culturally and by the State
correction system, into female roles.

Freud

The next milestone on this road is the writings of
Sigmund Freud (1973, originally written in 1925 and 1931).
Lombroso's and Freud's understanding of the concept of the
born criminal is quite different. Lombroso distinguished
between born criminals and other people, but Freud saw
everyone as a potential criminal in the sense that all human
beings are born with immoral and anti-social instincts. The
other main difference is that for Lombroso the criminal was
a product simply of hereditary factors, whereas for Freud it
was a mixture of inherited factors and the effect of external
experiences. So, Freud recognises that although all humans
are born with criminal designs, most will learn to control them;
it is those who do not learn such control who end up as
criminals. For Freud, the inability to learn social habits is
partly hereditary and partly related to up-bringing. His
successors often argue the human personality is shaped by
its social environment alone and that heredity plays no part,

but Freud places a large par of his argument on heredity. Here, it is intended to focus upon Freud's theory of female criminality.

As with a large portion of Freud's work, the central tenet of his theory tends to be sexual; that is, that the explanation or motivation for the female criminal is largely sexual neurosis. Due to the lack of a penis the female feels, and often is, inferior, better suited to the less demanding destiny of being wife and mother rather than breadwinner. He says that a woman, whilst she is still a child, recognises that she has inferior sexual organs and believes this to be a punishment. She then grows up envious and revengeful. The feminine behaviour of most women can be traced to their lack of penis. They become exhibitionist and narcissistic, and so try to be well-dressed and physically beautiful in order to win love and approval from men. Freud argues that the genetic differences between men and women lead to a difference in sexual functions which make women passive and masochistic, as their sexual role is receptive :

> It is perhaps the case that in woman on the basis of her share in the sexual function, a preference for passive behaviour, and passive aims is carried over into her life to a greater or lesser extent....

He further argues that women generally do not develop a strong conscience. Men develop one as a result of controlling their Oedipal complex. An Oedipal complex is a man's or boy's incestuous love for his mother which is repressed due to a fear of a jealous reaction from his father. The fear is that the father may ultimately castrate the son—this is the most feared punishment. As a result, boys generally by the age of about five develop a very strong super-ego or conscience. As girls and women cannot be castrated, they do not possess the fear necessary to overcome the Electra complex (their desire for their father and hatred of their mother). Normally this would lead to a higher crime rate for women, but due to the passivity (mentioned above) and their very strong desire for love and affection, particularly from their fathers or other men, they are controlled. They do not break men's laws for to do so would lead to disapproval and a withdrawal of male love and affection. Their problem is two-fold. Due to their preoccupation with envy, they are self-centred and concerned only with trivial personal and family matters: and because of a weak super-ego they cannot understand justice. They thus should play no part in production and property ownership.

In Freud's world, deviant women are those who attempt to become more like men, those who compete or try to achieve acclaim within the masculine spheres of activity, or those who refuse to accept their 'natural' passivity. These women are driven by the desire to claim a penis, which leads to aggressive competition. This ultimate desire is, of course, hopeless, and they will end up by becoming 'neurotic.' Such women need help to enable them to adjust to their intended sex role. The birth of a child would be seen as particularly therapeutic as the baby is seen as a substitute for a penis, according to Freud.

Like Lombroso, Freud mostly ignores, social, economic and political factors : unlike Lombroso, who centred his theory on physical characteristics, Freud's theory uses psychology and mental disease to explain female criminality. Nevertheless, the concept of a well-adjusted woman is based very much on traditional ideas of sexuality and society. It thus suffers from the same sex and class problems as the earlier theories, but was probably more demanding because of its 'scientific' basis.

Pollak

Pollak's theory was sex-based. He was doubtful that women commit as little crime as the official statistics showed. He thus advanced a theory of 'hidden' female crime. Pollak follows Freud in explaining female crime by reference to sexual neurosis. Women are traditionally shy, passive and passionless, but can simulate a sexual orgasm to hide their true feelings. They can take part in sex without any physical passion, and they can learn to hide their monthly menstruation. All this means that within the sexual sphere they learn to manipulate, deceive and conceal—this, he claims, decides the inherent nature of women, making them likely to be the instigators of crime which is then actually perpetrated by men. Where they do themselves commit crimes, there are related to their feminine nature and explained either on psychological (mental) grounds (for example, shoplifting is the result of kleptomania, an uncontrolled urge to steal), or on sexual grounds (for example, soliciting for prostitution or sexual blackmail). Other crimes committed by women can be hidden and underhand, for example, poisoning or infanticide. In so far as this description of female crime is valid, he seems not to have considered the possibility that lack of social, political and economic power may forced women into taking an underhand or manipulative way to enforce change, and so better their position and standing in society.

Lastly, Pollak claimed that women appeared less before, and were more leniently treated by, the criminal justice system because they were differentially treated by all officers of the law. This preferential or, as he saw it, chivalrous treatment arose from the fact that men generally had a protective attitude towards women. Men thus disliked making accusations against women because they did not want women to be punished. This chivalrous treatment, he claimed, stretched from police through the jury to the judge, and thus resulted in a great under-conviction of female criminals. This is a thread picked up by much later writers, although in rather more refined form.

Modern Applications

Each of the above theories seems to assume that women are more or less totally different from men in every respect: biology; psychology; needs; desires; motivations. They often link criminality in women to old, unquestioned popular assumptions about problem women—usually associated with their breach of the societal norm of wife, mother and homemaker. Implicit in such views are concepts of women as sources of evil, causing the downfall of mankind: their criminality is then represented as more destructive of social order than anything man could do. This almost pathological fear of female non-conformity and criminality is reminiscent to the 'witch-hunts' of history, which, as Heidensohn suggests, is a powerful and recurring popular image of 'deviant women as especially evil, depraved and monstrous...used by "scientific" criminologists...as the basis of their theories, theories which ...not only had a stigmatising effect, but have also had unfortunate consequences for the treatment of women offenders'. However, Heidensohn may provide us with one of the reasons why female criminality is so feared : women are relied upon to maintain order and to continue present societal structures, so deviance from this role is seen as especially threatening. The socialising role of women in the family and in society is also limiting on them, because it means that they are expected to, and often do, have a far greater stake in conformity. In addition, since the pressures of these roles limit their opportunities to offend, such action by women becomes viewed as more peculiar, and hence less acceptable, than it would be for men.

In studying male criminality, it was clear that mental illness or strong psychological problems were useful explanations only in rare cases where the mental problem was clear. In female criminality, it has been assumed that a wide range of crimes can be explained by such mental factors and that the sexual basis of the mental problem is strong, whereas it was absent in explanations of male criminality. In male criminality, even sex crimes are generally explained on some basis other than the sexual. Even rape is very rarely associated with an incomplete resolution of the Oedipal complex; more often it is said to be a crime of power or violence which just happens to assume a sexual element. In court it is often ascribed to sexual frustration (usually caused by the female dressing or behaving in a 'provocative' manner) or to drink and is thereby more understandable. Female criminality is, however, often explained in clinical or sexual way. Campbell discusses how shoplifting, traditionally a female crime (although in fact more males than females commit it), has frequently been connected with both mental problems

and sexuality. The sexual nature is interesting, as it is a crime which does not obviously possess any sexual elements. Female shoplifting has often been attributed to kleptomania despite the fact that such a mental disease is very rare. Campbell also refers to perceived sexual nature of shoplifting: women are supposed to obtain sexual excitement from the act; or perform the crime to still repressed sexual desires; or in order to be punished for such feelings. The prevalence of these ideas, until at least the 1960s partly continued because of the number of single, divorced or widowed women who performed such acts; the possibility was ignored that this particular group faced unusually harsh economic and social stresses.

Gibbens and Prince also studied shoplifting and explained male lower-class youthful shoplifting by reference to the gang or peer group and/or the desire to appear fearless and masculine. In the case of the small number of middle-class boys, they suggested that they suffered homosexual tendencies which meant that the reasons given for women would apply to this group too. Women were seen to commit these acts due to depression, resentment, to keep up appearances and meanness. The first two of these reasons have clear mental and clinical applications and are postulated with the little proof of their validity. The last two do appear to have a more socially based reasoning, although 'keeping up appearances' is something which may turn on a sex-based theory, the desire to attract a male partner.

Several psychologically based pleas have now emerged for the legal defence of women. The most interesting addition to this catalogue is the use of post-traumatic stress syndromes; the one most applicable as a defence is the battered woman syndrome; whilst the rape trauma syndrome has been used as a tool to back up both the defence and the prosecution cases. Similar syndromes have been clinically discovered in both men and women but are more frequently used in the courts in cases involving women. In the case of battered woman syndrome the defence is to a charge of murder and the claim is that what may look like a premeditated crime—

or at least one in which self-defence and provocation as presently defined would be difficult to use—can be psychologically explained. Some have attacked the use of, and the need to use, such defence and suggest that the traditional defences such as self-defence should be forced to take account of women's culture and experience; or that in assessing the reasonableness of the accused's actions and beliefs they should be explicitly subjective (how would a person in her circumstances and with her emotional condition assess the situation?). If these approaches were taken there would be less need to use psychological defences, particularly the syndromes which rather stretch and alter the legal concepts which they are used to prove.

The resurgence of women's sex roles and their treatment by the criminal justice system is evident in the treatment which women obtain from the application of the criminal law. The actions of criminal women are, as mentioned above, often viewed as having breached the idea of the female role in society, justifying, some claim, subjecting them to increasing sanctions as they move through the system. Although most studies do not find a gender bias in sentencing amply documents a criminal justice system which is generally biased against women, possibly because they are lien to it. Furthermore, for young female offenders, the system seems to want to try to show them the error of their ways, ostensibly to help them, by applying welfare approaches to resocialise them. These welfare models are more invasive of their private lives than those applied to young males, and treat such women more as sexual miscreants than as criminals.

From the above, it should be clear that clinical and sexual reasons for females criminality have been accepted even where those crimes have no clear sexual basis. In the case of male criminality, such explanations were rejected even where the crime appeared to have a very real sexual link. There would appear to be different standards being applied to explaining male and female criminality.

Learning Theories

Sutherland argued that criminality was the result of normal, learnt behaviour and claimed that criminality is not innate, but is learnt from interaction with other persons; the learning process includes both the motives for its commission and the methods of carrying it out. Criminality will result if the definitions favourable to law-breaking outweigh those unfavourable to it. In modern industrial societies, people are encouraged to pursue self-advancement and are not inculcated with a sense of social responsibility. As a result, although some still learn that the pursuit of aims by legitimate means is the morally acceptable way to behave, many at all social levels will learn that the achievement of the goal is the only important factor: they thus learn both legitimate and illegitimate modes of this end. In general, Sutherland and Cressey maintain that their theory is of general application and applies to rich as well as to poor, and to women as much as to me. The class equality continues throughout the book, but gender equality wavers under the need to explain why the male crime rate is so much higher. Sutherland does this by excluding females from this absorbed pursuit of self-interest. He argues that females of all classes and ages are socialised into the same sex role: they are taught to be nice rather than egotistical. Women, on this interpretation, seem to be excluded from the pursuit of wealth which pervades the rest of society.

Although not referring to any innate trait in women, Sutherland implies that women are more law-abiding because they are excluded from the dominant and, he seems to say, male culture. He avoids the potential clash between this and his claim to disprove innate criminality by arguing that differences of gender explain different socialisation of males and females. Because of their sexual difference, girls and boys had different capabilities and interests which are channelled and developed through different training and education, which leads to differential behaviour. Southerland might have been better stricking to a strict application of his original theory. The criminality of females is likely to rest upon their access to deviant or criminal inputs than on their gender. Sutherland removes from women the education necessary to criminality or to competitive law-abiding behaviour. He only allows them learning which fits their perceived roles as mothers and careers; any criminality has to arise out of this. More recently Giordano and Rockwell have revisited the link between differential association and female crime and concluded that this is a decisive factor. Although many women have suffered social deprivation or physical abuse without turning to criminality, they suggest that all female criminals had firm associations with positive depictions of deviant lifestyles. From a young age many of the women were 'immersed' in these definitions. From mothers, fathers, aunts, cousins and siblings who might be caught up in these activities. From this Giordano and Rockwell contend that learning theory and differential associations may explain much female criminal activity.

Sex Role Theories
Introduction

After the Second World War, this general line of thought is further developed through what are often referred to as the masculinity (or masculinity/femininity) theories. These centre not on sex itself, but on a recognised and accepted role for each sex. Under this approach, proper socialisation is explained purely as a function of the individual's physical sexual nature: maleness gives rise to masculinity and femaleness to femininity. It is only when this 'natural' process breaks down that women become criminal. These writers generally portray women as passive, gentle, dependent, conventional and motherly, a picture of woman that is not different from that painted by many of the biological determinant theorists. In these later writings, similar behaviours are being considered, but the role is learned. Gender roles are among the strongest learnt social roles in our society and, although not entirely static, they remain fairly constant although they may vary widely between different ethnic groups.

Masculinity/Femininity Theories

The American sociologist Talcott Parsons (1947 and 1954) explained the different levels of delinquency between males and females as being due to the basic structure of American society and families. The father is the breadwinner, and he works outside the home in order to provide for the family. The mother is involved with the care and upbringing of the children and looking after the home. Boys see the different functions performed by each sex and realise that they are expected to emulate the father, who is largely absent during their upbringing. They feel that they need to prove independence from the mother and acts as unlike her as possible. Parsons argues that her role is clearly less prestigious than that of the breadwinner and therefore the boy, wishing to become important, assumes that passivity, conformity and being good are behavioural traits to be avoided. This leads to an aggressive attitude which can lead to anti-social, rebellious and criminal activities. Girls, on the other hand, have a close adult model, the mother, to emulate which allows them to mature emotionally and to learn slowly and surely to become feminine.

Grosser uses this analysis and applies to explain juvenile delinquency. Boys see they must become future breadwinners and so become interested in power and money, which might lead them to steal to provide, and to fight to obtain power and prestige. Girls see they must become the home-makers, and so close relationships are more important to them. Girls are more likely to participate in sexual promiscuity than criminality; any criminality will be committed to win the affection of men, such as theft of clothes and make-up which may make them more attractive to the opposite sex.

This thesis was taken up by Cohen, first to formulate his theory on male delinquency, and secondly to argue that, although it is true that girls are essentially law-abiding, there are some who will break the law. He further argued that such law-breaking, when it did occur, was related to their feminine role in that it was either sexually promiscuous or directed at the task of finding an emotionally stable relationship with a man. He argued that women would avoid masculine aggressive behaviour.

Reiss similarly claims that the sexual activity of females may lead to criminality. Young girls may be willing to participate in sexual activity, both because by having a close relationship with a male they obtain prestige among their peers, and because they consider it necessary to maintain a close relationship with the boy. However, if complications, such as pregnancy or sexually transmitted diseases develop, the young girl will lose all prestige both from her male and female peers. Loss of prestige in this way may lead to criminal activity. Here criminality is the result of sexual behaviour which arises due to the need to fulfil a particular sex role—that of having a relationship with a male, which may also involve other type of criminality such as stealing clothes and make-up.

Dale Hoffman Bustamante notes that females are rewarded for conforming behaviour, where males, although being taught to conform, are often rewarded when they breach the rules. She argues that this teaches men, but not women, that though conformity is generally desirable, it can be rational to breach the rules in some cases. Women are shown that the only way forward is by conformity. She notes that media images can also be influential: male heroes can be portrayed as rule-breakers or benders (cowboys in Western movies, police in adventure films); heroines, at least until recently, have generally been pictures as girlfriends mothers and housewives. She says that sex role skills are important as they dictate what type of crime an individual will be capable of committing. Women are less likely to use weapons because they rarely learn how to use them, but they may use household implements to threaten their victims. This is also consistent with the fact that female crimes of violence are often committed against family members or close friends. Property crimes, she argues, often take the form of forgery, counterfeiting or shop-lifting which may arise from the stereotyped role of women as paying the bills and doing the shopping. She notes that amongst children and teenagers in America, girls and more likely than boys to be arrested for the juvenile crimes to 'breach of curfew' (which is an offence in some States in America) and 'running away.' This she explains by saying that girls are more likely to be noticed if they are out alone than are boys, and parents are more likely to worry about their daughters than they are about their sons.

The sex-role stereotyping is so strong that in some cases even where a theory is being postulated which runs counter to this idea, a feeling of the sex role may be present. Smart proposes a feminist critique of explanations but at points she lapses into sex role orientation. For example, she explains receiving stolen goods, when committed by women, in terms of a passive act carried out for a loved one, and the goods are likely to be hidden somewhere in the house. The offence is thereby ascribed to relationships and to passivity, both of which fit in with sex-role stereotypes.

Masculinity/femininity theories are based upon behavioural theories, social learning theories, control theories, and they are sometimes related to biological theories.

Empirical Testing of Masculinity/Femininity Theories

However the masculinity/femininity based theories arise, they all argue that criminality is inexorably connected to sex. Such theories have more recently undergone a certain amount of empirical testing. In 1979 Cullen, Golden and Cullen reported that they had tested 99 men and 93 women. The test was a self-report study of both delinquency and self-perceived 'masculinity' (it did not test for 'femininity'). The masculine traits used were independence, objectivity, dominance, competitiveness and self-confidence. Subjects were asked to choose their positioning on a four point scale for each trait (from 'to a large extent' to 'not at all'). Possession of high masculinity was linked to greater criminality both of males and females, but males, committed more crimes than females even when matched for masculinity. The conclusion to be drawn is that abnormal levels of 'masculinity' alone cannot explain female crime.

Again in 1979, Widom conducted a study which used tests of both masculinity and femininity traits. She studied 73 women awaiting trial and 20 controls, matched for status, race and education. Widom split her samples into four categories: (1) androgenous—high masculinity/high femininity; (2) masculine—high masculinity/low femininity; (3) feminine—low masculinity/high femininity; and undifferentiated—low masculinity/low femininity. Masculinity was found to be a very poor predictor of criminality, but femininity was found to be inversely related to law-breaking. Thus, high femininity led to conformity but low femininity led to criminality.

A further piece of research reported in 1979 by Shover et al., looked at over 1,000 people and tested them for masculinity and femininity traits. Unfortunately, the questionnaire was arguably rather unsophisticated, involving a subjective analysis of what is understood by 'masculinity' and 'femininity,' concepts which are inherently difficult to define exactly or at all. The main virtue of the test was that it was applied to over 1,000 people. Any judgements on the value of the results need to balance the defects of the tests against their substantial scale.

The researchers found that masculinity traits were largely unrelated to either property or aggressive crimes. They did find, however, that women were more likely to be aggressive if they were less feminine, that is, there was an inverse relationship between femininity and aggression. (These and other tests are more fully dealt with by Naffine.)

Evaluation of Masculinity/Femininity

The three studies surveyed provide very inconclusive results. They neither prove nor disprove the hypothesis that increased 'masculinity' leads to crime. While there is some suggestion that the female crime rate is inversely related to femininity, this is by no means proven, nor is it necessarily a causative relationship. Because the male is so much greater than the female crime, rate, any tests which seem to suggest that masculinity leads to crime and femininity leads to law-abiding behaviour are understandably attractive at first glance. But the tests all confront the difficulty that, both theoretically and empirically, there seems to be no unexceptional criterion by which to measure 'masculinity' and 'femininity.' Even so, it may be cautiously suggestive that these tests question the correlation between masculinity and crime, but do find an inverse relationship between crime and femininity. The implication is that masculinity is an unreliable indicator but that a very 'feminine' woman may be less likely to commit crime than is her less feminine counterpart.

Many doubt whether even such tentative implications have much validity. The constructs of masculinity/femininity are themselves seen as patriarchal and thus are rejected by many feminists. In particular, their use as an explanations of crime is challenged because one of the defining elements of femininity is usually given as conformity. Partly as a result of feminist writings, a newer field studying masculinity and its connection to criminality is beginning to emerge. This links crime, particularly violent crime to masculinity. It is uncertain whether any female 'masculinity' is innate or socially conditioned, but it is the case that the re-socialisation of women towards femininity has played a large part in punishing them for straying from their role of conformity. Bosworth argues that in the past prisons were one of the social methods of restricting women and trying to teach them 'good' and 'bad' femininity. Similarly, Erricson discusses the role of child welfare work in trying to curb boys' criminality whilst not subduing their masculinity but working to alter girls back to the path of 'virtuous' femininity. It may be difficult to establish identities of femininity and masculinity and even harder to establish whether if any exist, they are innate or socially learnt, but it does seem that punishment regimes have been using such a distinction to try to socialise females back into accepted feminine roles whilst leaving masculinity unaltered and merely trying to persuade men and boys back to law-abiding behaviour.

Strain Theories

The strain theory as applied to men discussed, which described the anomic theories of Durkheim and the way they were adapted and almost completely altered by Merton to explain the American way of life. In Merton's analyses, individuals are taught to desire certain things such as material success, but the legitimate means of achieving this—education and thence employment—are either not available or have only a limited relevance for bulk of the American people. Those with limited opportunities were then frustrated into committing criminality to obtain the goals. This formulation was adopted by Cohen to explain male lower-class and youthful criminality but, as seen above, females were excluded from this form of strain: the only thing which they ought legitimately to desire was a mate or male companion, and therefore their criminality would revolve around that aim. In Cohen's scheme the whole of American culture is basically gendered; ambition, wealth, rationality and control of the emotions are the outward signs of a successful person, but only a male persons. For women, success is to form a close relationship with a successful man. A lack of ambition, inactivity, irrationality and emotional instability are signs of a failed and defective male; they are the very identity of women. The other main proponents of the strain theory, Cloward and Ohlin, also relegate women to a position which excludes them from the main masculine culture. Because women are not subjected to financial pressures, they do not suffer strain in the same way and so have no need of criminal gangs or cultures to redress the balance.

As Box has pointed out, females have increasingly become economically marginalised. More women are now the only, the major, or the joint breadwinner and therefore the pressures or strains of economic requirements are increasingly placed upon them. As women often inhabit low paid and insecure areas of employment, or are unemployed, they have tremendous pressures upon them to provide. Within this context it is instructive to note that women are more likely than men to be poor. From the official social security statistics over a number of years it is clear that two thirds of adults supported by the social assistance income support scheme are women; while the Family Expenditure Survey reveals that women are over-represented in the lowest deciles, both on the basis of their individual incomes and when taking account of the incomes of other household members. In the latter, case, two-thirds of adults in the poorest households are women. This is not a peculiarly British situation: in the whole of Europe (expect the Netherlands) Eurostat figures show that female-headed households suffer much higher rates of poverty—this is particularly so in the UK, Ireland, Portugal and France. These increased strains may help to explain some of the increased female criminality, especially in the traditionally male criminal areas. Applying strain theory to females could, however, predict too much criminality since they are the most economically marginalised so if they were also to enter the competition for success one might expect their criminality to exceed that of men. Some of the reasons for the lack of such an immense increase in female criminality may be found in Tittle's control balance theory. However, there are certain offences which have risen dramatically and which are associated with female poverty: evasion of payment for television licences is probably the most dramatic example.

There is no doubt that to view the criminality of women as related only to their desire for a partner is too narrow. Clearly, women play a real role in society in general, and often fall under similar strains to those suffered by men. If there is a vast difference in their criminality, it must be ascribed to some other reason.

Control Theories

Theorists in this school claim that it is not necessary to explain criminality, as this activity is natural. What is to be explained is conformity: why don't more people break the law? Here its specific relation to female criminality needs to be considered.

In 1958 Ivan Nye argued that delinquent behaviour is natural, whereas conformist behaviour has to be learned, first through childhood socialisation, and later through prohibitions and punishment inflicted by social institutions. The difference between male and female criminality is, according to Nye, generally explicable by the fact that girls, and later women, are subjected to much closer socialisation than their male counterparts. They are often more severely punished for minor transgressions of social rules. It is because of this close learning process that girls accept and live by conforming behaviour more completely than do boys. Delinquency results when there is a lessening of social control.

Hirschi set out the main thesis of control theories, whereby society controls people by means of our methods: attachment to conventional and law-abiding people; commitment to conventional institutions such as work, school or leisure activities; involvement in these same activities; and belief in the conventional rules of behaviour. These should lead to conformity. This idea is a set out as a gender-neutral idea, but Naffine suggests that for a number of reasons it remains a male-gendered theory. First, she notes that if Hirschi was really interested in conformity he would have studied females, as the largest and strongest conforming group, to see why they were law-abiding, and yet he studied men. Secondly, Hirschi sets out as factors of conformity the traditional male role idea of breadwinner, such as responsibility, hard work, commitment to employment and making a rational decision to remain law-abiding rather than risk all of that. Conformity in males is thus depicted as a positive, but females are said to conform because the passive nature—conformity has become negative. Naffine claims that Hirschi alters the nature of the conformity because he conceives it as male rather than female. When the theory has been used to explain female conformity, the element of conformity is altered and has been devalued.

Control theory does not necessarily involve this strong

gendering and negative view of the female. It is clear that some other tests have not included such factors. For example, Hindelang ran a replica of Hirschi's study but included females. The finding was that the control theory could predict criminality in both girls and boys, although the prediction for males was slightly stronger than for females. This suggests that the positive view of conformity could be attached to female as well as male behaviour. However, the greater conformity of women seemed to come from their being denied full access to the outside world of work, which was seen as being kept largely by men for men. Women were controlled, more closely in the home and almost forced to conform, as their opportunities were very narrow.

Certainly Box viewed the control theory as gender neutral and as a useful tool to explain the greater conformity of females than of males. He argued that greater social bonding, a stronger perception of the risk involved in delinquency, and greater support for conformity among peers all make for more conforming behaviour and make the choice of conform rational and intelligent, a positive choice. Historically, Nye explained low female criminality by reference to women's close control in the family and society. Hagan also sees family socialisation as important, but notes that in some respects upbringing has altered and that this may explain changes in crime rates for women: in patriarchal families, girls, in contrast to boys, will be socialised as home-makers and away from risks; whereas egalitarian families increase the propensity of girls for risk-taking and so of their likelihood of turning to crime. Similarly McCarthy *et al.*, found that girls brought up in less patriarchal homes were more involved in common forms of criminality whilst boys in such homes are less involved in criminality. Where the power-control relationship between parents was more equal it thus had a beneficial effect on boys and a detrimental effect on girls. Interestingly Hagan and McCarthy suggest that in youths living on the streets where the controlling influences had been removed, the crime involvement by gender was similar, though they might be involved in differing forms of criminality (young women in prostitution, young men in stealing food and serious theft).

Braithwaite links the power-control relationship with labelling to suggest that the lower criminality of females is also explained by the different effect that labelling might have. In patriarchal homes young men are encouraged to have a period of independence, sexually and in other ways, before setting to head their own patriarchal units whereas women are socialised from one male-dominated household into another with no expectation for sexual or other independence. They are less likely to be criminal and stigmatised and easier to reintegrate into society and conformity if they do stray into criminality. Hagan and McCarthy state that they replicated this in a re-analysis of their data concerning street youths. If this holds true for most female offenders, it would seem that would be most likely to respond positively to reintegrative and community punishments. It is thus particularly unfortunate that as noted by Worrall and McIvor these sentences are considerably underused in the case of female offenders. McIvor found that the underuse meant women were unnecessarily sent to prison, albeit for short periods. Worrall suggests that because of underuse by the courts, community service for women is more difficult to organise. These and other factors led to a doubling of the female prison population between 1990 and 1998, mostly for very minor infringements, such as television licence evasion. It is against this background that it seems a reasonable judgement to argue that the disposals most likely to lead women away from further criminality, reintegrative and community punishments, are vastly underused.

Heidensohn proposes control theory as offering the best account of female criminality or, more particularly, female conformity. She argues that women are controlled in the home by their caring role of mothers and wives. She sees this role as being reinforced by social workers and health visitors stressing the rights and welfare of the child, through the idea of community care for the elderly and disabled, and through the way society assumes dependency of women in certain areas. She notes that although it is obviously a simple fact that women are dependent, the legitimation of the position by the State helps both to perpetuate this position and to control their behaviour. Even if they are at work, their free time is often constrained by having to perform the household tasks as well as their jobs, while because they are often in the least secure employments they are deterred from behaviour which might jeopardise their position. Lastly, male violence also acts as a very real control; domestic violence may keep them in their place in the home, and street violence also tends to keep women in the home, especially when their presence on the streets at night may actually be taken as being a temptation to prospective attackers (as in certain rape cases). Heidensohn, while confirming this thesis, also considers the changes that have and may come about as women attain positions of control in criminal justice.

The already mentioned work of Tittle concerning control balance might also be used to analyse gender differences in offending. He notes that in most areas of their lives women are controlled, often very heavily. As he sees control deficit as one aspect of deviant behaviour, this would appear to predict that women would be heavy offenders, but he notes that large control deficits results in submissive behaviour rather than predatory offending. Also, as women's lives less frequently motivate them towards deviance they tend to be law-abiding. This theory and its possible use in explaining gender differences in offending needs to be more closely considered.

The way in which controls act in our society generally means that females have less opportunity to take part in criminal behaviour and are possibly more at risk if they so do. This make criminality a less rational and available choice in the case of females than it is in the case of males. The argument here is that it is not women's natures which make them more conforming; it arises rather in the way others control them, together with fewer opportunities. This will be discussed again in connection with female emancipation and its effects on criminality.

8
Destructive Organisational Psychology

Most crime involves people dealing with each other at some stage in their criminal activity. It is most common in property and commercially driven crime although that can include activities as varied as vice, paedophile networks and fraud. Furthermore, these interactions between people may be as casual as a person selling a stranger in a pub some CD's he has pirated; as formal as a gang leader giving instructions to his team on how they will rob a bank; or as structured as a criminal Triad organisation initiating noviciate members and training them up through their ranks. All these transactions are in one sense or another aspects of criminal organisations.

Of course, some forms of crime are integrally linked to existence of legitimate or illegal organisations. The world-wide distribution of illegal drugs, for example, the smuggling of contraband goods, unlawful trading in banned or controlled products, or international fraud and corruption, all depend upon networks of contacts that have, in various ways, to be managed and controlled. Offenders in prison are also often part of networks that can be used to weaken the prison authority. To investigate and undermine all these activities it is often as important, if not more important, to understand the organisational frameworks that support them rather then to focus entirely on the key individuals who carry out the illegal activities.

The task of law enforcement agencies the world over is to reduced the effectiveness of criminal networks and organisations and, wherever possible, to destroy them or to prevent their emergence in the first place. In order to do this it is necessary to understand how organisations work, what makes them productive and efficient and enables them to continue to exist? This will then provide the insight to reduce their productivity and make their existence problematic.

There is considerable understanding in the psychological and sociological literature of the processes that keep organisations working. The proposal here is to turn that knowledge on its head. Usually organisational psychologists are concerned to strengthen the businesses and networks they are studying, but in the context of criminal investigations the objectives are the very opposite. Police officers and detectives want to destroy the organisations they are examining in order to reduce or remove the criminal activities that they support. This may be thought of as the development of an 'anti-organisational psychology.' A destructive organisational psychology that seeks to find the vulnerabilities in the teams and networks that make up criminal transactions and then exploit those weaknesses to serve the objectives of the legal process.

From the perspective of a destructive organisational psychology there is a vast literature to be raided for insights into how normal, legal organisations work and the difficulties they have in maintaining their activities. Most of this literature provides pointers to what can go wrong with even the most efficient, legitimate group of people trying to earn their daily bread. Many of the problems that non-criminal organisation face are also faced by illegal ones. Indeed, the nefarious nature of the organisation can often aggravate their problems, making criminal organisations even more vulnerable to the difficulties all organisations face.

The Nature of Organisations

The nature of organisations, their very essence, is a product of why they exist and of the mathematical consequences of a number of people working together. Therefore any organisation, legitimate or illegitimate, will share this essence and have many characteristics in common. Of course, no two organisations are identical and there will be many important differences between criminal organisations and between them and non-criminal ones. For simplicity, though, in what follows it will be the similarities they all share that will be emphasised.

These similarities stem from two central aspects of all organisations. One is their objective. The second is their structure. In other words, first, the reasons why the organisation exists, what it is there for, and secondly, how it goes about achieving those objectives, it component parts and how they are related.

Organisational Objectives and Job Satisfaction

If a person can achieve a task or set of tasks on his or her own without the assistance of anyone else then no organisation is necessary. Alone rapist or a murderer killing his spouse can often achieve their goals without recourse to any help from other criminals. But as soon as a task is identified that requires two or more people the basis for an organisation exists. This may be as few as two offenders setting out to rape a victim together because they can control her better that way, or hundreds of people around the world involved in a paedophile network.

If the group is to continue in existence at all as an entity its members must have some shared objectives and an understanding that their objective is shared. This may be a confused and poorly articulated objective may well have many levels and aspects to it. For example, the two rapists may share on objective of showing each other how determined and 'masculine' they are, and be very unclear about a particular victim. But they will not achieve anything if one of them assumes they are going to rob a bank and the other thinks they are going to frighten girls in the park.

A crucial aspect of these objectives is that the members of the organisation gain some benefit from their involvement. There are always personal objectives as well as organisational objectives to keep people with at least the minimal level of involvement in an organisation. In the psychological literature these have often been referred to as 'morale' or 'job satisfaction' or job motivation. These are the basic reasons people have for continuing to be part of an organisation and to function within it. An important discovery from decades of study of legitimate organisations is that, contrary to popular belief, financial benefit is not the sole, or evens necessarily the primary, motive for people being part of any organisation. Social benefits from mixing with others, status benefits from being recognised as part of a group, or sheer interest in the job itself, have all been shown to be more powerful as job motivators in some jobs than the financial rewards on offer.

The debates in the literature as to be essential motives for staying and working in an organisation are very relevant to considering illegal organisations because in many of them the financial benefits are small and short lived, especially when set against the risks involved. There may often also be huge disparities in distribution of financial gain between different members of a criminal organisation that could cause great disaffection. Thus although there has been little systematic study of the clarity of objectives and motives for being part of criminal organisations, it seems very likely that many people stay as part of them because they are coerced to do so, usually by fear and intimidation. It may also be the primary way in which they gain any social standing and any sense of belonging to a community or family.

Structure and Leadership

The second inevitable component that is the essence of an organisation is that it will have some structure. The people who make it up will have different, but related roles within the activities of the organisation. These roles may be fluid and each may carry out the full range of activities in which the group or network engages, but at any point in time the various tasks that the organisation needs to have done in order to achieve its objectives will have to be divided amongst its members. This process gives rise to differentiation within the organisation and often to the emergence of different groups and sub-groups.

Such differentiation itself requires management and guidance. This may be achieved through discussion and the emergence of a consensus but it often requires some direction from one or more individuals, in a word, leadership. The notion of leadership, like that of motivation, is a complex and hotly debated one within the realms of organisational theory. But the relevance of these debates to considering criminal organisations lies in the attention they have drawn to the many different forms of leadership that any group, team or network requires. Leaders are not required merely to issue instructions. They are needed to devise plans, to obtain knowledge and information as well as to keep people participating in the organisation. Criminal groups, like non-criminal ones, are likely to have different people taking these different leadership roles. This, of course, has important implications for how such an organisation may be disabled. Removing the person who has the important information, or who coerces the other members to stay within the group may be more effective than arresting the person who plans and gives instructions, who may be the most difficult to convict in court.

Organisational Vulnerability : Communication

An Organisation is nothing without communications between its members and with its supplies and 'clients'. Communications are fundamental to the two aspects explored earlier, objectives and structure. People need to be informed of what the objectives and tasks of the organisation are and to be kept involved in its activities. The assignment of roles and the processes of leadership all depend not only on communications between the different individuals and groups but also on some of those individuals having knowledge of the communication process itself.

Non-criminal organisations constantly battle to maintain and improve the efficiency and effectiveness of their communications. Weaknesses in this aspect of their activities are frequently chronic problems with which they struggle. This is almost invariably their Achilles' heel. For criminals this vulnerability is more parlous. They have to keep their contacts confidential and secret wherever possible. This makes them less effective and more prone to confusion and misinterpretation. Therefore many of the vulnerabilities of criminal organisations can be traced to the various weaknesses that emerge from problems generated in aspects of their communication processes.

The Vulnerability of Size

The organisational psychology literature is replete with studies that show that broadly speaking, the larger an organisation the more problems it has. Larger organisations are less efficient than smaller ones. Their staff is less satisfied with their working situation and more likely to indicate this through high turnover and absenteeism rates. Many explanations have been put forward for these consistent findings but some of the most obvious have direct implications for the investigation of criminal organisations— communications, control and alienation.

The Vulnerability of Size 1 : More Communication

As messages are passed between more people there are more opportunities for confusions to occur. As a consequence the larger an organisation the more likely are its communication processes to be weak. For a criminal organisation this also means the more opportunity there is for unwanted leaking of information. The implications for law enforcement therefore are to establish the extent of a criminal network as fully as possible. The larger a network the more likely are there to be weak, in the sense of confused or ambiguous, communications between aspects of it. These weak links can be utilised for intelligence sources or as opportunities for disruption.

The clandestine nature of communication process creates more possibilities for confusion. A person buying an illegal drug has no way of determining who the supplier is to their dealer nor where the supplier's stock originates. The country of manufacture that is required by law to be marked in all products sold legally has no place in illegal market. One interesting consequence of this is that criminal networks probably rely much more on published accounts of matters of relevance to them than is often realised. A notable example is the way the upsurge in the use of particular recreational, illegal drugs often follows very public banning of them. It is only through the public outcry against the drugs that illicit users find out about their existence. Conventional television advertising campaigns are not an option for the producers of 'ecstasy' or 'crack cocaine'.

These communication problems will also mean that misinformation, rumour and superstition will be rife amongst criminal networks. They will be very prone to misinterpreting what has happened and exposed to misleading information. A fact that well-informed police officers around the world have always taken advantage of.

The Vulnerability of Size 2 : Less Effective Control

Along with the problems of extended communication any increase in size also puts greater demands on the mechanisms of control. This is particularly problematic for criminal organisations both because of their need to keep their activities secret and because of the importance that coercion often has in maintaining those activities. Knowing who is doing what is the key to control and clandestine communications make this much more difficult to determine.

The problems that increase in size poses for effective control can be better understood by recognising that leadership requires an understanding of who is communicating with whom. The mathematical implications of this are that the more people involved the more of the organisational effort that is required to monitor communication processes themselves. Consequently the less time and energy there is available for the directly 'productive' activities of the organisation.

As criminal networks grow, therefore, the greater the possibility that 'maverick' offshoots will form who are not strongly under the power of any 'boss.' These may be the downfall of the central group or may be the source of new criminal activities. This proliferation and growth has particularly important policy implications for international law enforcement agencies as it can help them to predict the forms of growth that crime will take as well as providing them with strategic opportunities for intervention.

The Vulnerability of Size 3 : Individual Alienation

As the communication networks grow longer and the messages become more ambiguous and less reliable there is a growing possibility that the concerns and goals of particular individuals are not being catered for by the organisation. This is the recipe for some members of the organisation not to feel involved with it or committed to it. These will typically be people who are the ends of communication chains and whose contacts with other members of the network are in low in frequency. They are the people who are most likely not to follow the instructions given to them or to provide information to people outside the organisation. Such people are good targets for intelligence activities and have potential as informants, even though their position in the communication network may mean that they have little detailed information.

The Vulnerability of Structure

Although two people may share tasks out evenly and play very similar roles in their dyad such equality is rare. Certainly the larger the group the more likely is it that the individual members will each have different functions and that the group as a whole will therefore have some identifiable sub-groups that each interact with each other in different ways. The most notable feature of these differences in interaction is that there will be unevenness in the distribution of communications. Some people will send and receive more than others.

The simplest way to consider organisational structure is the degree of hierarchy it exhibits. In a strongly hierarchical structure the chains of command are long and a very small proportion of individuals carry responsibility for the actions of the organisation as a whole. This can lead to a strong direction for the organisation, including careful monitoring of the actions of everyone within it. It is the classic structure for a military organisation that needs to be able to respond to complex, challenging situation with all the resources available to it in a focused and concerted way. But the long chains of command, or communication routes that such a hierarchy requires is enormously vulnerable to breakdowns and ambiguities in those communications. There is therefore a tendency for these hierarchies to become very 'flat' when the communications are under pressure, through the need to keep them secret or because of the risks of confusions. 'Flat' in the sense that few people keep in touch with as many people in the network as possible, so that the layers of command are reduced.

This 'flattening' of an organisation can have further problems. The people in the key, 'central', position become bombarded with information and demands for contact. The flow of information therefore becomes very uneven because the people in the central positions do not have the time or resources to deal with every contact. They hoard the information they receive and people at the periphery do not know what is happening. This can add to confusions and the generation of alienated groups outside of the central leadership.

One way of attempting to deal with these difficulties is to create a more open organisation in which everyone can keep in contact with everyone else. But such open structures can cause further problems for criminal organisations. They increase the risk of secret information leaking from the network and of the loss of control by the central figures as other individuals and groups have more opportunity to influence the course of affairs.

The sorts of problems that criminal organisations have which derive from aspects of the organisational structure therefore often can be understood in terms of the demands on the criminal 'leaders.' Indeed, this is undoubtedly one reason why notorious criminal leaders become of such interest to the factual and the fictional media. They can be readily portrayed as tragic heroes. If they are able to survive for any length of time they must have some remarkable management skills, but these skills are doomed to lead them to eventual failure as the forces of law eventually overtake them. The great demands on the individuals who 'lead' criminal groups or steer nefarious networks stem from the many different capabilities that are required of them They need to have enough background knowledge to understand what their group or network is doing and to have enough specific information to be able to give effective instructions. However, they also need to be able to motivate their subordinates in some way, whether negatively through coercion or positively through promised rewards. Demands for trust and loyalty are only likely to be successful in very tight knit groups that have long established family ties or ethnic minority connections.

On top of these direct management skills leaders need to be aware enough of what is going on within their group to maintain the secrecy and focus of the group. To some extent, of course, the criminal nature of the activities facilitates this in the same way that a known enemy keeps an army on its toes. Pressure from law enforcement can strengthen the resolve of a criminal group and increase the power of its leadership. However, the overload that can be placed on the leadership by the structural processes can be the major cause of the group or network collapsing.

To deal with these demands leaders in many groups of any size will have recognised lieutenants who help them to cope. These individuals may be trainee leaders themselves to people who have specific functions to do with the control of the group. By understanding these processes police intelligence analysts may be able to identify the potential vulnerabilities inherent in a criminal organisational leadership. For example if the network has grown rapidly in recent weeks it is very likely that the leaders are not fully aware of all that is going in within the network and that any central figure is very dependent on the information given to him by his 'lieutenants.' It is also likely that many of the more peripheral people feel very separate from the 'core' of the group and are either attempting to gain admittance or seeking ways of becoming more separated. Police contact with such individuals could therefore take advantage of these vulnerabilities.

Reciprocal Anarchy as an Organisational Strategy

The many difficulties that face criminal groups, teams and networks in forming effective organisations and maintaining effective leadership does have the consequence that very few criminals are really part of organisations in any formal sense. The clear management positions, strict chains of command and specific roles that would be expected of a legitimate organisation are far less likely to be found amongst criminals than a shifting set of loosely knit allegiances and changing patterns of communication. The much publicised criminal organisations such as 'Hells Angels' and 'Chinese Triads' and the 'Mafia,' so enjoyed by Hollywood, are very rare indeed against the general mass of much more anarchic criminal activity. Even which they do exist they are likely to survive only for a relatively brief period as recognisably structured organisations. All the pressures considered above will lead to change and collapse and reconstruction in relation to changing demands.

Indeed, it is this anarchic, network quality of criminal organisations that can make them so difficult to investigate and destroy. A strictly structured organisation can be readily understood and described and can be destroyed by removing crucial individuals in the network, but a fluid, flexible, opportunistic pattern of activities can easily be reconstructed if some of its members are removed. Also no one will know exactly what the network does or how and so obtaining clear intelligence on the network can be very difficult indeed.

Destroyers of Morale

One approach to destructive organisational psychology of crime is to tackle the reasons people have for being part of criminal organisations rather than only using the more conventional law enforcement approach of seeking to destroy the organisation directly. This has some parallels to the psychological warfare strategies that are used to undermine enemy populations. This approach does require some understanding of why people join and continue membership of criminal networks and of the weaknesses within those networks that can lead to their members being confused or misinformed about their network or its activities.

If people only remain within a criminal group because of pressures that are brought upon them then removal of those pressures are crucial. This is widely recognised by law enforcement agencies throughout the world in their witness protection programmes. But can also be extended by ensuring that rapid police action will minimise the risk of coercive violence. Once an area of a city becomes a 'no-go' area for the police or other forms of protection from violence, whether it is in shanty towns in South America, or caused urban guerrillas in Europe, then scene is set for organised crime to emerge.

A further mechanism for reducing morale and commitment to a criminal organisation in to reduce any self-esteem that members may gain by belonging to it. This requires that the status and kudos of the criminal organisation be challenged at any opportunity. If its members see themselves as a heroic team of freedom fighters attempts should be made to change the perception to a gang of callous thugs. This may be done in one to one contact with the criminals as they come into police contact or through the accounts of their activities that are portrayed in the media. The confusions in the communication process can be utilised here, as many criminals in the organisation will not have first hand knowledge of the actions of other people in the group.

The third process is to encourage feelings of alienation and separateness from the other members. Reducing the ability of criminals to communicate with each other with increase the likelihood of some of them feeling less involved with the organisation and will also feed the confusions in their communications with others. Out of this process, sub-groups of more isolated offenders may be identified who can then help to undermine the whole criminal organisation.

Myths of Organised Crime

In conclusion the points made in this essay can be summarised as challenges to a number of myths that seem to circulate amongst police officers about organised crime.

Because police officers themselves usually have only limited experience of how organisations work, namely experience of police forces, they have a tendency to assume that any other network of people will be managed in a similar way. But many studies of criminal groups, including those reviewed in the present volume, show that whilst there is often some element of organisation to criminal networks, in that there is some degree of role definition and rules of how to carry out activities, this is usually far less rigid or stable than for legal organisations. In general then it is a myth that large networks of criminals are 'organised' in anything like the same sense that a police force or university is organised.

9
Media and Criminal Psychology

This is far too simplistic a view for some theorists who claim that the media is being used as a convenient scapegoat by parents, teachers and society of deflect the blame away from them. A judge recently threw out a case against 25 media companies after a 14-year-old school boy shot dead three girls at a prayer group in 1997. The victims' parents claimed that the 'one hit, one kill' pattern used by the young killer mimicked that of video games. The judges however commented that 'Tragedies such as this simply defy rational explanation, and courts should not pretend otherwise.'

In this chapter we take a critical look at research into the effects of the media on antisocial aggressive behaviour, including some recent work on the effects of violent video games. We consider the conditions under which children may be most susceptible to the influence of media violence and the factors that contribute to its influence.

Finally we take a brief look at research on the effects of pornography, especially violent pornography and whether this can contribute to crime such as rape.

Introduction

There is no doubt that children are exposed to great deal of media violence. Eron estimated that by the end of primary school a child is likely to have seen 8,000 murders and more than 100,000 other acts of violence on television and video. Such has been the concern regarding the possible relationship between media violence and violence within society including the possibility of 'copycat' crimes, that this has been the focus of several public commissions and reports designed to influence social policy.

The debate about the extent of media influence is not a new one: many years ago Bandura, a major proponent of Social Learning Theory, expressed the view that viewing of violence could encourage imitative aggression in children. His research (for one piece of which see Classic Research), paved the way for many studies investigating the possible link between media violence and violence within society. Such research, however, is beset with methodological problems and various methods have been used in an attempt to obtain some answers. Before looking at the research itself, we will describe and evaluate each of these methods.

Methods Used to Investigate Media Influences

There are four main methods by which the link between media violence and aggression has been investigated.

1. Laboratory Experiments

These are investigations carried out in a laboratory or similarly controlled environment and usually compare two matched groups on their level of aggression when one has been exposed to some form of media violence (such as film clip or video game) and the other has been exposed to something similar and equally engaging but with no violent content. The participants are then given the opportunity to aggress (or so they believe), by, for example, pressing a button marked 'hurt' to deliver a painful stimulus to another person (the pain is never delivered) and the level of aggression between the two groups is compared. Sometimes, in addition to this, a repeated measures design is used in which levels of aggression are rated before and after viewing violent material.

This method has the important advantage that, being experimental, it can establish cause and effect. However, such studies have been criticised for their lack if ecological validity; there is a world of difference between pressing a button marked 'hurt' or a noisy buzzer and being deliberately cruel to others following exposure to media violence in a natural setting. Doubts have understandably been expressed about whether what is found in the laboratory will occur in real life. Another serious problem with this method is that it only measures very short-term effects. Ethical concerns have also been voiced. There is, in the eyes of some, an encouragement to be violent by providing such an opportunity. An example of such a study is that of Bandura.

2. Field Experiments

These are experiments that are carried out in a more natural setting, such as the home of the participant or a boarding school. They have greater ecological validity than laboratory studies but, like the latter, they are looking only at short-term effects. Another problem is that since it is difficult to control extraneous situational variables, such as how much other violence the children witness or who they associate with, there can be less confidence is judging cause and effect. Examples of this type of research include that of Leyens *et al.*, and Parke *et al.*, in which an institutional setting was used.

3. Natural Experiments

These are studies carried out in a real-life setting in which the independent variable (the degree of exposure to violent media) exists already and is not therefore controlled and carefully engineered by the investigator.

These studies have a reasonably high level of ecological validity but it is impossible to clearly establish cause and effect since other factors and changes will also have an effect. These are few opportunities to conduct such investigations but recently one has become available: that of the island of St. Helena.

4. Correlational Studies

These studies compare the level of aggression expressed by individuals (by using personality tests, self-ratings or crime statistics) and the amount of media violence experienced to see if there is a positive correlation between the two variables. Some such studies have been conducted over many years, following individuals from childhood through to adulthood, so they have the advantage of looking at very long-term relationships; others measure short-term effects. Their main limitation is that of all correlational studies: they cannot establish cause and effect. When a positive correlation is demonstrated it could be to the fact that experiencing media violence causes aggression but this is not the only possible explanation. It may be that aggressive children (and adults) seek out violent films and games or that children brought up in a violent household and subculture are exposed to media violence but it is the general upbringing rather than the media influences which cause the high levels of aggression. Examples of such studies are those of Eron *et al.*, Eron & Huesmann, and Phillips.

Studies Investigating the Effects of Media Violence

Early laboratory studies of the effects of viewing violence were conducted by Bandura, the founder of Social Learning Theory. He demonstrated in many laboratory studies that children imitate aggressive models. His famous Bobo doll studies in which young children watched an adult either beat up the large inflatable doll or simply play non-aggressively with other toys, showed that young children imitate aggressive acts and learn from the models new ways of aggressing. The study on Classic Research demonstrated this, and also showed that if a person is seen to be punished for acting aggressively then children are unlike to imitate them. This an important point because much media violence is seen to rewarded, either directly or indirectly. The 'good guys' often use violence to get their own way and are hailed as heroes (or very occasionally heroines) for so doing.

How Do Children Respond to TV Violence?

Aims

1. To observe children's responses to seeing a television presentation of an aggressive model who is seen either to be punished, rewarded or to have no consequences for the behaviour.
2. To see how many of the novel aggressive responses the child will imitate when induced by rewards to do so.

Method : This is an experimental study with a carefully controlled independent variable, that is, whether the model is punished, rewarded or no consequences occur.

The participants were 33 boys and 33 girls aged between 3 years 6 months and almost 6 years. The children were assigned randomly to one of three treatment conditions of 11 boys and 11 girls.

The children viewed the televised film on their own. The film lasted five minutes and involved a character called Rocky being abusive to an adult-sized plastic Bobo doll. The content of the film is described in the paper as follows:

"First, the model laid the Bobo doll on its side, sat on it, and punched it on the nose whilst remarking. 'Pow, right in the nose, boom, boom.' The model then raised the doll and pommeled it on the head with a mallet. Each response was accompanied by the verbalisation, 'Sockero...stay down.' Following the mallet aggression, the model kicked the doll about the room, and these responses were interspersed with the comment, 'Fly away.' Finally, the model threw rubber balls at the Bobo doll, each strike punctuated with 'Bang.' This sequence of physically and verbally aggressive behaviour was repeated twice."

The ending of the film differed according to the conditions. There were three of these:

(a) Model-rewarded condition: the model was given drinks, called a "strong champion" and congratulated

on the aggressive performance.
(b) Model-punished condition: the model was given a good telling off, called a bully, spanked with a rolled-up newspaper and threatened with a more serious spanking if it happened again.
(c) Non-consequences condition: no extra ending was added to the basic film.

After viewing the film, each child spent 10 minutes in the test room, which was equipped with a Bobo doll, balls, a mallet, dart guns, farm animals and a dolls house. Two observers, who did not know which condition the child had been assigned to, recorded their behaviour and noted the number of imitated behaviours they performed.

After a short break, the children were offered a sticker and juice for each physical or verbal response they reproduced. They were asked to show what Rocky did and what he said in the film.

Results : Children in the no-consequences and the model-rewarded condition imitated significantly more aggressive behaviours than the model-punished group. There was no difference between the no-consequences and the model-rewarded groups.

In the second part of the study, when children were offered rewards to recall the behaviour of the model, there was no difference between the groups. They could all repeat a considerable number of the aggressive actions. The use of positive incentives had completely wiped out any previous performance differences.

Conclusion : Although the administration of punishment reduces whether or not children imitate aggressive behaviours, it does not influence the degree to which they learn them.

Correlational Studies
Longitudinal Studies

Eron and his colleagues conducted a longitudinal correlational study of a large number of children over more than twenty years. Although the findings may be somewhat dated they are worth considering because the length of the study permits conclusions about long-term effects of television violence. At the beginning of the study, in 1960, Eron, *et al.*, measured the TV violence level of what the children watched and the aggressive of 875 seven and eight year olds and found a positive correlation between the two. Ten years later, with 475 of the original sample remaining, they measured the same two variables and found a negligible correlation. However, when during the teenage tears the level of violence viewed and the amount of aggressiveness were compared, an even stronger positive correlation was found in the boys, though not in the girls. Furthermore, the more television violence the boys had watched at age eight, the more likely they were to have been convicted of violent crimes at age 30. The methodological problems inherent in such longitudinal studies applied in this case: only 55 percent of the original sample were available, so they may not have been representative. It is also quite possible that those participants who were predisposed to be aggressive sought out violent television programmes to watch or that a common factors, such as harsh parental punishment, produced children (and, later, adults) who were both aggressive and enjoyed watching others suffer. Nevertheless, while recognising the limitations of the correlational method, the researchers concluded that watching TV violence can cause aggression in later life.

Correlational Studies

Huesmann proposes that the cumulative effect of media violence does not only reveal itself in crime statistics but is implicated in general antisocial behaviour such as inconsiderate driving and the use of harsh corporal punishment on children. The pervasive influence of violent television, argues, Huesmann, is to make all forms of aggression more acceptable.

Eron maintains that television violence teaches children attitudes that condone violence and offer example of specific aggressive behaviours, such as giving someone a good thump, as a way of solving problems. Television violence differs in important ways from that shown in films, fairy stories or at the theatre because these are perceived as fantasy. Not only is a great deal of television violence quite realistic but a child sees a great deal of it—in many homes the television is on most of the time.

Somewhat different correlational research was conducted by Phillips who investigated whether there was an association between violent crime and the newspaper and television coverage of 18 heavyweight boxing matches. He found that homicide death rates rose after each of these boxing matches, peaking at about three days afterwards. Phillips even found that murders of white males increased after the defeat of a white boxer and homicides of African-Americans increased following the defeat of an African-American fighter.

Not all correlational studies show a relationship between viewing violence and aggressive behaviour. Over a three-year period. Milavsky *et al.*, found only a small association between viewing violent television and levels of aggression. They concluded that the influence of violent television was extremely weak compared to the family and social environment, a point to which we will return. Hagell & Newbury compared the television and video watching habits of 78 young offenders with those of a school control group and found that the delinquents reported watching no more violent television and having fewer television sets or video records. They were also less able to name favourite television programmes and had more difficulty naming a television character they emulated. They were typically to be found on the streets getting into trouble than indoors, watching television. Significantly, though, they tended to come from chaotic, deprived, unhappy homes.

Fields Studies

A classic field study on media violence was conducted by Leyens *et al.*, in a correctional home for boys. The amount of aggression shown by the boys was measured both before and after a week of watching either violent films (such as

Bonnie and Clyde and *The Dirty Dozen*) or non-violent ones. Those boys who watched the violent films showed considerably more aggression in the week after watching them than in the week before whereas those had seen the non-violent films showed no increase at all.

Parke *et al.*, conducted a similar study, also on juvevile offenders, in three different institutions. These boys were split into two groups matched on the amount of aggression shown in the course of one week. On each of the next five days they were shown either non-violent or violent films, all judge to be equally exciting. Trained observers coded the amount of violence the boys showed during the days of the study and found that the boys watching the violent films were more aggressive than those who had watched neutral films. In addition to this, the boys who had seen the violent films were more likely to give what they believed to be an electric shock to opponents in a game when provoked by them.

Both of these studies used a sample of delinquent boys, so their findings cannot be generalised to most youngsters. They do, however, demonstrate that media violence may increase the antisocial tendencies of youths who are already very aggressive.

A Natural Experiment : The St. Helena Study

Recently an opportunity arose to investigate the effects of the introduction of television to a small community. The island of St. Helena became the site for a natural experiment when satellite television was first transmitted to it in March 1995. Before and after television was introduced video cameras as were installed in two school playgrounds, filming children aged between three and eight during the lunchbreaks and playtimes. Analysis of the videos before the introduction of television showed that the great majority of the children were well adjusted and hard working; in fact the three and four year olds were considered to be among the best behaved in the world.

So did this change after the introduction of television?

Not at all. Even though the violent content of the programmes was slightly higher than in the UK (46 percent as opposed to 41 percent) and there was no watershed, the amount of hitting, kicking, pushing and pinching was just the same after the introduction of television as it was before. Teachers also rated the children as just as hard-working and co-operative as they had ever been.

Conclusions to be Drawn

So what we can conclude from all of these findings? Obviously the issue is a complex one and much as the popular press may like to draw simplistic conclusions and even more facile solutions, psychologists and media researchers have a responsibility to weigh up the argument in a rather more considered fashion.

One major problem that besets any attempt to assess the effects of media violence is outlined by Livingstone:

> "Almost irrespective of the academic legitimacy of claims for media effects, such claims tend to be addressed within a context in which the mass media are constructed as a scapegoat for, or deflection, from, broader cultural and political anxieties (concerning, say, childhood, sexuality, crime, unemployment or the underclass). The urgency of this moral and political agenda complicates, or even undermines, careful assessment of the academic research literature."

Certainly much of the research indicates that exposure to excessive violence can affect *some* viewers some of the time. Huesmann & Malamuth comment that the great majority of field and laboratory studies indict media violence as a factor in the development of aggressive behaviour. Nevertheless, it is only one factor and even the researcher most convinced of the detrimental effects of media violence would not argue that exposure to it alone would be sufficient to make a person behave aggressively. Cumberbatch argues that right from the time of 'Penny Dreadfuls' the media has been used as a scapegoat. He considers that the link between media violence

and criminal acts is greatly exaggerated and founded more
on moral panics fuelled by newspaper hysteria than on factual
evidence. He lists some of the criminal acts, including the
Hungerford massacre, that were supposedly the result of
copycat crimes (as documented in a Panorama programme)
and argues that none were supported by convincing evidence.

It is plain common sense to note that ordinary people
do not go and murder and maim simply because they
watched a gruesome film the night before. Most of us just
chat about it to our friends. After a 'Media Watch' we will
look at what factors interact with media violence to
enhance or inhibit the effects of media violence.

TV Wrestling in the Dock Over Death of Girl, 6

The death of six-year-old Tiffany Eunick has shocked
America. The little girl's alleged killer is a boy of 13 who is
said to have pounded her skull until it was flat, and to have
beaten her so badly that her liver was split.

Her attacker's line of defence has caused further alarm.
Lionel Tate, one of the youngest defendants to face a murder
charge, claims that his actions were inspired by professional
wresting on television.

Tate's assertion puts the flamboyant and aggressive
image of wrestlers such as Hulk Hogan and The Rock next
to him at the dock of the Florida court where his tribal began
last week. Central to his defence is her lawyer's claim that
the killing was the result of the boy copying moves he had
seen in bouts televised by the Worldwide Wrestling Federation
(WWF).

According to his lawyer, Jim Lewis, the teenager—who
weighs almost 10st but has the mental age of an eight-year-
old—was incapable of distinguishing between the mock
brutality and phoney persons of the WWF and the real harm
he was capable of inflicting. The defence calls Tiffany's death
a "horrible accident".

Although at least four other children have died in
incidents linked to copycat violence from wrestling shows,
the Florida case is the first to put the blame squarely on the

effects of television. It comes at a time of growing concern about the impact of screen violence on children and teenagers.

A report released last week by David Satcher, the United States Surgeon General and the country's most senior public health official, stated: "A substantial body of research now indicates that exposure to media violence increases children's physically and verbally aggressive behaviour in the short term."

The allegations are being vigorously countered by the WWF, which is shown in Britain on Sky TV. The federation is suing Mr. Lewis for defamation after remarks he made on television chat shows. The WWF, which insists that children can distinguish between screen fiction and reality, has also successfully blocked attempts by the boy's defence team to force star wrestles including The Rock—otherwise known as Dwayne Johnson—to give evidence during the trial.

The issue of media violence is particularly sensitive in America after a series of violent rampages by children and teenagers, including the 1999 Columbine High School massacre in Denver, in which 12 pupils and a teacher were shot by two pupils who later killed themselves.

An unsuccessful attempt to sue the video-game industry for $33 million (£22 million) was made by the parents of three children killed by another armed pupil in Paducah, Kentucky, in 1997. The killer, Michael Carneal, 13, claimed to have been influenced by violent videos, films and internet sites.

Last week's report by the Surgeon General was originally commissioned by President Clinton in the wake of Columbine. It found that violence in children was usually the result of a combination of factors, which poverty and abuse were the most significant.

While it concluded that children became more aggressive after watching some television programmes and videos, the report noted that this behaviour did not usually translate into violence against others, except among children who were already disturbed.

A separate study by Stanford University in California,

published this month, compared the actions of two primary school classes, one of which had been discouraged from watching television for almost two weeks. The research team found that the group that cut down its viewing by more than a third was almost 50 percent less likely to engage in aggressive playground behaviour than other pupils.

Factors that Mediate the Effects of Media Violence
Individual Differences

One of the most important individual differences in susceptibility to media violence is the level of aggression already shown by the individual. The relationship between aggression and viewed violence is by no means a one-way street; Bushman showed that people who are habitually violent seek out media violence and are more affected by it. Bushman conducted a series of experiments in which he compared the responses of aggressive and non-aggressive individuals after watching violent films. He found that, compared to non-aggressive individuals, the aggressive ones felt more angry and were likely to seize an opportunity to aggress against others.

Other studies indicate that aggressive children not only watch more media violence but are more likely to identify with violent characters and believe that the violence they see on television reflects real life.

Family and Social Influences

These children are more likely to be involved in crime if they are raised in families in which aggression is the norm. There are more important models for the child than the media—parents, teachers and peers all provide powerful models of behaviour and children brought up by parents who use reasoning rather than corporal punishment are less prone to behave aggressively after watching violent television. In general, media effects are insignificant in changing behaviour in families who do not rely on aggressive behaviour to discipline their children or settle arguments amongst themselves. Conversely, the greatest effects are shown by people who, as children, had frequently been frustrated, were habitually victims of violence and who had seen aggression used as the main means of getting one's own way.

The researchers of the St. Helena study point put that their

> *"results do not contradict the claims that children* **learn** *aggressive behaviours from their television viewing. But they suggest that learned aggressive behaviours need not necessarily be* **practised**. *Whether or not they are* **practised** *depends upon* **the extent to which young viewers are watched over and cared for in the home,** *school or community. What is evident on St. Helena is that good parenting and schooling, alongside a strong sense of community, have contributed to creating an environment which prevented television from exerting a negative influence upon young children." (emphasis as original)*

The researchers go on to suggest that perhaps it is not only the media that has become a scapegoat but families and schools as well. May be the culprit is 'urban apathy,' which, they argue, fosters uncaring attitudes in our young which inevitably have an impact have on our crime statistics.

The Context and Content of the Message

Research as far back as Bandura's has demonstrated that the content of the actual media message is an important variable upon its effect on others, as are the circumstances in which the violence is shown. Comstock & Paik have reviewed data from a very large number of studies using a variety of methodologies and they conclude that media violence has the greatest effect under the following conditions :

> when aggression is shown as an effective means of succeeding
> * when any negative, painful effects of the aggression on the victim are not shown and the violence is justified because it is in the support of 'good'

* when the aggressor is an ordinary person in an everyday situation
* when viewers watch in a state of arousal because they are, for example, excited, angry or frustrated.

The amount of exposure people have to media violence can also have an effect on attitudes which in turn influence behaviour. When people are exposed to media violence over a long period of time they become *desensitised* to its effects and are more accepting of it in everyday life. Gerbner *et al.*, used the term **cultivation** to describe the fact that when we are exposed to the mass media we begin to construct a social reality which is false, even though we perceive it as true to life. For example, if we are constantly shown scenes of late-night muggings, we may be afraid to go out at night for fear of being attacked. If we see the world as a dark and dangerous place we may overestimate the chances of our being victimised, perceive harmless interactions, as threatening, and retaliate aggressively rather than risk getting hurt.

Research also demonstrates that viewing justified violence increases the likelihood that it will be imitated. In many films and television programmes the 'good guys' often bring the 'bad guys' to justice by beating them to a pulp or killing them. Viewing acceptable violence can make violence more acceptable.

The Effects of Violent Video Games

Despite the fact that playing video games has been a popular entertainment for children and adolescents for a number of years, until recently research into its effects was sparse. It is now, however, attracting the attention of a growing body of researchers.

Video games differ in important ways from television. The player or players are actively engaged in the action and can change the course of events. As Bowman & Rotter point out, video game paying is an active two-way communication medium. Another difference is that unlike television, which is watched by all ages, video games are almost exclusively designed for the young.

In the 1980s few video games had a violent content but this changed dramatically in the 1990s with the introduction of many games featuring destruction and killing. Nowadays the violent games tend to dominate the market. Dietz sampled 33 popular games and found that nearly 80 percent of them were violent in nature and, rather worryingly, over a fifth of these portrayed violence towards women. It is hardly surprising then that concern has been expressed that they may encourage aggression. Indeed the adverse effects of such games could be greater than that of television because of the active involvement of the players. Of particular concern is the argument that some video games encourage racism and sexism by providing children with a world populated by the worst of such stereotypes.

Do Video Games Increase Aggression?

The argument as to the effects of playing violent video games on aggression is as contentious as that of the effects of more passive entertainment, with some researchers arguing that it increase aggression while others (e.g. Griffiths) arguing that the case is by no means proven. Emes has expressed the Freudian view that video game playing is cathatric and as such may be a useful means of coping with pent-up and aggressive energies.

We shall review a small sample of the available research before looking in more detail in the Research Now section at a very recent study designed to test a theory concerned with the way in which video games affect players both in the short- and long-term.

A series of correlational studies looked at the relationship between measures of aggression (including self-reports, teachers ratings and peer reports) and video game playing habits. A positive correlation was found in three out of four of these studies. However, we need to remember what has been pointed out several times already: that aggressive youngsters may seek out violent games to play. This, coupled with the fact that there was no record made of whether the games played were violent or non-violent, means that we cannot conclude from these studies that playing the games was the cause of the aggression ratings.

Wiegman & Van Schie argue that intense engagement with a violent game can increase the aggressiveness. They reviewed 12 studies, all of which showed that playing violent video games is liable to increase aggression in the players. However, Griffiths points out that there are at least 11 others that have not yielded the same results.

Several experimental studies have used a design in which children play either a non-violent or violent video game and are then assessed on aggressiveness. Many of these studies demonstrate that levels of aggression are significantly high after playing the violent games than after playing the non-violent ones. However, there is a very important confounding variable not controlled in these studies. The games played were not matched on difficulty, enjoyment or excitement. As pointed out by Anderson & Dill and Bushman, violent materials tend to be more exciting than non-violent materials, so the effects could have been the result of higher excitement levels induced by the violent games. Thus the crucial difference between these studies and that of Anderson & Dill in Research. Now is that the games used in the recent resarch have been matched on these key variables. We will now take a look at this research.

Do Violent Video Games Cause Aggressive Thoughts and Behaviour?

Aims : The general aim was to investigate video games violence effects and broaden the understanding of media violence in general. Specifically, the aim was to begin laying down empirical evidence to test the GAAM formulation.

Method : There were two studies which used different methods, a correlation and an experiment, chosen because these were considered to have strengths that complement each other and surmount each other's weaknesses.

Study 1 : the correlation

The variables to be correlated were long-term exposure to video game violence and a set of other variables, the most important being aggressive behaviour and delinquency, both aggressive and non-aggressive.

There was a total of 227 participants, 78 males and 149 females, all psychology students.

Participants completed self-report questionnaires to measure

* aggressive behaviour
* delinquency
* irritability and trait aggressiveness
* the amount of time spent playing video games in general
* the amount of time spent playing violent video games.

Study 2 : the experiment

A pilot study was conducted to select two video games, one violent, one non-violent. The games selected were Wolfenstein 3D and Myst: this pair were chosen because they produced no difference in physiological measures, difficulty, enjoyment, frustration and action speed (however, Wolfenstein was rated more exciting than Myst). It was important to control for physiological arousal to avoid this becoming an extraneous variable.

Wolfenstein has a blatant violent content, realism and human characters. The human hero can choose from an array from an array of weaponry; the goal is to kill Nazi guards and thereby advance through the levels to the ultimate goal of killing Hitler. Myst is an interactive adventure game designed to be non-violent. It is a fast-paced, thinking game in which players attempt to align geometric figures as they fall down a computer screen.

There was a total of 210 participants, 104 females and 106 males, all psychology undergraduate.

Participants were matched on high or low irritability, then divided by gender and each group was then given either violent or non-violent video games to play. The procedure was that each participant played the game three times, twice in the first session and once in second session approximately a week later. In the first session, they completed and affective measure (how they felt), a world view measure and a cognitive measure (what they thinking).

After playing the game for the third time, participants played a game in which they had the opportunity to give an opponent a blast of noise (no noise was actually administered). All games were arranged so that all participants won and lost the same number of contests. This noise level was used as a measure of aggression.

Results

Study 1: There was a positive correlation between the amount of time spent playing violent video games and both aggressive personality and delinquent behaviour. Both aggressive and non-aggressive.

Study 2: The participants who played a violent video game behaved more aggressively towards an opponent than did those who played a non-violent video game.

Conclusion : In the short term playing a violent video game increases aggression, presumably by encouraging aggressive thoughts. The researchers suggest that longer term exposure might alter the person's basic personality structure, making them more likely to have aggressive thoughts and feelings and to behave aggressively. Because of the active nature of these games, this effect is probably stronger than that of watching violent television and films. Consumers and parents of consumers should be aware of these potential risks.

G.A.A.M. : General Affective Aggressive Model

This new model is designed to describe a multi-stage process by which aggressive personality and certain situational variables lead to aggressive behaviour. It integrates existing theories, such as Bandura's Social Learning Theory, and the data derived from the researchers' own studies (described previously in Research Now). It explains the processes that are involved in both the short-term effects and the long-term effects of video game violence.

Whether an aggressive response is made depends on the person's usual mode of responding. Well-learned behaviours (called, in this model, scripts) come to mind relatively easily and quickly and are expressed fairly automatically. People who score high on aggressive personality have a relatively well-developed and easily accessible array of aggression scripts that are easily activated by relatively minor provocation. What is more, aggressive people have cognitions (thoughts) that encourage violent reactions, such as thinking that there is more violence than there really is, and that the best way to solve problems is to use aggression.

In sum, playing a violent video game primes aggressive thoughts, including aggression scripts. The short-term effects of both an aggressive personality and playing a violent video game have the short-term effect of increasing aggressive responses.

Study 2 in Research Now was designed to test the short-term effects of violent video game playing and, by showing that participants who played a violent video game behaved more aggressively than those who played a non-violent game, it supported the GAAM model.

Long-Term Effects

Taken together over a long period of time these effects change the individual's personality. Habitual video game players can become more aggressive in outlook and behaviour than they were before the repeated exposure. As the person becomes more aggressive, their whole social environment changes. Their interactions with teachers, parents and non-aggressive peers worson and the they seek out more delinquent peers with whom to associate.

Study 1 in Research Now was designed to test this part of the model and by demonstrating a positive correlation between a person's level of exposure to violent video games and their aggressive behaviour, it was supportive.

The Media Encouraging Antisocial Behaviour

+ Correlation longitudinal studies show a consistent positive relationship between the amount of violent television watched and levels of aggression.

+ Laboratory and field experimental studies also show that watching violent television and films or playing violent video games can cause certain people to behave in an aggressive and antisocial manner.

− Correlations do not show that viewing media violence *causes* aggressive behaviour. People who are aggressive may seek out violent programmes to watch, or a third factor. Such as a violent family, may be responsible for the connection.

− The media are being used as a convenient scapegoat so that more deep-rooted problems in society can be absolved of blame.

− Psychodynamic theorists argue that viewing aggression may be *cathartic* and therefore reduce violent behaviour, not increase it.

The Effects of Pornography

Pornography, defined as material intended to arouse sexual excitement, causes as much if not more concern than non-sexual material does, especially with the highly publicised amounts of it to be found on the Internet. Poronography is widely available: 'top shelf' magazines are sold in virtually every newsagent, video rental shops carry sexually explicit material to cater for a range of sexual appeities and, expensive though they are, phone-sex lines are widely used.

Pornography can be non-violent or violent in its content and this is a crucial difference. Violent pornography graphically depicts a violent, degrading form of sexual activity, mostly directed towards women and children who are raped, beaten or even killed. In some of this material, the women are shown as enjoying forcible sex. For our purposes, we will concentrate on research that investigates whether watching such material is liable to increase the likelihood that men will commit sexual crimes; such research is mainly concerned with violent pornography.

Methodological Problems

Researching the effects of pornography on behaviour is riddled with methodological problems. Some social psychologists have conducted experimental research based on the same design as that used for laboratory studies of media violence. A typical design would involve male participants being divided into two matched groups and while one watched pornographic material, the other viewed non-sexual footage. The two groups are then compared by, for example, measuring their attitudes to various forms of sexual violence, such as rape. We have already considered the drawbacks of this type of methodology, and they are even more acute when investigating the effects of pornography. Firstly, young college students are not representative and do not necessarily respond to pornography in the same way as other men. Secondly, the situation in which the sexual material is viewed is far removed from that of real life. Being shown in pornographic film in a psychology laboratory is hardly the same as, for example, deciding to sit around with a group of mates and a few beers to enjoy a bit of filmed sex. Last but not least, there is no way that any direct behavioural measures can be taken. All researchers can do is assess attitudes, and attitudes do not predict behaviour. Just because an individual may comment that a girl was 'asking for it' does not mean he intends to 'give it to her.'

Other methods carry their own inherent problems. Correlations of real-life events, such as investigating whether rapists and other sexual offenders watched some pornography prior to committing the crime, do not tell us anything about cause and effect. Even if such a relationship exists, it does not reflect the way the majority of people behave, nor does it demonstrate that watching the pornography caused the perpetrator to commit the crime. Most rapists have not viewed pornography prior to the rape; those who have might have raped even if they hadn't seen the film. And clearly, just because a man sees some pornography does not mean he will then commit a sexual offence. Many, many men look at pornographic material but few of them commit sexual offences.

Investigations into the Effects of Violent Pornography

One effect that pornography may have is to make men or more likely to believe in so-called 'rape myths', that is, the belief that women really enjoy and want to engage in non-consensual sex. Zillman & Bryant investigated the longer term effects of watching pornography. Student participants watched 18 or 36 non-violent pornographic films over the course of six weeks while two control groups saw either neutral films or no films at all. Watching pornography reduced the physiological arousal the students had to new pornography and these experimental participants were *less* aggressive than controls when provoked by a same-sex confederate. However, when asked to give their judgements on a rapist, the groups who watched pornography recommended a lighter sentence than the control groups did. This applied to both men and women. The men who had viewed considerable amounts of pornography also expressed more negative attitudes women in general.

In a field experiment designed to investigate the effects of violent pornography, Malamuth & Check showed male students either two films, *Swept Away* and *Get Away* in which women are seen to enjoy forced sex, or two neutral films. When compared on a 'rape myth acceptance scale,' there was a non-significant difference in their attitudes, with the pornography group very slightly more likely to accept them. However, this group did show a slightly greater (though not very large) acceptance of interpersonal violence against women.

Malamuth suggests that violent pornography is particularly dangerous when viewed by men who already have violent attitudes towards women and who are particularly sexually aroused by viewing this type of material. Demare *et al.*, in survey of male college students found that those who reported watching violent pornography admitted to having used force in sex, to having anti-women attitudes and to say that, as long as they were guaranteed to get away with it, they would rape a woman.

In an analysis of 217 studies of media violence, Paik & Comstock found that violent pornography had a stronger effect on aggression, especially male-to-female aggression, than any other type of violent material.

As with other forms of media violence, it seems to be more dangerous when viewed by already aggressive and disturbed individuals. Some researchers believe that violent pornography is particularly arousing to known rapists and that these effects are particularly pronounced when the victim seems to enjoy the abuse.

One particular concern with respect to pornography is that it reinforces prejudices against women. Even more worrying is the possibility that it leads certain women to believe that they should endure being hurt during sex, that it is 'normal' for men to want to do this and that requests to engage in this sort of sexual activity are reasonable.

Violent Pornography and Sexual Crime

Perhaps unsurprisingly, the relationship between violent pornography and sexual crime is not straightforward. Certainly no direct causal relationship can be inferred as demonstrated by cross-cultural studies. In Japan where extremely violent pornography is available, rape is rare, whereas in India where pornography is banned and films are not allowed to have any sexual content, there is a high incidence of rape. There is a multitude of other social factors that need to be considered when assessing the conditions under which sexual crimes take place. Nevertheless, it is probable that very violent pornography is extremely dangerous. Feldman draws our attention to a content analysis by Dietz *et al.*, of detectives magazines, referred to by the researchers as 'pornography for the sexual sadist.' As Feldman reports:

*"A content analysis of contemporary detective
magazines revealed covers which juxtapose erotic
images with images of violence, bondage and
domination. The articles themselves provide lurid
descriptions of murder, rape and torture. The
magazines publish advertisements for weapons, and
for burglary and car-theft tools. With the aid of case
histories, the authors illustrates how these
magazines might facilitate the development of
highly deviant sexual fantasies. It may be that
socially isolated individuals with a strong tendency
to ruminate about deviant fantasies, and in some
cases to act on them, make particular use of the
magazines described by Dietz et al., but there seems
no information on this crucial point."*

Index

A

Adult Criminality, 155
   Criminal, 182
African-American Women, 132
Age Rations in Crime, 162
American Psychopath, 146
   Police, 162
Anger Management, 37
   Management Assessment, 40
Atomic Bomb Radiation, 14
Autonomy, 7
Autonomic Nervous System, 77, 171, 180

B

Behavioural Science Investigative Support Subcommittee, 85
Beyond Trait, 186
Biological Theories of Crime, 174
Bond, Thomas, 82
Bratton, William, 43
Britain's Violent Jail, 31

C

British Crime Survey, 23, 82, 133
   tradition, 71
   system, 72

California Psychological Inventory, 180
Cambridge Study, 124, 130
Canter, David, 85
Central Nervous System, 121
Chicago School of Sociology, 179, 192
Civil Rights, 34
Classic Research, 67
Coleman, Alice, 53
Crime, 1
Criminal Law, 2, 6, 9, 15
   Justice, 70
   Justice System, 71, 76
   Record Office, 125
   Network, 136, 149
   Culture, 136
   Organisation, 137
   Career, 140
   History, 141
   Intelligence, 147, 194

U

United States, 105, 152, 157
United State of America, 132

V

Villain, 138

W

Western Society, 182
Wilson, James Q., 176
Wing Behavioural Checklist, 39
Wolfenden Committee Report, 11

Wolfenden Report, 19
Wolfenden Committee on Homosexual Offences, 70
World War I, 167
World War II, 167

Y

Yochelson, 193

Z

Zero Tolerance, 42, 44
Zero Tolerance Charitable Trust, 46
Zillman, 99

❑ ❑ ❑